ADVANCE PRAISE

"Nyck Walsh's book is a must-read for any therapist, counselor, or helping professional, but especially for those of us who are neurotypical and likely have no idea how it feels to move through the world as a neurodivergent person. This book has helped me to better identify and support clients who are neurodivergent, and to better support my own nervous system. I believe this book should be mandatory reading in all counselor education programs."

—**Tajah Schall, MA, LPC,** therapist at Culturally Relevant Counseling and former chair of the Somatic Counseling master's degree program at Naropa University

"From beginning to end, *Neurodivergent Somatics in Therapy* guides the reader through a nonjudgmental framework, validating the embodied, intersectional experiences of neurodivergent people and providing the language to name them. Clearly written, deeply engaging, and accessible far beyond its target professional audience, Nyck Walsh has written a book that is crucial for any therapist serious about critical reflection, understanding their complicity in systems of marginalization, and committing to more liberatory, anti-oppressive ways of practicing. It is the book I would want to represent my story to this field."

—**Kieran Rose,** consultant and academic researcher at www.theautisticadvocate.com, and author of *Autistic Masking: Understanding Identity Management and the Role of Stigma*

"Every chapter of this book feels like a safe space, offering guidance with grace while honoring diverse ways of thinking, knowing, and processing. Nyck Walsh embodies the anti-oppressive values he describes, modeling inclusion, compassion, and justice on every page. With practical tools for therapists and powerful challenges to entrenched norms in somatic psychotherapy, this book invites readers to expand and embrace more liberatory approaches to practice. Bold, brave, and deeply humane, *Neurodivergent Somatics in Therapy* arrives at a time when it is needed most, offering an essential and affirming resource for therapists and clients alike."

—**Wendy Allen, PhD, LPC, BC-DMT,** associate professor and director of dance/movement therapy at Lesley University

"*Neurodivergent Somatics in Therapy* invites critical reflection and action for equitable, effective practice in neurodivergent-affirming counseling. Rather than objectifying and 'fixing' clients, this book centers the power of client self-knowledge when it's invited, activated, and supported through the therapeutic counseling relationship. It invites the counselor into an ongoing exploration of self-knowledge, including relationship to the diversity of clients within ND-affirming counseling, as well as practices of dismantling oppression in support of all clients, counselors, and communities. A timely, heartfelt, and practical work."

—**Carla J. Sherrell, EdD (she/her),** educational, counseling, justice, and equity consultant; former associate professor, Graduate School of Counseling and Psychology, Somatic Counseling Department, Naropa University

NEURODIVERGENT SOMATICS IN THERAPY

NEURO-DIVERGENT SOMATICS IN THERAPY

An Anti-Oppressive Model for Whole Person Care

NYCK WALSH, MA, LPC
FOREWORD BY MORÉNIKE GIWA ONAIWU, PHD

Norton Professional Books
An Imprint of W. W. Norton & Company
Independent Publishers Since 1923

Note to Readers: This book is intended as a general information resource for professionals practicing in the field of psychotherapy and mental health. It is not a substitute for appropriate training or clinical supervision. Standards of clinical practice and protocol vary in different practice settings and change over time. No technique or recommendation is guaranteed to be safe or effective in all circumstances, and neither the publisher nor the author(s) can guarantee the complete accuracy, efficacy, or appropriateness of any particular recommendation in every respect or in all settings or circumstances.

Any URLs displayed in this book link or refer to websites that existed as of press time. The publisher is not responsible for, and should not be deemed to endorse or recommend, any website other than its own or any content that it did not create. The author, also, is not responsible for any third-party material.

Copyright © 2026 by Nyck Walsh
Foreword copyright © 2026 by Morénike Giwa Onaiwu

All rights reserved
Printed in the United States of America
First Edition

For information about permission to reproduce selections from this book, write to Permissions, W. W. Norton & Company, Inc.,
500 Fifth Avenue, New York, NY 10110

Frontis and part opener art © oxygen / Getty Images

For information about special discounts for bulk purchases, please contact W. W. Norton Special Sales at specialsales@wwnorton.com or 800-233-4830

Manufacturing by Versa Press
Production manager: Gwen Cullen

ISBN: 978-1-324-08291-0 (Paperback)

W. W. Norton & Company, Inc., 500 Fifth Avenue, New York, NY 10110
www.wwnorton.com

W. W. Norton & Company Ltd., 15 Carlisle Street, London W1D 3BS

Authorized EU representative: EAS, Mustamäe tee 50,
10621 Tallinn, Estonia

1 2 3 4 5 6 7 8 9 0

To the sweet, sensitive, fierce, stubborn, and determined neurodivergent little boy in me who is finally home after decades of not being allowed to exist. I offer this to you.

To my Pops, who showed me that it's never too late to come home to ourselves. I offer this to you.

To my Dad, who as my ancestor, has offered me the sweetest gifts of repair and homecoming. I offer this to you.

CONTENTS

Acknowledgments ix
Foreword xi
Introduction xv

Part I

Chapter 1: An Introduction to the Neurodiversity Paradigm and Important Terms 5
Chapter 2: Accessing Identification and Attributes of Autism and KCS/VAST 24
Chapter 3: An Introduction to Autistic and KCS/VAST Culture and Communication 40

Part II

Chapter 4: Pleasure/Neutrality: Prioritizing Parasympathetic States 59
Chapter 5: Client as Self-Expert: Boundaries as a Form of Differentiation 99
Chapter 6: Client as Self-Expert: Dismantling Ableism 128
Chapter 7: Global Permission: Accommodations and Executive Function Supports 160
Chapter 8: Global Permission: Questions to Dismantle Normativity in the Counseling Office 198
Chapter 9: Global Permission: Transitions, Ritual, and the Sacred 231
Chapter 10: Pleasure/Neutrality: Joy! 269

Appendix 295
Epilogue 305
References 309
Index 313

ACKNOWLEDGMENTS

GRATITUDE

This book has come into form on the stolen lands of many Indigenous peoples, including the Agawam, Pawtucket, Naumkeag, and Massachusett, the Abenaki, Maliseet, Micmac, Passamaquoddy, and Penobscot, collectively called Wabanaki, the Pennacook and Mohican, and the Ute, Arapaho, Cheyenne, Apache, Comanche, and Shoshone. I acknowledge the ongoing devastation of colonization, and I deeply honor and express gratitude for the Indigenous wisdom that is steeped in these lands and waters.

Thank you to the Earth and to all of the land, water, trees, plants, and animals who have offered me such nourishment, wisdom, care, and protection.

Thank you to my ancestors, including the Transcestors, Autistic ancestors, and KCS/VAST ancestors. May this book honor your journey and create more safety and spaciousness for the future ancestors.

Thank you to my spirit team and protectors; you've been supporting me and keeping me alive long before I even knew your names.

Thank you to every client I have ever had the privilege of working with. I am who I am today because of you. Thank you for all that you've taught me and for inviting me on your journey.

Thank you to all of my teachers, mentors, therapists, coaches, practitioners, and colleagues who I've learned so much from and who helped me grow into who I am today. I am so grateful for your wisdom.

Thank you to all of the activists and advocates who came before me, who are invested in social justice, and who gave language to the neurodiversity movement. I am so grateful to be part of this collective of humans.

Thank you to my community, which has shown me that it can be safe to be me, that I can be authentic and be loved, that I can make mistakes and be forgiven, and that I belong.

Thank you to Dr. Carla Sherrell, whose teachings and wisdom have profoundly influenced and informed my orientation as an anti-oppressive, social justice counselor.

Thank you to Mama Walsh and Pops, who have loved me like their own child and helped me heal in ways I couldn't have imagined. I know my parents are deeply grateful to you.

Thank you to Atlas and Tuck, who provide endless sensory delight.

Thank you to Kaden Walsh, who believed in me and my work more than I could have imagined, who encouraged me to take myself more seriously, and who contributed invaluable language to help me turn my bottom-up processing into a tangible model.

Thank you to Griffin, fellow trans, queer, ND, somatic-oriented, Earth-suit wearer who finds humaning as simultaneously bizarre, complex, wild, and delightful as I do. I don't know how I would have gotten through these past few years without your care, support, and allyship.

Thank you to Tajah Schall, Rachael Collins, and Griffin for your editing support, solidarity, insight, wisdom, and love, including when terror took over and I wanted to pretend that I never wrote this manuscript.

Thank you to Deborah Malmud and the team at W. W. Norton for calling this project in and supporting me every step of the way. Thank you for believing in me and in this work and for your investment in a new way forward for the counseling field.

FOREWORD

Although it is an enormous honor to have the privilege of writing the foreword for this important book, I recognize that there are readers who will never see it. For a long time, I myself typically skipped what publishers call the "frontmatter" in my eagerness to get straight to the main content. It wasn't that I found those auxiliary portions of the book unimportant; I assumed they had a purpose or else they would not have been included. However, I perceived them as being somewhat of the literary equivalent to a preview for a movie or a show, and being that I had already committed to reading said book, I felt that I didn't need further convincing.

And since you have this book in your hands (or on your device?) I'm assuming you don't need convincing either. Which is good, because (1) I'm not skilled at marketing anyway, and (2) I'm writing this to both thank and encourage you.

"Thank me for what?" you might be wondering. There are many things that I could list, but I'll stick with the primary ones in the interest of preserving time (and word count). I want to thank you in advance for seeking out this book. As you might have already gleaned (and if you haven't, you will soon), this ain't no ordinary therapy book. Bursting with intentionality, candor, empathy, and vulnerability, it is as much about (and for) *you*, the reader as it is about the clients you work with. As Nyck states, "While it offers a modality of how to engage in therapeutic work, it is much more than that. It is a foundation for how we can approach the work of counseling that transcends any one particular modality. It is a framework for how we can take our existing theoretical orientations and apply them in an anti-ableist, anti-oppressive, neurodivergent-affirming way." This is vital, and the very fact that you are willing to embark on this journey is a testament to how passionate you are about doing the hard work to be able to show up for your clients authentically. This isn't something required of you to maintain licensure. It isn't something you're getting paid to do. It's something you have chosen to do. For that, I thank you. Thinking of my first stint with a therapist as a terrified multiply neurodivergent Black queer AFAB preadolescent, I wish a book like this had existed that could have guided the well-meaning yet, completely ineffective therapy sessions.

I remember it so vividly. One day, a few months before my 12th birthday, I was summoned during math class to the office of my middle school. My father was waiting there, and he notified me that I was leaving school early that day to meet with a therapist. Unbeknownst to me, my parents had discovered and read my personal journal, which contained very detailed plans to end my life, and utilized the employee assistance program through my mother's employer to find a therapist and make an emergency appointment. As I had no idea they knew anything, I was very confused about why I was being taken to a therapist. Already inundated with a negative perception of myself, I didn't consider that they were trying to help me. Instead, I assumed that I must have done something wrong that made my parents displeased with me. I was determined to "fix" whatever was broken about me so that they could be proud of me again.

After that first visit, I started attending therapy sessions weekly after school. The therapist, an older white man, was kind, but he didn't get me at all, and the sessions felt like a cross between school and a clinic visit. Moreover, I was frightened that if I was honest about my struggles that I would be placed in an inpatient psych ward. Or that they would blame my parents (Black immigrants to the United States who are neurodivergent themselves) for not being able to curb my suicidal ideation, and maybe my brothers and I would be taken away by Child Protective Services. Thus, I quickly learned to parrot the things I knew he wanted me to say, to smile on cue, and to force eye contact and keep my body still.

I "graduated" from therapy within a matter of weeks—according to the therapy notes, my depression was "in remission" and there were no lingering suicidal ideations. That was untrue. The only thing that had changed was that I learned how to camouflage myself better, and I honed that skill for years. I did indeed end up in an inpatient psych ward several years later, involuntarily unmasked by a period of intensive burnout.

Having shared this, I hope it's clearer why in addition to thanking you, I want to encourage you to take the lessons in this book to heart. To lean in, truly examine yourself, make space for reflection and growth, and find within yourself the courage to both learn and unlearn. Therapy is a helping profession, and most people enter it to help, not to cause harm. But the reality is that many people in my community do experience therapy-related trauma. Or, like in my case as a youth, we just don't feel safe being our true selves, and therefore we don't get an opportunity to benefit as we should from it.

But there's so much more than just that. The field alone can be extremely hostile to us. After all, as Nyck states, "According to the pathology paradigm, 'there is no such thing as a joyful Autistic person.'" We are confronted with language that stigmatizes us in the very place where we are seeking support. We are further dehumanized by "treatment plans" whose very name is an that implication something is wrong with us. We are often expected to engage in ways that are exhausting and counterproductive. Bureaucracy is often a problem as well. Those of us whose intersections include racialized identities frequently experience invalidation of our experiences which complicates things even more, placing us in the uncomfortable position of having to self-advocate in a setting where we are supposed to be building trust.

Many of us avoid therapy (assuming one has the privilege and resources to even be able to access therapy) for these and related reasons. Those who have taken the leap of faith that is necessary to pursue therapy deserve to have their wholeness honored and to have a safe environment to do so. And that's where you come in. Anti-oppressive work is not easy, but it is of immense value, and we are worth it—you, me, and your clients. I pray you will be encouraged as you incorporate the lessons from this book into your practice as well as your life.

I leave you with an idiom from my culture that I find empowering, "Odò tó ńṣàn kì í b'ojú w'ẹ̀hìn" which translates to "A flowing stream never flows backwards."

—Morénike Giwa Onaiwu, PhD

INTRODUCTION

Welcome, I am so glad you are here! What a gift it is for me to get to share my passion with you. I look forward to embarking on this journey together. As we begin, I want to spend a few moments addressing some overarching elements of this book to set the foundation of our time together. I know it can be tempting to skip over an introduction out of eagerness to "Just get to it." How valid! I urge you to take the time to be with me here. While you may notice some anticipation, excitement, wonder, or nervousness, may we honor the timing and process of this unfolding, trust in the scaffolding of content, and allow this to be an invitation to come home and be with ourselves.

First: I want to name that while there are many ways to diverge from neurotypicality, what is known as the dominant neurotype in the dominant culture of the United States, this book will specifically focus on two neurotypes: autism and attention deficit hyperactivity (ADH). ADH is medically known as ADHD. KCS and VAST (kinetic cognitive style and variable attention stimulus trait) are more affirming and accurate alternatives for this neurotype that will be described further in Chapter 1. ADH, KCS, and VAST all refer to the same neurotype. Because this book is as much a philosophical approach as it is a model for how to be with clients and with ourselves, I think it could be applied to many forms of neurodivergence, but I want to let you know early on what to expect.

Second: As a social justice counselor invested in unpacking power, privilege, and oppression, I understand that my sociocultural identities directly inform my lived experience. Both my privileged and marginalized identities influence who I am as a person and as a counselor. I have a few thoughts on this topic. To begin I'd like to share what my identities are: I am a white U.S. citizen, queer, trans, speaking Autistic, KCS/VAST, highly sensitive, empathic, middle-class, master's degree–educated, cultural Jewish person invested in a Free Palestine. I am both able-bodied (in terms of physical ability) and disabled (in terms of what it means to be an Autistic and ADH/KCS/VAST person in this society). I learned how to mask at an early age, and I have access to a plethora of spoken verbal language, the privileged communication style in the United States. This means that I hold privilege within the Autistic community. Also, no matter how oppressed I may feel as a trans or multiply neurodivergent (ND) person, my white body affords me a great deal of privilege.

Next, while I actively work to examine and dismantle this privilege in the ways that I can, it is profoundly important for you to also learn from, listen to, and/or read other diverse voices on neurodiversity and ND-affirming approaches to life and counseling, namely racialized and nonspeaking Autistic, ADH/KCS/VAST people. No two Autistic or ADH/KCS/VAST people are identical, and the influence of culture and race is a vital component to the neurodiversity movement. Unless we are looking at and acknowledging intersecting identities and how intersectionality amplifies oppression, we are perpetuating a whitewashed neurodiversity movement. All too often, I hear Black, Indigenous, Latinx, Asian American, Pacific Islander, and Southwest Asian and Northern African people speak of the racism they experience in Autistic spaces in particular.

I'm going to be really explicit: *The white, speaking Autistic, and ADH/KCS/VAST experience is not a universal Autistic and ADH/KCS/VAST experience.* As a collective, we need to stop pretending that it is and be aware that dismantling racism, white supremacy, colonization, capitalism, cisgender-heteronormativity, and patriarchy are just as important as dismantling the notion that neurotypicality is the only right way to be human.

Welcome to my fire.

As we go, I will offer insights, ideas, and knowledge from

many different people I have learned from and been influenced by. In accordance with what I just described, I will share their sociocultural locations that I am aware of when I introduce them to you. This choice is an intentional one and is directly related to my effort to express how vital a diversity of perspectives and lived experience is. When I am aware of a person's pronouns, I will offer them.

One of the people who has profoundly influenced my development as a counselor, particularly as a social justice counselor invested in anti-oppression work, is Dr. Carla Sherrell (she/her). Dr. Carla is a Black, same gender loving scholar, counselor educator, social justice leader, clergy candidate, and my former professor at Naropa University in the Somatic Counseling Psychology department. Her name will appear many times throughout this book. So much of what I learned from her is embedded in how I approach ND affirming care. For example, just as she offered consistent reminders and encouragement to be gentle with ourselves as learners about anti-oppression and anti-oppression counseling, you will notice me offering the same encouragement to you. I will also honor her teachings by offering, as she did, prompts throughout our journey to notice what is present for you somatically in relationship to anti-oppression learning and invitations to slow down, pause, or make other shifts, if doing so would be helpful. While this book is expressed through me, it very much is an expression of collective wisdom that is so much bigger than me.

I am also aware that our identities can unfold and change over time, and I feel sensitive to the ways that a book is a static object that cannot account for this evolution of self. For instance, awareness of and access to language around gender identity, pronouns, sexual orientation, and neurotype can change. Something similar can be said around racial and cultural identity, specifically for people who are white passing and have had their multiculturalism or multiracial identities erased due to how they were raised and kept themselves safe and the impacts of systemic oppression.

As I aim to deconstruct systems of oppression and colonization, it is essential that I remind you of your own wisdom, insight, and contributions, just as I share my own wisdom, insight, and contributions in the following pages. From my places of oppression and trauma, I spent too much of my life discounting my ideas when they differed from someone else's, particularly from someone in power or with authority. This created a lot of internal conflict with regard to my passion for learning and taking in information.

I now have a better understanding of how oppression creates hierarchies around knowledge and wisdom. I think this is why I've avoided calling myself an *expert*. No matter how much I know, the more that I learn, the more I realize how much I still don't know! I urge you to honor your own brilliance and intuition and to not discount your own ideas. At the same time, when you notice that you disagree with me, I encourage you to stay connected to your internal experience and be curious. Perhaps you can ask yourself:

- Is this my privilege pushing back on things I wish weren't true or don't want to believe?
- Do I have a different way of relating to this idea that is a better fit for me and my clients based on my lived experience and sociocultural locations?
- Can I give myself permission to not agree with everything Nyck says?

Another note on language. Even though I am Autistic and KCS/VAST, because this book is intended for counselors of all neurotypes, whether that be Autistic, ADH/KCS/VAST, another type of neurodivergent, or neurotypical, I will generally write in the third person. A lot of thought and counsel went into this choice, and it was not an easy choice to make. This choice is not intended to distance myself or to center the neurotypical gaze, but to be the most accessible to the broadest audience. There will certainly be times when I overtly include myself in the writing.

I also use the word therapist and counselor interchangeably. I use the word client to refer to the people we are in service to. I also really appreciate the words practitioner and participant, respective alternatives offered by Dr. Jennifer Mullan (she/her), a Black Panamanian, multiracial author of the national bestselling book *Decolonizing Therapy: Oppression, Historical Trauma, & Politicizing Your Practice.*

I've chosen to use the word *racialized* in place of BIPOC. I've learned that some folx of color find the term BIPOC to be a form of erasure or minimization. Black folx, Indigenous folx, Latinx folx, Asian American and Pacific Islander folx, and folx of Southwest Asian and North African[1] descent all have profoundly diverse experiences, cultures, histories, and relationships to systemic oppression. When I am referring to a particular racial or ethnic group, I will be specific; otherwise I will use the word racialized.

I have chosen to capitalize the word Autistic whenever it is being used to describe a person or group's identity. This is an intentional choice to convey deep respect to a marginalized community, to honor our agency, and to express my support for the reclaiming of Autistic empowerment.

I've heard other authors name the ways that once a book is in print, it doesn't account for how the field or work is ever changing and ever evolving because it is a static object. I feel acutely aware of this myself. I recognize that the neurodiversity movement is very much a growing, evolving field, and the language I use today may not be the best or preferred language in times to come. I also recognize that as a person, author, and counselor, I am continually learning, growing, and evolving; as such, my work will continually grow and evolve too.

---

[1] I learned the term Southwest Asian and North African (SWANA) from Mahyar Nili (she/they), a trauma-informed, holistic, somatic, neurodiversity-loving, Islamo-friendly, invisible illness/disability understanding, Muslim SWANA therapist of color. SWANA is a more affirming and accurate term for people whose lineage is from what has been commonly referred to as "Middle Eastern." The term "Middle Eastern" stems from U.S. imperialism and colonization.

I also want to address how I envision this book being used. While it offers a modality of how to engage in therapeutic work, it is much more than that. It is a foundation for how we can approach the work of counseling that transcends any one particular modality. It is a framework for how we can take our existing theoretical orientations and apply them in an anti-ableist, anti-oppressive, neurodivergent-affirming way. It is not an attempt to alienate other approaches, but rather to offer a lens through which these other approaches can be applied to reduce harm and better meet our clients.

Along those lines, this book addresses how we can apply this framework both in our work with clients and also with ourselves. As counselors, our body, nervous system, intellect, and intuition are our greatest tools. As such, many of the chapters to come are divided into three sections: an overview of the topic, working with clients, and working with ourselves. This is an honoring of our own wholeness as counselors, human beings who have a sacred helping role.

While it may feel radical to tend to your humanness on your learning journey, I think this is a key part of ND-affirming approaches as I understand them. It is my intention that this book creates a ND-affirming learning experience for you that transcends cognitive pathways alone. As such, here is a key to explain symbols I use throughout this book: This will be our very first list together. This makes me giddy!

KEY: SYMBOLS AND TOOLS TO SUPPORT YOUR JOURNEY

- When I am offering an explicit experiential, kinesthetic learning opportunity to take what you are reading and integrate the cognitive with your felt sense or embodiment, I will use this icon of four trees on two hills:

Introduction xxi

> When you see that icon, it might be helpful to have a journal, art pad, or something nearby that you could use to write, draw, or doodle your thoughts, impressions, reflections, integration, and so on.
> - When I offer questions or ideas for reflection, I use this black diamond bullet point: ♦
> - General lists will use an unshaded circle as a bullet point, as in: o
> - I sprinkled reminders along the way to encourage you to check in with yourself, to notice how you are doing and what you may be needing, and to honor your own pacing.
> - I also name when transitions are approaching, and use four asterisks (****) to indicate a transition within a section.
> - Each section also ends with a recap summarizing what was covered.

There is a lot in the following pages. I encourage you to think of this as a journey we are taking together. On your journey, you may find yourself on a side quest, needing breaks, wanting to speed up or slow down, or desiring to engage with others in connection around the content. All of that is valid and good. While each chapter does build on the one before it, please honor whatever makes this experience the most accessible, digestible, and engaging for you and your learning style. If reading the chapters in the order they are presented doesn't work for you, feel free to play with and explore what order is a better fit for you.

As part of honoring your wholeness, no matter what your neurotype, I encourage you to take a moment and gather some sensory delights to have with you on this journey. Think cozy, pleasurable, or whatever engages your senses and supports you to be present. We'll be spending time in later chapters exploring how diverse sensory delights can be. In the meantime, consider food, snacks, beverages, comfy clothes, pleasant sounds, smells, textures, visuals, weight, movement, and anything else that may be nourishing to your system. This could also mean the absence of undesired input. There is no right or wrong way to engage with sensory delight!

Okay, I think that's all for now. Thanks again for being here with me. When you are ready, I look forward to joining you in Chapter 1!

NEURODIVERGENT SOMATICS IN THERAPY

PART I

CHAPTER 1

An Introduction to the Neurodiversity Paradigm and Important Terms

In the first three chapters of this book, I will lay out the foundation on which the rest of this book sits. To begin, we will cover an overview of the neurodiversity paradigm, contrast it with the pathology paradigm, and discuss what language to use and to avoid. I will also offer alternatives to the medical languaging of the ADHD (attention deficit hyperactivity disorder) neurotype. In the meantime, they are kinetic cognitive style (KCS) and variable attention stimulus trait (VAST). In Chapter 2, we will explore the validity of self-identification and qualities or attributes that might suggest that a client is Autistic and/or ADH/KCS/VAST. In Chapter 3, we will learn more about these two neurotypes specifically, including Autistic and ADH/KCS/VAST communication styles and culture. Before transitioning to the second part of this book, I will introduce the model that I have created for what I believe is the standard of care for quality neurodivergent-affirming, anti-ableist counseling.

Depending on how you were trained in graduate school, coupled with the continuing education you've been engaged with around neurodiversity, this content may be new for you, or it may be rather familiar. If you are new to my work, even if you are not new to the neurodiversity paradigm, I strongly suggest you still take the time to read these foundational chapters. I have been told many times by folx who are already working in the realm of the neurodiversity paradigm that they were surprised by how much they learned from this initial content. There is nuance to how I share this content that directly influences my approach to this work.

For people new to this content, you may be surprised to discover that the neurodiversity paradigm and neurodivergent-affirming counseling are anti-oppression work. That being said, some of what we cover in these first three chapters may be challenging to read, discover, or integrate. You may wish some things weren't true. You may be surprised by what you learn. This is why I present this content in as neurodivergent-affirming a style as possible. This is also why in the introduction I encouraged you to invite in sensory delight as much as possible, both in these beginning chapters and throughout the rest of this book.

While you may likely be reading this book because you are in the mental health profession and want to simultaneously increase your effectiveness while reducing harm with ND clients, you are also very much a human being reading too. Or as some Autistic and ADH/KCS/VAST folx like to joke, Earth-suit wearing beings that pass as human! That said, I want you to care for your wholeness here, including both your counselor self and your noncounselor self. You get to have needs and preferences. When I teach this work, I make a point of emphasizing that I approach this very differently from what we are accustomed to in "professional" trainings. That means centering who you are as a learner and reminding yourself that you also matter as an individual. That means bringing your wholeness along for the ride, to include body and mind. Or as Dr. Margaret Price (she/they), a white, genderqueer femme, disabled scholar and author likes to say: *bodymind*.[2] The two are inextricably linked and deeply interconnected.

---

[2] While Dr. Price popularized this term in the area of disability studies, bodymind was previously used by Shigenori Nagatomo, in *Attunement through the Body*, and Babette Rothschild, in *The Body Remembers*.

Whether you are an already identifying ND therapist, a questioning therapist (as it relates to your neurotype), or a neurotypical (NT)/neuronormative therapist, this content may impact you in unique ways. For some, it may feel deeply personal. For others, it may remind you of loved ones, clients, and community members, but may not touch you viscerally. And for yet others, you may feel disconnected from the content, but are curious to get an inside perspective from the lived and professional experience of a multiply-ND therapist. In any event, we all get to play with sensory delights, practice staying connected to our present moment experience, and noticing when we have needs to tend to that may involve taking a break, putting this away, or slowing down to allow for more integration. Our practice and learning are always strengthened when we open ourselves to diverse experiences, so regardless of where you sit: welcome.

If you haven't already, now is a great time to gather some sensory delights! Examples include, but are most certainly not limited to: beverage, snack, meal, fidgets, yummy smells, music, candle, cozy things, weighted things, or any forms of movement that do or don't require anything extra than your body. You may also want to reduce sensory input from your environment. As we go throughout this chapter and the rest of the book, I encourage you to track your own present-moment experience as you remember to. I will also offer occasional prompts for you to check in and notice how you are doing, what you might need, and encourage you to meet that need as you are able.

OVERVIEW OF THE NEURODIVERSITY PARADIGM

Despite many misperceptions, the term neurodiversity emerged collectively from members of the Autistic community and cousin members of the Autism Rights movement (Botha et al., 2024). Similar to how ecological diversity is innate and essential to the thriving of ecosystems, the concept behind neurodiversity posits that neurological diversity is natural and innate to human populations. Rather than the previously held notion that there is one superior or so-called "right" way to be human, also known as NT or neuronormative, there are actually a multitude of neurotypes, all equally valid and inherently good, or even perhaps, value neutral. Having a brain, body, and mind means that we have a neurotype. Some people's neurotype matches the dominant culture's expectations, while others diverge. Those who diverge are known as *neurodivergent*, a term coined by Kassiane Asasumasu (she/they), a biracial, multiply-neurodivergent Autistic advocate and activist. What matters most is that, in truth, there is no biologically inherent hierarchy of neurotype. Said another way, there is no one right way to think, perceive, process, socialize, engage, be, communicate, or experience being human.

With the introduction of language to describe neurological variation, and in response to the oppression faced by neurodivergent people, the neurodiversity paradigm or the neurodiversity movement was born. Neurodiversity joined the movement for equal rights, protections, awareness, supports, and celebration of difference, along with racial diversity, gender diversity, sexual orientation diversity, ability diversity, and so on. The neurodiversity movement recognizes that the basis of oppression faced by neurodivergent people stems from white supremacy, colonization, capitalism, neurotypicality, cisgender and heterosexual normativity, patriarchy, and more. Therefore, while there are many seemingly distinct diversity movements, they all have roots in white supremacy, colonization, and capitalism.

There are a vast number of ways to diverge from neurotypicality. A few examples include but are certainly not limited to: Down syndrome, Autism, ADH/KCS/VAST, posttraumatic stress (I avoid the "d" for disorder), complex posttraumatic stress, learning disabilities, traumatic brain injuries (TBI), bipolar, obsessive-compulsive, schizophrenia, epilepsy, multiple sclerosis, what are known as personality disorders, and so much more. Neurodivergences can be innate, like Autism, or acquired, like trauma or traumatic brain injury.

Neurodiverse refers to multiple neurotypes among two or more humans, such as Autistic and NT; ADH/KCS/VAST, Autistic, and NT; or Autistic and ADH/KCS/VAST, to name only a few of seemingly limitless possibilities. *Neurodivergent*, however, refers to one human who diverges from neurotypicality.

As a tenet of the diversity movement, there is ample advocacy and energy being poured into not just awareness of neurodivergence, but also effort to create greater access for individuals and communities to the accommodations and supports they need in order to exist and ultimately, to be well and thrive. It is about decentering neurotypicality, dismantling neurotypical privilege, and recognizing that not all people have the same needs, even looking at how spaces and environments are designed in support of people with sensory sensitivities.

Asasumasu coined the term neurodivergent to encompass all forms of diverging from neurotypicality, not any one specific neurotype. Over time, many people have come to relate neurodivergent (ND) as synonymous with autistic. This is not accurate, though. Throughout this book, I will name the specific neurotypes I'm referring to: Autism and ADH/KCS/VAST. Sometimes I will use the abbreviation ND rather than writing out both neurotypes. While this book focuses on the autistic and ADH/KCS/VAST neurotypes, its anti-oppressive, anti-ableist nature makes the philosophy well suited to many neurotypes.

While I'm choosing to focus on these two neurotypes, much of this book also applies to the *highly sensitive* neurotype and to those who identify as *empaths*, a lived experience of feeling, sensing, and/or knowing what others experience as though it is their own experience. Within the Autistic community, there are mixed opinions on whether or not highly sensitive is its own neurotype, or if it is a more socially acceptable label for someone who is actually Autistic. Some are adamant that not all Autistic people are highly sensitive, while others argue that using the label highly sensitive is a way to avoid the social stigma associated with autism. Similarly, with the term empath, some Autistics believe that word is a way of coding social stigma with a lofty spiritual label. I don't have a stance on this; I honor people's choices, especially informed choices.

I have been steeped in neurodivergence for many years now, both through my lived experience and in my career. It is easy for me to forget that the mainstream is significantly less versed in the neurodiversity paradigm and all things neurodivergence related. As a social justice counselor and activist, I am being explicit that this book is not about creating more boxes for people or labeling for the sake of adding labels. It is about reaching as broad an audience as possible so that we can create more support and reduce harm, regardless of how someone may articulate their neurotype. I am not here to argue over the language someone most identifies with, but to provide as much clear, thorough, and accurate information as I can to the mental health profession, which has a long way to go before being generally effective and not harmful to ND clients.

THE PATHOLOGY PARADIGM

This may be a great time to connect with your sensory delights. This is not pleasurable for me to write about, though it is absolutely necessary. You will hear me offer similar words multiple times throughout this chapter. Even though it is uncomfortable, history and the truth are still just that: history and truth. I like to qualify that I love my profession as a therapist and can't imagine having a different career in this life. That said, the origins and foundations of the mental health field and western psychology are deeply problematic and need to be named. Only by knowing these roots can we truly dismantle them.

It would be easy enough to just refer to the pathology paradigm as the prevailing paradigm that the mental health field and western psychology is founded upon (as are the medical field and others), one that is rooted in seeking out deficits and disorders and fixing them; said another way, it is the medical model. The pathology paradigm views autism and ADH/KCS/VAST as disorders and deficits, and as such, the only response is to cure, fix, or change them. Said another way, that means to contort people with these neurotypes to look, act, and communicate as closely to NT people as possible. Any variation from neurotypicality is viewed as an innate flaw that must be fixed or obliterated. People are seen as either whole or broken, and the only way to be whole is to be the socially dominant identities in the United States: white, cis-heteronormative, able-bodied, neurotypical, Christian, male, wealthy, and capitalist. Anyone who falls outside of those limited criteria is expected to effort their whole lives in order to be as close to the dominant identities as possible.

Ugh. Please take care of yourself and stay engaged with me as you are able to.

The pathology paradigm is characterized by the *Diagnostic and Statistical Manual* (*DSM*). This is considered to be the holy book of western psychology and is filled with disorders and deficits. For many counselors, this book was the foundation of graduate school. This book is steeped in the dominant sociocultural identities and locations mentioned above; it is the essence of white supremacy, colonization, and capitalism. Many are unaware of the horrifying history of this book and some of what has been contained in this book throughout time. Please stay connected with yourself and care for yourself as needed as we continue on. There are many I could share, but for the sake of our nervous systems and brevity, I'll only share two.

- In 1851, a white U.S. physician coined the diagnosis "drapetomania." I don't even want to share his name because I do not believe he is worthy of being named. He believed that enslaved Black people who wanted to be free were afflicted with madness. I feel rage pulsing through my body.
- Up until 1973, homosexuality was in the *DSM* and was labeled "sociopathic." My feels would be feeling even if I wasn't queer, but wow, being queer certainly ups the intensity.

I share all this *not* to hate on our profession, but to make sure that we are awake to reality and deeply understand why the neurodiversity paradigm is essential to the well-being of our clients. This is about understanding the intersections at play, the ways racism, particularly anti-Black racism, is tied to ableism, is tied to homophobia, is tied to transphobia. More to come.

Let's all take a moment to care for ourselves however we may need and are able to in this moment. I'm going to honor my impulse to stand and stretch, and then I'll return to share about language.

Recap: The Neurodiversity Paradigm vs. the Pathology Paradigm

- The neurodiversity paradigm recognizes that there are vast multitudes of neurotypes among human populations, and there is not an actual hierarchy or so-called "right" neurotype. We do, however, live in a culture where the dominant and privileged neurotype is neurotypical (NT).
- As a part of the diversity movement, the neurodiversity movement is working toward creating greater access to accommodations and support for those who need them.
- People who diverge from the dominant neurotype are known as neurodivergent (ND), a term coined by Kassiane Asasumasu. There are vast ways to diverge.
- In this book, we will be referring to two specific divergences: autism and ADH/KCS/VAST, although much of the content also applies to those who are highly sensitive, empaths, and other forms of neurodivergence.
- The pathology paradigm is rooted in looking at what's broken, identifying deficits and disorders, and fixing said problems. Western psychology and the *DSM* are rooted in white supremacy, capitalism, neurotypicality, cis-heteronormativity, able-bodiedness, wealth, and Christianity.

LANGUAGE TO USE AND TO AVOID

My stretch break happened to also include a piece of chocolate. How was your break?

As we continue, I'm reminded of a quote from Kieran Rose (he/they), The Autistic Advocate, a white Autistic man from the United Kingdom and coauthor of *Autistic Masking: Understanding Identity Management and the Role of Stigma*. I find it so valuable: "Autistic people are not broken NT people. [We] are perfectly whole Autistic people." When I heard this, it was such a lightbulb moment, even in its simplicity. You know how you can hear something hundreds of times, and then all of a sudden one day, you hear it as though you heard it for the first time? That was totally me when I heard him say this.

The irony of this section is that I do therapy in such a way that centers and prioritizes permission, and I continually offer my clients invitations, rather than directives. At the same time, however, language holds a great deal of power, and that power can be deeply harmful. This section is about gaining knowledge to reduce harm, and as such I will essentially be writing directives, or at least what I believe is best practice. You may notice some internal pushback about what I'm about to share. I invite you to notice it, be with it, and consider that even your internal reaction there may still be validity in my words.

First off, within the Autistic community, there is a preference for identity-first language. This is different from the person-first language that so many of us learned to use in graduate school. Unlike something someone may have, like a broken arm, neurotype is embodied and embedded throughout the bodymind; there is no separation of a human from their neurotype. Instead of "has autism" or "on the spectrum" (though some people in the community don't mind that phrase), it's "So and so is Autistic." If this language feels new or foreign to you, practice saying it aloud if you are able. You can make up a name or refer to someone you already know.

Let's actually try it. We can use me as an example: "Nyck is Autistic." I encourage you to notice how your body responds as you state that fact. "Nyck is Autistic." If you feel yourself tighten or contract, notice that, take a break if you need to, then say it a few more times. As Dr. Nick Walker, Autistic scholar and author of *Neuroqueer Heresies: Notes on the Neurodiversity Paradigm, Autistic Empowerment, and Postnormal Possibilities*, likes to say, "Autism is not a bad word." You may not realize how ingrained that socialization is within you. Just as getting used to they/them pronouns can take practice and repetition, so too can using identity-first language for an Autistic person. One more time: "Nyck is Autistic!" This time with joy!

Before we continue, I need to offer a note about language as it relates to identity. While I'm providing you with general rules that I'd like you to digest and implement, when it comes to people in marginalized sociocultural locations, only they have the power to claim what their identities are. What I mean is it is your job to ask your clients specifically what language they prefer to use to express their identities. It is *not okay* for us to tell people what language they need to use to identify themselves. That is an individual choice. Even as we continue and I offer words to use and to avoid, you may have clients who use words on the avoid list. What I do in those situations is share about that specific language and give them the knowledge to choose for themselves what feels most in alignment for them.

One more note on identity-first language. Someone I love to learn from is Tiffany Hammond, perhaps better known as Fidgets and Fries, author of the *New York Times* bestselling book *A Day With No Words*. As a Black Autistic person and mama, she generously shares about her and her Autistic sons' relationship to language and identity. Some days, she and her son Aidan prefer identity first. Other times, they prefer person first. Her son Jojo chooses person first. As Black folx in the United States, their Blackness is often noticed and responded to before their neurotype. Especially as a white therapist, it would not ever be okay for me to tell a client "you have to use identity-first language." Instead, what might be okay is to express genuine curiosity and ask my client if they are willing to share about their language preference as a way for me to better know and understand them.

Moving on. For the sake of simplicity, I'm going to offer a basic chart, and then I'll share more details.

Table 1.1

Language to Avoid	→	What to Use Instead
ASD & Autism Spectrum Disorder	→	Autism or Autistic
Asperger's	→	Autism or Autistic
High-functioning/ Low-functioning	→	Refer to specific support needs
Non-verbal	→	Non-speaking
Diagnosed	→	Identified/Realized/Discovered
Pathological Demand Avoidance (PDA)	→	Persistent Demand Avoidance (PDA) or Persistent Drive for Autonomy (PDA)
ADHD	→	ADH (mediocre alternative) or Kinesthetic Cognitive Style (KCS) or Variable Attention Stimulus Trait (VAST)

ASD AND AUTISM SPECTRUM DISORDER → AUTISM OR AUTISTIC

Let's start with the first "No!" Autism is not a disorder; it is a distinct and valid neurotype. I know that autism exists in the *DSM* as "Autism Spectrum Disorder," which is often abbreviated to "ASD." Just don't. My body has a visceral response to these words that is hard to describe. I think it's the energy of the historical and present-moment trauma associated with the autistic neurotype. The prevailing narrative is that "It's better to be anything but Autistic." We have the power in our profession to change this. We can, from here on out, change our language, no matter who we are talking to. I get that dealing with insurance companies may be the one time this cannot be avoided. Otherwise, omit it from your vocabulary (sorry to any PDAers who did not appreciate my directive). It's autism from here on out.

ASPERGER'S → AUTISM OR AUTISTIC

Next: Asperger's. You may have clients who use this to identify themselves, and they likely don't know the history behind this word, so you can respectfully share it with them. Asperger's was in former versions of the *DSM* and was known as *cringe* "high-functioning autism." In the *DSM-V*, it got lumped into the autistic umbrella. When Steve Silberman first wrote the book *Neurotribes* about the history of autism, less was known about Hans Asperger than we know at present. The man credited with naming this neurotype was a Nazi.

Because of the stigma associated with autism, versus "Aspies" (short for Asperger's) being *merely* quirky and more likely to pass as NT, some Autistic people hold dear to the term Asperger's. This may be especially true if they came into their Autistic identity when Asperger's was commonly used. But when most people learn the history, both what I have already shared and what I'm about to share, they are often shocked and disturbed. Consider that your trigger warning for what's about to come next. Sensory delights, anyone?!

HIGH-FUNCTIONING/LOW-FUNCTIONING → REFER TO SPECIFIC SUPPORT NEEDS

High-functioning/Low-functioning: I really dislike talking and writing about these terms. Oftentimes, the more basic level of these terms is only what is shared, but as I've said, knowing the history of things helps us to better understand the why and be more invested in dismantling. I'll start with the aspects that are harder to digest and lesser known, then get to the more practical aspects. As we learned in the term before this one, we now know that Asperger was a Nazi. He wasn't the potentially noble fellow we thought he was when *Neurotribes* was published. During the Holocaust, the kids in Asperger's care were divided into two groups. One group was deemed "high-functioning" and were known as the little scientists. They were perceived as very verbal, having high intelligence, and very likely to contribute something *gag* "meaningful" to society. *These people were allowed to live.* Ah, deep breath (that's more for me than you, but if a deep breath would be supportive for you as well, I encourage it).

The other group was deemed "low-functioning." They were the kids who were likely nonspeaking, perhaps had intellectual disabilities rendering them "not smart" in the eyes of professionals, and were less independent. They were perceived to be "burdens" on society, rather than "meaningful contributors." *These people were killed.*

I notice a lot of energy pulsing through my system as I feel this and share this. I'm inviting the energy to be present with me, to flow as it chooses to, to remain open in the face of this pain and horror. It can be so easy, even habitual, to contract in the presence of emotional and historical pain. I'm allowing my breath to keep me connected to myself, present. In this presence, I am aware of many other genocides that have happened and are currently happening, many other groups of humans who have been sacrificed.

I notice I'm sweating now. My body is processing all of this energy. It wouldn't be authentic of me to not acknowledge others whose cellular memory knows this history, too, particularly in relation to the United States. I would like to acknowledge and honor the Indigenous peoples of Turtle Island, Black people, Palestinians, and Jewish people. Many other groups have also been profoundly oppressed. My heart is feeling called to my grief altar at the moment (in Chapter 9, we will explore the topic of ritual and the Sacred).

I encourage you to tend to yourself as you choose to. I notice myself calling on my ancestors and expanding my heart connection with the land I am on at the moment, which is the stolen land and the waters of the Wabanaki. I do not expect my body to be able to hold this energy by itself; it is too vast and historical. I will, however, allow it to move through me. I will go put my feet on the Earth so that I can feel deeper connection to what holds us in all of it, the beauty and the horror.

Having spent some time outside, then bouncing and jumping up and down a bit while making sounds and feeling my weight, I am ready to return. I feel grateful to have taken and shared a moment of support for my deeply empathetic, justice-sensitive self, allowing the fullness of my sensitivity to exist and be cared for. Please know that if you did not feel impacted by the previous paragraphs as I did, you are not any better or worse than me, just different; this is all the more reason why we need neuro-affirming approaches that honor *all* people.

Big exhale. Moving on to the practical elements of functioning labels. They are also harmful because they negate who a person is and what they actually need. For those considered "high functioning," they effort to pass as NT, often negating their very real but perhaps less obvious support needs. There is no such thing as "a little Autistic." This is where differences in support needs arise. The term high-functioning, similar to Asperger's, is often used to distance oneself or one's children from the stigma of being Autistic.

Those deemed "low-functioning," may be nonspeaking and have a variety of support needs related to things like eating, dressing, toileting, and communicating. This functioning label perpetuates a harmful narrative of infantilizing and dehumanizing these Autistic people. Their intelligence, wisdom, skills, capacity, and wholeness get completely overlooked.

As we integrate the use of support needs, let's avoid replicating the message of functioning labels. Instead of high support needs or low support needs, let's refer specifically to the types of support needs a person has.

NONVERBAL → NONSPEAKING

People who do not use what we think of as verbal language spoken from their body to communicate often use other forms of communication such as sounds, gestures, pictures, spelling, and other augmentative and alternative communication devices (AAC) that use words and pictures. While still deemed controversial in the eyes of mainstream science and those embedded in the pathology paradigm, telepathy is another common form of communication for nonspeakers. Telepathy is most simply defined as reading minds, yet is much more broad in scope. *The Telepathy Tapes*, a podcast hosted by Ky Dickens, an award winning filmmaker, interviews neuroscientists who study telepathy in nonspeakers and features many nonspeakers who share about their lived experiences with telepathy. Calling someone nonverbal perpetuates the infantilizing mentioned above and is inaccurate. Nonspeaking is more affirming and accurate.

DIAGNOSED → IDENTIFIED/REALIZED/DISCOVERED

Diagnosis insinuates something is broken and needs to be or can be fixed; it is the pathology paradigm. It also requires someone with particular sets of credentials to make said diagnosis. Neurotypes are innate and value neutral, therefore they are identified, realized, or discovered. As we will get to in Chapter 2, self-identified or self-realized is equally valid.

I dream of a future when neurotypes are talked about at an early age and doctors or psychologists no longer play a middle person or gatekeeper role. Just like I didn't go to a doctor or therapist to tell me I was queer or trans, I hope we get to a point when other people don't have authority over one's neurotype either. Maybe we'll also get to a point where no kid, teen, or adult ever has to come out, because cis-heteronormativity and neurotypicality are no longer perceived as the default way of being. Wanda Sykes, a Black queer comedian, did an awesome spoof on this theme where she talked about "coming out as Black" to her parents.

To avoid any possible misunderstanding, I want to be clear that plenty of Autistic and ADH/KCS/VAST people need support for their co-occurring medical or mental health symptoms or conditions. This is valid and real. This is completely separate from a medical professional having the power to affirm or deny one's sense of self.

PATHOLOGICAL DEMAND AVOIDANCE (PDA) → PERSISTENT DEMAND AVOIDANCE (PDA) OR PERSISTENT DRIVE FOR AUTONOMY (PDA)

At present, PDA is known as a subtype of autism and is not in the *DSM* in the United States. It has been much more widely studied in places like the United Kingdom and Australia, though it is more commonly talked about in the United States now too. While some degree of demand avoidance is common for all Autistic people (I'd say ADH/KCS/VAST too), PDAers have what is sometimes called a nervous system disability. Their nervous system is so acutely attuned to threat that the presence of a demand, whether from someone external or from oneself, is perceived as a threat. An example could be having an assignment due. At the same time, even so-called pleasurable demands, like "Let's go on a hike this afternoon"—whether external or internal—can register as a threat. While anxiety is common for many Autistic and ADH/KCS/VAST folx, PDAers have even more pervasive anxiety. Anytime their autonomy is in question, their threat response can get signaled.

Given that *pathological* is literally in the name, I think it's pretty obvious that this name is from the pathology paradigm. The PDA community has reclaimed it as either Persistent Demand Avoidance or Persistent Drive for Autonomy. You may see other deviations as well.

ADHD → ADH (MEDIOCRE ALTERNATIVE) OR KINESTHETIC COGNITIVE STYLE (KCS) OR VARIABLE ATTENTION STIMULUS TRAIT (VAST)

First off, this term is totally inaccurate, plus it is deeply harmful. How this neurotype appears in the *DSM* is "Attention Deficit Hyperactivity Disorder." This screams pathology paradigm. While the Autistic community tends to give a lot of pushback when people use language like ASD or spell out the acronym, I've noticed much more acceptance of the use of ADHD. I don't think that's okay. While there is less intense societal stigma with this neurotype than with autism, it still gets plenty of invalidation and shame. As a mediocre alternative, I've been using the abbreviated letters ADH to bring awareness to this term being problematic. Even better options are the following two other alternatives that have been suggested; hopefully we can get enough traction with these to create a systemic shift. These alternatives are kinetic cognitive style (KCS), coined by Dr. Nick Walker, and variable attention stimulus trait (VAST), coined by Drs. Edward Hallowell and John Ratey, coauthors of *ADHD 2.0*. Both of these shift the focus from deficits to a whole person perspective that includes ample strengths. When I've shared these terms with clients, it's almost as if they intuitively sense the innate accuracy of these terms.

Here are some ways that clients may trade out the term ADHD or even ADH for one or both of these affirming alternatives: some people refer to themselves as kinetic, while others refer to themselves as KCS, as VAST, or as KCS/VAST. From now on, instead of ADH, I will refer to this neurotype as KCS/VAST.

Let's now address the inaccuracy. If you are or you know anyone who is KCS/VAST, then you know full well that when it comes to an area of passion or interest, there is no shortage of attention. There is a plethora of attention, also known as hyperfocus. The perceived lack of attention shows up when there is a lack of interest. Both this neurotype and autism are interest-based systems, meaning that focus and attention are directly tied to engagement of interest. Kinetic, in **KCS**, and variable, in **VAST**, both refer to these differences in how attention is distributed. Attention stimulus in **VAST** refers to the impact of sensory and other input from the environment on a person. Both cognitive style, in **KCS**, and trait, in **VAST**, refer to this as a neurotype, rather than a disordered way of being.

Also, there is a transition component here that often gets

missed. When a KCS/VAST person is deeply engaged with something, there is a period of time required for them to disengage their attention, shift attention, and then reengage with something else. Monotropism is another way to describe this vortex of attention or singular focus and the need for transition time both into and out of that state. This focused attention can also be referred to as a flow state or hyperfocus. Both neurotypes are monotropic in nature. Multiple Autistic people are credited with the concept of monotropism, including Dr. Dinah Murray, Dr. Wenn Lawson, and Mike Lesser; Jeanette Buirski, Dr. Murray's friend, named the idea.

So far, there has been a lot of emphasis on the autistic neurotype, with seemingly less on KCS/VAST. I want to point out that these two neurotypes share a great deal of overlap. First off, depending on what studies you look at, research shows anywhere from 30–80% of Autistic people are also KCS/VAST. I've seen some people suggest that KCS/VAST belongs under the autistic spectrum umbrella. Both neurotypes have a sensory component, a social component, and executive function challenges, and they are monotropic. There are also many other co-occurrences that people with these neurotypes deal with, including physical ones like Ehlers-Danlos syndrome (EDS), hypermobility, food sensitivities, postural orthostatic tachycardia syndrome (POTS), sleep differences, autoimmune conditions, migraines, and so much more. There is also a greater likelihood of co-occurring depression, anxiety, bipolar, obsessive-compulsive, trauma/complex trauma, or what we call personality disorders, which are starting to be better understood as unique and creative behavioral responses to complex trauma.

One more thought about this neurotype. While KCS/VAST is commonly associated with low dopamine levels or having fewer dopamine receptors, this is not the whole truth. I first learned about this from Janae Elisabeth (she/they), a white Autistic researcher and ND advocate who is well known online as Trauma Geek. Rather than low dopamine being an innate trait, dopamine gets converted to noradrenaline and then adrenaline, which is associated with a stress response. Due to oppression, trauma, and being forced to focus on things that are not of interest (rather than on dopamine-producing interest-based activities), dopamine gets depleted in order to produce adrenaline.[3] This will become especially relevant in Chapter 4 when we explore prioritizing parasympathetic states.

We've reached the end of this chapter. Now is a great time to check in with yourself and notice if there is anything you want or need including a break, the bathroom, food or drink, movement, rest, stimming, or something else. When you are ready, I'll meet you in Chapter 2 about identification and attributes of autism and KCS/VAST.

Recap: Language to Use and to Avoid
- See Table 1.1 for a summary of the language to use and to avoid.
- Bear in mind that it is up to marginalized folx to choose what language they use to articulate their identities. They hold that power, not us as counselors.
- From now on, instead of ADH, I will be using the term KCS/VAST to articulate that neurotype.

---

[3] If you'd like to learn more, an interesting article to read is "How Chronic Stress Feeds Suffering by Eating Up Our Dopamine" by Gary Sharpe, published in *Mad in America* on March 22, 2024.

CHAPTER 2
Accessing Identification and Attributes of Autism and KCS/VAST

Welcome back. Now that we have established the language we will be using and avoiding and why, we're going to use that foundation to explore the importance of identification and especially the validity of self-identification. Gaining language for one's neurotype(s) can be an essential part of self-knowing, self-validation, and dismantling internalized oppression. We will also learn more about how Autistic and KCS/VAST people present across sociocultural locations. The list I provide is intended to broaden our scope of what we previously thought autism was and wasn't and to notice the similarities and differences with KCS/VAST. We will continue to wade through the impacts of systemic oppression on the psychology field and on our clients directly. Please continue to care for yourself in any and all ways that you may need or want to, including honoring your own pace.

SELF-IDENTIFICATION

I'm going to focus on autism in this section. Self-identification is absolutely just as valid for people with the KCS/VAST neurotype, and getting a KCS/VAST external identification is often more accessible than for autism.

We have already discussed the challenges with the *DSM* and western psychology, but there's more specific to the autistic neurotype that we'll get to now. Autism is depicted in the *DSM* based on the experience of a very limited subpopulation: white, cisgender, heterosexual, middle-to-upper class boys in distress. On the one hand, this is not actually all that surprising given what we have already talked about. On the other hand, this leaves out a vast number of people and explains why the only widespread view of autism that most people have is what is known as the stereotypical presentation.

The holy book of psychology that is intended to be a guide for mental health of all humans (I wish you could see my snarky smile in this moment) has eliminated a huge segment of the population: all racialized people, women, nonbinary people, transgender people, gender nonconforming people, intersex people, bi/gay/asexual/pan/queer people, poor people, and people in states of pleasure or neutrality. No wonder it's a novel concept to the masses that someone can be Autistic and joyful, or Autistic and Black, or Autistic and poor, or Autistic and a woman.

Given these primary factors:

- How much sheer lack of information or misinformation is out there.
- Waiting lists for assessments from psychologists and neuropsychologists can be upwards of a year or more (and they still may not know anything about nonstereotypical presentations).
- Prevalence of misidentification or incomplete identification: oftentimes anxiety, depression, bipolar, obsessive-compulsive, trauma, personality disorders (particularly borderline for people assigned female at birth), and/or KCS/VAST are given. While any of these can co-occur with autism, they could be incorrect or incomplete. Unidentified Black Autistic kids are much more likely than their white unidentified Autistic peers to be identified as having oppositional defiance or a conduct disorder instead of autism.

- The enormous costs of assessments (they can cost upwards of $5,000 or more, and those fees often are not covered by insurance).
- No one knows anyone better than they know themselves, so people who have long histories of masking and working tirelessly to blend in with NTs are often told profoundly harmful things like "you can't be Autistic, you make eye contact" or other absurdities like "you have a job, you can't be Autistic" or "you have friends, you can't be Autistic."

Self-identification of autism is completely valid and just as valid as any medical or psychiatric identification.

It's easy for me to get fired up about this. I've worked with so many clients over the years who've researched tirelessly about autism, only to finally work up the courage and finances to get an assessment and then be denied their Autistic identity. On top of the trauma of living as an unidentified Autistic person for potentially decades, they endure more trauma from the medical and psychology fields. By the time they make their way to my virtual office, having endured way too much, usually within the first hour of knowing them, I'm like: "It's obvious to me that you're Autistic!"

This may leave you wondering, "If the *DSM* is so problematic and incomplete, why bother labeling the neurotype at all?" Great question, to which I have an answer. Keep reading. If you could see my face, you'd see me smiling.

For some people, it's the only way to get their support needs met. For others, especially later identified people assigned female at birth, who may have spent decades being invalidated in their challenges, blamed for their challenges, and isolated, receiving an Autism identification can be a full-on game changer. Having language for one's neurotype can both be a profound relief or source of liberation and a source of tremendous grief, maybe even rage, and everything in between.

> "You mean it's not my fault?!"
> "There's a reason I am the way that I am?!"
> "I'm not broken?!"
> "Who am I, then?"

The potential onslaught of thoughts and feelings can be deep and vast. At the same time, with language comes information, validation, access to knowing oneself, identification of support needs, and hopefully, getting those support needs met.

This is where we, ND-affirming, anti-ableist therapists come in to help them reframe their life through this new Autistic lens and help them identify and access the support they need. What this also means is that imposter syndrome is likely. In fact, I've known a lot of people, whether medically or self-identified, who navigate ongoing cycles of imposter syndrome. It's hard not to in the dominant U.S. culture that labels any challenges we face as a moral failing based solely on our own efforts or supposed lack of effort. We get so accustomed to blaming ourselves that it's easy to feel that "Autism is just an excuse."

Oh, I feel the heartbreak in that statement. Both I and so many clients I've worked with over the years have echoed that sentiment. Talk about oppression in action. Part of my own unmasking journey has involved gaining access to my anger and rage, something I wasn't allowed to feel or express growing up in my family of origin. Needless to say, anger and rage come to visit quite often these days, this moment being no exception. It's a truly valid reaction, if I do say so myself.

Have you checked in with yourself lately? How are you doing? Would you like to pause, move, play, eat, drink, or take a break? When you're ready, there's some more to cover in this section.

When it comes to identifying autism in the United States, there's a misnomer out there that only PhD or PsyD credentials have the authority. For master's level therapists, there are many states in which it is very much within the scope of their license to offer this identification to clients. Each state regulates this differently, so they may need to do some research to see what their state allows. Some clients may want us to validate their neurotype for them, while others may come to us already confident in their neurotype. In any event, there is a myriad of support we can help clients to access as their therapist. Over the years, I've written many letters for clients helping them to access accommodations at work or in higher education.

That said, there are some caveats where master's level credentials fall short.

- When it comes to accessing government funding, particularly disability funding, a doctoral level identification is required. From what I've seen, this is similar for state or county funding that may offer grant money to Autistic people. It's best to check what is available and what the requirements are in your area.
- To access an individualized education plan (IEP) in the public school system, generally a doctoral level identification is required. Sometimes the school district will provide and fund this, though it may not be as comprehensive as an out-of-school assessment.
- Some people have been so deeply conditioned to believe that only doctoral level credentials are worthy or valid that they may choose that extra validation in order to take the identification seriously.

Of equal importance to note, there are times when medical or psychiatric identification could be harmful. I share this so that you can be fully informed and use this information as you counsel clients (both adult clients and parents) about their choices regarding external identification versus self-identification. These next bullet points are steeped in oppression; please tend to yourself as you need to:

- At the time of this writing, the U.S. government has made a number of alarming and offensive statements about the Autistic community. It is hard to know how this will unfold over time. They have been using a lot of erasure-type language, creating a lot of concern about safety for Autistic people. When accommodations and support needs can be met without having an Autistic identity on public or private record, it may be safer to do so. This is not possible for so many people. This is heartbreaking to write. What is unfolding on the national level is the antithesis of a ND-affirming approach to autism.
- Also at the time of this writing, there is a massive backlash toward trans people. There are states that will not allow trans Autistic people to access gender-affirming care. These states view autism as a preexisting condition that disqualifies them for gender-affirming care. There are also situations where health insurance will not cover gender-affirming care if it is documented that a person is Autistic. Some individuals (depending on their support needs), are forced to choose between accessing potentially lifesaving accommodations for their autism *or* accessing potentially lifesaving gender-affirming care. My heartbreak is shifting into anger. I'm envisioning the emoji with the bursting red cheeks and deeply furrowed brow. Grrrr. More to come on this in the section "The Intersections Between Queerness, Transness, and Neurodivergence" later in this chapter.
- Here's another anticipatory "Grrrr." I know what I'm about to share, so I'm letting you know in advance. Custody cases are another situation where having it on file that someone is Autistic could be deeply harmful. There have been many cases in which parents have lost custody over their children because the parent is Autistic. Oh, I feel the rage growing; now the emoji has smoke blowing out its ears.

I think we deserve a break after that. I'm going to opt for some movement to allow this intensity to flow through me as it needs and wants to. So much profound injustice. Talk about *sacred rage* as Dr. Jennifer Mullan, who I introduced in the introduction, calls it. This is collective and ancestral rage, sheer aliveness pulsating through me that is so much bigger than me, that is yearning to be tended to.

* * * *

Wow, that was deeply restorative. Once I stepped away from writing, the pause helped me to identify that I actually wanted rest more than active movement. I opted for legs-up-the-wall pose with my hands interlaced under my head. This helped me to connect with the ground beneath me and the Earth that holds me. Thank you, parasympathetic nervous system, for showing up! I'm way more sleepy than I previously realized. Generations of oppression is exhausting. It makes me want to appreciate you all the more for taking the time to read this book and educate yourself about how you can be an even better ally to the Autistic and KCS/VAST communities.

I'd like to check in with you. I wonder how you are doing and what you noticing for yourself? You may be having a totally different experience than me, and that is totally okay! We've reached the end of this section. Please honor your pacing.

Recap: Self-Identification
- The *DSM* portrays a particularly limited scope of autism, namely that of white, cis-het, middle-to-upper class boys in distress.
- There is no accounting for racialized people, women, nonbinary people, transgender people, gender-expansive people, intersex people, bi/gay/asexual/pan/queer people, poor people, and people in states of pleasure or neutrality.
- Self-identification is valid and just as valid as external identification.

- Identification provides much-needed language to help a person understand themself, including to reframe their life through the Autistic lens, identify support needs, and hopefully be able to access those needs.
- There are many barriers to accessing doctoral level external identification, and sometimes such external identification can even be harmful.
- In many states, master's level clinicians can provide external identification.

POSSIBLE QUALITIES OR TRAITS THAT COULD INDICATE A PERSON IS AUTISTIC

Before I share the list that I've come up with, I want to mention that many of these qualities also apply to KCS/VAST. I'll point out some differences along the way, and the reality is that there are way more similarities than differences between these two neurotypes. This list transcends what exists in the *DSM* and encompasses many nonstereotypical qualities.

For starters, there is *no* one way to be Autistic. When I read my first book about autism 15 years ago, this was true. It is still true today. As the saying goes, "When you've met one Autistic person, you've met one Autistic person." We are a beautifully diverse neurotype. Also, autism is so much more than a particular subset of behaviors; it is a different *bodymind*. Lastly, given that only one tiny subset of the Autistic population is represented within the *DSM* and that by the time people reach adulthood they have often learned a multitude of strategies for existing within the neurotypical (NT) world, it is essential that we have a broader picture of what autism is. Please note: not everyone will identify with every one of these characteristics.

- They report a lifetime of anxiety, sometimes depression too.
- They report feeling different or misunderstood.

- They have specific sensory needs, preferences, and aversions.
  - The sensory component of these two neurotypes is extremely important and can often be overlooked or downplayed. Each person, Autistic or KCS/VAST, has their own unique sensory profile that likely includes a combination of sensory seeking and sensory avoiding. I feel like Autistic people are more commonly known for their sensory overwhelm, while KCS/VAST people are more known for their understimulation. This is not entirely true, though, as both neurotypes can and do experience both. The sensory world can be a source of deep distress; it can also be a source of euphoria and joy!
  - There are eight senses that are essential: in addition to sight, sound, taste, touch, and smell (to which not all humans have access), we also have three more. Proprioception is about knowing where we are in space, where our body ends and the air or environment begins. Deep pressure, containment, and touch can help us access this knowing. Interoception is inner body awareness, which includes cues like hunger, thirst, need to rest, need to eliminate, or any other body sensation. Vestibular is connected to the inner ear and balance and is accessed through rhythmic movements like rocking, swaying, or spinning.
- They have some degree of discomfort, confusion, and/or anxiety when it comes to being social with other humans.
  - Autistic people have their own unique communication style, including body language, that is often misunderstood by non-Autistic people (more on this when we talk about the double empathy problem). For KCS/VAST people, it's less that they don't understand NT communication, but more that their

tendency toward having many thoughts at once and taking in so much at once makes them more likely to miss certain cues or communication.
- They can be easily overwhelmed and when they are really distressed or overwhelmed they may melt down, shut down, explode, implode, or self-injure.
  - This looks different person to person and across the two neurotypes. While this is certainly not true of everyone, there seems to be a trend (based on how the binary genders are socialized) that assigned male at birth (AMAB) people tend to express their distress more externally and seemingly, more obviously. Oftentimes, assigned female at birth (AFAB) people tend to internalize more often, making their struggles seem invisible to others. Self-harm, such as cutting, counts in the meltdown category. Racial identity and racism also directly affect how people are allowed or not allowed to express their overwhelm.
- Certain things just don't make sense to them, and they don't know why. Alternatively, things that are obvious to them may be not at all obvious to others.
- They may or may not make eye contact.
  - For some Autistic people, eye contact is actually more distracting than it is connecting. Possibly due to less synaptic pruning, Autistic people take in vast amounts of information at any given moment, and it is too much to filter. Not making eye contact can provide less input, which often results in *more* focus.[4]

---

[4] While this may be considered "common knowledge" these days, I first came to really understand the relationship between eye contact and autism when I read Temple Grandin's book *The Autistic Brain: Helping Different Kinds of Minds Succeed.*

- They are easily distracted or have a hard time staying focused, specifically when something isn't interesting to them.
- They have some sort of movement, sound, or other behavior that they engage in repetitively that helps them feel more relaxed, present, engaged, or safe. This is called stimming and is an essential part of self-regulation.
  - Stimming is a wonderful thing! It's a part of Autistic innate brilliance that the bodymind knows how to regulate itself as needed. Stimming can be fun, playful, creativity enhancing, relaxing, or energizing. There are endless ways to stim! A lot of people are trained out of their more visible stims as a way to appear more NT or less "weird," which is really sad. The more well-known Autistic stims are rocking and flapping, but they can be big movements or barely visible.
  - Both neurotypes stim, but oftentimes it's referred to as fidgeting for KCS/VAST.
  - It is my perception that stimming has more stigma associated with it, while fidgeting is somewhat more socially acceptable. That said, there is still plenty of judgment out there about engaging in repetitive movement. White supremacy prefers people to have "quiet hands and bodies." Ick!
- They may seem really intense or deep.
  - Small talk may be a struggle.
- They may report a history of feeling disconnected from other humans, lonely, or misunderstood and have a deep longing for connection with others.
- They need alone time.
- They are extremely passionate about certain topics or areas of interest. This is sometimes referred to as *special interests/SPINs*, but that can have a condescending connotation, so I choose to say *passions*.

- Autistic people may have the same passion for years, even decades. Their depth of knowledge about the topic is likely profound and nuanced. It's common for KCS/VAST people's passions to change more frequently. These are not absolutes by any means. Due to oppression, many KCS/VAST people get accused of "not following through," "losing interest too easily," or "jumping from thing to thing." Whether long term or short term, these passions are not just valid but important and vital to that person's aliveness and well-being (more on this in Chapter 10, Pleasure/Neutrality: Joy!).

  o They prefer routines and can seem rigid.
    - A primary difference between the two neurotypes is that Autistic people tend to crave sameness, predictability, and knowing what to expect. KCS/VAST people, on the other hand, tend to crave novelty as part of producing more dopamine for their brain. This is also why their passions may change more frequently, because once the novelty wears off a passion may no longer be as interesting.
  o They may relate to the terms *highly sensitive person* or *empath*.
  o No matter how much self-growth work they've engaged in, some things just don't change.
    - Many times, unidentified Autistic and/or KCS/VAST people are long-term clients who may be on a perpetual journey to try to change who they are. They may be deeply invested in the narrative that "This is a *me* problem, and if I just try harder, I'll be 'normal' like everybody else." They may change therapists multiple times to try to find someone who can finally help fix them. They may try to induce their therapist into believing their narrative; together you may find yourselves in cahoots with their belief that they

are "broken" and you can be the hero they've been searching for. Turns out, you just might be! But not in the way they anticipated. You may be the person to finally help them accept that they aren't broken, they're Autistic and/or KCS/VAST!
- They have a hard time with executive functions such as being on time, managing all the different responsibilities of life/home/adulthood (e.g., cleaning, laundry, groceries and cooking, bills, scheduling appointments), staying organized, advocating for themselves, navigating new situations, and so on.
  - Sometimes called "adulting" for people who are adults. Both neurotypes have varying difficulties with this. For kids this is most often obvious with things like the state or disarray of their room or challenges at school. Much more to come on this in Chapter 7 on accommodations and executive function supports.
- The more they heal from trauma, the more sensitive they become.
  - Let's use an example of a particular loud sound, say a siren. With trauma work, one would suppose that over time the sound of the siren and the memories associated with it would get integrated into the system and be less disturbing. The person may never like or have an affinity for that sound, but the trigger may diffuse or get easier to tolerate. For Autistic and KCS/VAST people, healing from trauma can make the unwanted loud sound even more difficult to deal with. Healing and unmasking can increase sensitivity, not lessen it.
- They may be easily influenced, a "chameleon" becoming like the others in their environment.
  - When I learned this, it was a total lightbulb moment for me. It was what I needed to move beyond

the perpetual (not cyclical at the time) imposter syndrome in my self-acceptance as an actually Autistic person. This is especially common in high-masking AFAB folx. They can feel that they have a diffuse sense of self or lack a sense of self, but it can also make them really adaptable. It is often not something that is done consciously, and it can very much be a survival strategy. You may hear clients refer to "becoming who the environment expects them to be." This can be a form of code switching, is tied to intersectionality, and is about passing as "safe enough" or "normal" in the presence of dominant sociocultural identities. It is deeply tied to masking (more to come on this).

- Regulating emotions can be really challenging.
  - Perhaps they tend to a feel a lot and frequently, and their emotions seem to shift quickly.
  - They may not know what they are feeling; it can feel more like a "jumbled internal indecipherable" landscape, also known as alexithymia (there's a lot happening inside, but I don't know what it is or why I feel it).
- They may experience heightened sensitivity to injustice, also known as justice sensitivity.
  - In children, this can present behaviorally as inflexibility in the face of real or perceived injustice, especially with siblings, peers, or people in positions of power. It can also present as deep distress over injustices like climate change, racism, homophobia, transphobia, eating meat, animal abuse, or abuse of any kind.
  - In adults, it may be more visible through activism and investment in social justice. Again though, there is deep distress over injustice, deep empathy for the abused planet, people, or beings on the receiving end

of injustice, and a profound internal drive to make right what is wrong, unfair, and unjust.
- They may be very sensitive to rejection, whether actual or perceived, or fear of possible rejection, also known as rejection sensitivity dysphoria (RSD).
  - This is being more talked about lately with KCS/VAST, though it's definitely a lesser known but important attribute of this neurotype. Rejection can signal a threat response and be a very real source of trauma.
- They have pattern recognition.
  - They tend to notice trends and connections among things or ideas and have a way of weaving together past, present, and future.
- They are curious about their neurology and find themselves wondering if they might be Autistic or KCS/VAST.
  - Just as straight and cisgender people don't tend to question their identities or spend months if not years researching queerness or transness, learning everything they possibly can, losing sleep over it, maybe even talking to every person who will listen about it, neither do neurotypical people when it comes to their neurotype. It just is. It's not a question.
- They tend to like or connect more easily with or gravitate toward other Autistic or KCS/VAST people.
- They have family-of-origin members who are also Autistic or KCS/VAST.
  - There is definitely a genetic component here. It's common for one person to be identified and then suddenly many others in the lineage get identified, too. Sometimes a child gets identified and then there is a trickle-up effect. Or an adult will get identified, then discover their child(ren) shares their neurotype, or siblings, parents, and other relatives.

As you read through this list, even more ideas may come to mind. Whether you are Autistic or KCS/VAST or love people who are, there may be aspects of who you are or relate to that didn't make it onto this list. These aspects are just as valid! Here is a great place to remind you of the wisdom and insight with which you came to this book.

We've reached the end of this chapter. Please notice what you may need or want to tend to within yourself before moving on to Chapter 3, an introduction to Autistic and KCS/VAST culture and communication. Ideally, once you notice what you are needing or wanting, may you be able to take yourself seriously and tend accordingly. I'll be here whenever you are ready.

Recap: Possible Qualities or Traits That Could Indicate a Person Is Autistic

- There isn't one for this section! The recap is to read the list I just shared, hehe.

CHAPTER 3
An Introduction to Autistic and KCS/VAST Culture and Communication

In this next chapter, we are going to focus on communication styles and tendencies of Autistic and KCS/VAST people. We will begin with exploring and unpacking the double empathy problem and how it is a direct expression of ableism. That will lead us into communication preferences and forms of self-expression, including how ND people may tend to express and receive care. We will end with the correlation between neurodivergence, queerness, and transness. While the diversity within and among these communities is vast, especially as it relates to intersecting identities, this chapter will offer more insight into how Autistic and KCS/VAST people express themselves and connect with others. This content will support you in growing relationships with your ND clients, and will be woven into the rest of this book.

DOUBLE EMPATHY PROBLEM AND ABLEISM

When I provide trainings on this content, I use the gifted visual aid of Em Hammond, better known as Neurowild, a white Autistic and KCS/VAST Australian speech pathologist and gifted artist who takes complex topics and makes them easily digestible and interesting. She uses squirrels and beavers to represent Autistic and non-Autistic people, respectively. The squirrels have a surplus of nut shells and the beavers are seeking nut shells to help build their dam. They link up to support one another, but when they try to communicate, a communication breakdown happens. It's as if they are each speaking different languages, but somehow, the squirrel takes all the blame for the miscommunication.

It's beautiful, concise, and sad all at the same time. Her art depicts what Dr. Damian Milton (he/him), a white Autistic British sociologist and social psychologist named the *double empathy problem* to describe communication differences between Autistic and non-Autistic people. Ableism, or systemic oppression of people based on ability/disability, posits that Autistic people are inherently lesser than non-Autistic people. In that vein, any cross-neurotype communication difficulties are blamed on the Autistic person. After all, autism has long been dubbed a social communication disorder.

What Milton's research discovered is that Autistic people do well understanding other Autistic people, and that non-Autistic people, also known as allistic, do well understanding other non-Autistic or allistic people. However, when Autistic and allistic people try to have a conversation, they *each* struggle to understand the other. The communication challenges actually go *both* ways. Autistic people have a hard time innately understanding allistic people, and allistic people have a hard time innately understanding Autistic people.

As I state many times throughout this book, other humans are a primary source of trauma for Autistic people. I think the double empathy problem is one part of a complex journey toward shifting this reality. As we reduce the historical hierarchy of neurotypes in the dominant culture and come to greater acceptance of neurodiversity, hopefully more non-Autistic or allistic people will make efforts to learn more about autistic communication and culture. For those of you reading who are allistic, deep gratitude to you for being here.

A final thought before we move on. What I've shared in this section is precisely why ND people need to connect with and be in community with other ND people of shared neurotype, no matter what their age. Children, teens, and adults all benefit from connecting with others of the same neurotype. It feeds their life force, normalizes who they are, and fosters a much-needed sense of belonging. The same is true for people across all forms of difference, be it race, culture, religion, gender, or sexual orientation. In a similar way that my whole system can more easily settle when I'm around other Autistic folx, the same is true when I'm around other trans folx. It becomes easier to breathe. *May we all have more access to breathing easier.*

As we reach the conclusion of this section and prepare to transition to the next one, may you take the time you need to digest this knowledge. Whether it resonates, feels sticky, or even controversial, may it serve to reinforce why our ND clients need ND-affirming support that is actively invested in reducing harm. When you are ready, I'll meet you in the next section where we will discuss culture and communication.

Recap: The Double Empathy Problem
- The double empathy problem, a theory created by Dr. Damian Milton, provides an accurate depiction of cross-neurotype communication challenges.
- Autistic people have an easier time understanding other Autistic people, and non-Autistic or allistic people have an easier time understanding other non-Autistic or allistic people.
- When Autistic and allistic people come together, they each have a hard time understanding each other; the miscommunication goes both ways.

A BRIEF OVERVIEW OF AUTISTIC AND KCS/VAST CULTURE AND COMMUNICATION

One of the most common complaints that I hear about NT communication styles is the plethora of subtext and the prevalence of indirectness. The U.S. dominant culture teaches that it is rude to be clear, direct, and to the point. We are supposed to be polite, which often means some version of: lie, omit the truth, avoid the truth, or pretend. Instead of being allowed to clearly state consent, as in "yes," "no," or "maybe," we are taught to be vague and wishy-washy. Instead of saying "no, I'd rather not spend time with you," we make up all kinds of excuses and hope the other person gets the hint. Or we go along with what others want, only to be some version of cranky, annoyed, and resentful the whole time, and then we blame them for it. I recognize that oppression has a lot to do with this. Folx in marginalized groups are often forced into these dynamics as a matter of safety, and these dynamics are the epitome of whiteness. Being a cis white male provides exemption to most of these societal expectations.

I've had a number of clients over the years express some version of, "I can't understand why I'm so often misunderstood when I literally say what I mean!" Literal communication is most natural for many ND people, yet NTs are trained to detect subtext and respond to that, rather than to the actual words expressed! This can be confusing for Autistic people.

Additionally, Autistic people are often deemed rude because the tendency is for direct and literal communication. If they are interested in something, they may express a lot of excitement. If they are not interested in something, they may express boredom, annoyance, disgust, or something else. How they show what they feel may look very different from person to person. Some may express it with words but not body language; others express with body language but not words; and others may use sounds, gestures, or technology aids. Oftentimes, the body language Autistics use is different from the body language allistics use; this is often cited as one of the reasons for the double empathy problem.

There is vast diversity of communication within and across the Autistic community; some have access to a plethora of spoken words from near infancy, others may not ever speak words from their mouth. Stimming is a valuable source of communication, no matter what their relationship to spoken words. I remember seeing a post on social media from Danny Wakefield (he/him), a transgender dad and activist, sharing his experience of being at the playground with his child. There was a visibly Autistic child flapping their arms. His child expressed curiosity and wondered what the other child was doing. He replied, "We all show joy in different ways. They look very happy to me." And then his child went over and joyfully started flapping their arms next to the other child. The two kids continued to play together for a while, sharing in such joy together. As far as I know, Danny is not Autistic; he is, however, an incredible human who is deeply invested in social justice and loving one another. What a beautiful example of honoring different forms of expression and not centering spoken communication.

KCS/VAST people tend to understand NT communication styles more readily or innately than Autistic folx. With so many thoughts happening at once and a plethora of constant input, or the distress of boredom in response to a lack of enough interesting input, their focus and concentration may show up differently. Direct communication and clear expectations are ideal for this neurotype, too. At the same time, the tendency for rejection sensitivity dysphoria is very prevalent among people with this neurotype. What that means is that rejection, whether overt, implied, or perceived, or fear of rejection, can have an intensely negative impact. On the other hand, positive feedback or praise can have an equal yet opposite effect. How that could play out in session is clients working hard to be liked, hiding when they get distracted or bored, or apologizing for what they call their "tangents" or "rambling." Offering genuine and generous reassurance, validation, and acceptance of clients is extremely important.

Throughout the rest of the forthcoming chapters, we will delve more deeply into how communication styles, preferences, and needs may show up in the counseling space. We will explore different ways by which we can meet clients where they are, whether they are external processors who benefit most from large chunks of uninterrupted speaking time; whether they do best with a lot of spacious quiet time to internally or energetically process; whether they prefer nonspoken communication forms such as text/chat function, art, play, movement, or dance; or whether they need a lot of external validation to support their internal validation. We will keep returning to the importance of explicit and collaborative communication, for us as counselors to not assume our clients' needs or preferences, but to co-create the experience with them.

When I'm leading trainings, I love to share a favorite piece of mine from Marcela Gonzalez, well known as Autisticamente Marcela, a Mexican-American Autistic mother, advocate, writer, and artist, and Amythest Schaber (they/them), well known as Neurowonderful, a Métis Autistic, multiply disabled writer, public speaker, artist, and activist. It is titled "The Five Neurodivergent Love Languages: Autistic Love." It is an Autistic take on Gary Chapman's work called *The Five Love Languages*. He describes them as: gifts, words of affirmation, acts of service, physical touch, and quality time.

To my knowledge, the five categories came from Amythest, and then Marcela added additional text and illustrations. It's just brilliant. I've had parents of Autistic kids see this and be amazed to realize these qualities were not unique to their child! Or that they had misunderstood how meaningful or important these ways of being in their child are. And, Autistic adults have shared how affirmed they feel in how they express care. I'm going to share each one and give a brief overview of how I integrate this into my therapy work. You will notice that these themes resurface throughout the remainder of the book as we go deeper into tangible application. I'd also like to add that while these were created with the autistic neurotype in mind, I think they apply beautifully to KCS/VAST people too.[5]

---

5 Here is a link to access this post: www.facebook.com/story.php/?story_fbid=529516288536203&id=100044335094112

- **Infodumping:** Some Autistic people prefer the term *monologuing* to describe their love of sharing information about their passions. This is a tremendous way to build rapport with clients by engaging them in infodumping. Especially for new clients who are likely dealing with heightened social anxiety in the presence of us, a stranger, inviting them to share about their passions is a great way to support co-regulation. It honors their communication style, supports their confidence, and dismantles the inherent power dynamics within the counseling relationship by centering them as the expert. Infodumping is also a great regulatory tool that can be used at any time in a session to support parasympathetic nervous system states.

  It is a gift when clients are willing to share with us something that is so important to them. It is important that we receive their sharing with respect and appreciation. I have learned so much from my clients on such a broad array of topics!

- **Parallel play:** Another way of saying coexisting together in the same space, but each person is doing their own thing. Doing "good" therapy does not require that we are actively engaged in process or conversation with clients throughout the entire session. Coexisting in the space together can be deeply therapeutic too. Having another nervous system present can allow for co-regulation, and this co-regulation can be passive and still very effective. This can look like taking intentional quiet pauses; engaging in independent activities in the same space such as art, movement, or games; and it can also be a form of body doubling. Given that our role includes being an executive function coach by helping clients with things like adulting, planning, and organizing, parallel play can be a great way to help clients get things done that they are having a hard time initiating or completing on their own. More on this in Chapter 7, on executive function supports.

- **Support swapping:** Thanks to executive function challenges, there's a lot that clients may need help with. There may be things they are good at and another person struggles with, so they can give each other the support they need. A great example of this is the struggle with remembering things and being on time. We can support clients by offering reminders about our upcoming session, whether that be the night before, an hour before, or whatever you and they decide is most helpful. I've had therapists tell me stories of significantly reduced missed sessions from clients when they implemented reminders an hour before the start time. Unfortunately, western psychology tends to deem this sort of thing as enabling or co-dependent. Having consent from clients to help them get the support they need to show up and be successful in their life is the antithesis of ableism. (Please note that I use the word *successful* very loosely, and I believe that each of us gets to define what that word means for us, not the institutions of capitalism, white supremacy, and colonization).

- **Please crush my soul back into my body:** Proprioceptive input at its finest! For some people, deep pressure can be calming, soothing, and like an antidote to sympathetic arousal. It can help people to feel more in touch with their body, feel less a sense of being lost in space, and feel safer and more grounded. Weighted blankets and stuffies are great for this, as are books and any other objects that are heavy that might be around. I've even had clients pick up and carry around their potted house plants when no other obvious heavy objects were available. Weight, pressure, and compression can be great ways to evoke parasympathetic states. Rolling up in blankets or hiding in teeny tiny spaces can also be great options. This can be a useful sensory tool in and out of session for people of all ages.

- **"I found this cool rock/button/leaf, etc. and thought you would like it"**: Autistic gift giving may be deemed unconventional, but it is no less meaningful or special. To come across something that reminds us of another and to share it is a beautiful expression of love. My Pops (i.e., second father), who has come into his Autistic identity since knowing me, knows I love rocks. One of his passions is to dig holes in his yard. I'm talking like 5 feet deep and 6 feet wide holes when he can! For him it's a form of meditation. What a cool stim! Sometimes when he digs he finds really cool rocks, and he will gift them to me. Even as I write this, I can feel the warmth and love in my heart that I feel in those moments.

    I've also brought shells to share with clients when I've traveled to meet them in person. It is a beautiful way to share my love of the ocean and nature with them, and a way for them to have a tangible object that represents our connection.

As therapists, we can use these love languages to grow our relationships with clients and support them on their journey. As we continue on our journey together throughout this book, these love languages will be woven into the concrete and tangible tools I offer you.

I notice I feel sweetly settled after sharing these love languages with you. It feels deeply affirming and celebratory of ND people. I'm going to enjoy this moment and take a few deep breaths here. I wonder how you are feeling and what you might be wanting or needing in this moment? When you are ready, I'll meet you in the next section on the intersections of neurodivergence, queerness, and transness.

Recap: A Brief Overview of Autistic and KCS/VAST Culture and Communication

- Directly communicating, being literal, and having clear expectations tend to be the most natural for Autistic and KCS/VAST people; this is very different from NT dominant communication.
- There is no one so called "right" way to communicate: all forms of communication are valid.
- The five ND love languages, created by Neurowonderful and Autisticamente Marcela are: infodumping, parallel play, support swapping, please crush my soul back into my body, and I found this cool rock/button/leaf/etc. and thought you would like it.
- We can use our knowledge of these love languages to support our clients and build secure relationships with them.

THE INTERSECTIONS BETWEEN QUEERNESS, TRANSNESS, AND NEURODIVERGENCE

As we complete our chapter on Autistic and KCS/VAST culture and communication, it is important that we address a theme that you may or may not have already noticed within and among Autistic and KCS/VAST communities; there is a greater likelihood of LGBTQIA2S+ identities and these two forms of neurodivergence. From the research I've seen, the likelihood of being transgender and gender expansive is highest for Autistic folx, but the overlap is still statistically relevant for transness and KCS/VAST folx.

Regarding language, I tend to use trans or transgender as an umbrella term for *not cisgender*; as in, does not identify with the binary gender they were assigned at birth that is based on their genitals. That said, not all gender-expansive folx use the term trans, so I want to explicitly name that there is a large population of nonbinary, genderqueer, and other gender-expansive or gender nonconforming folx within the autistic and KCS/VAST neurotypes.

There is also a great deal of overlap of queer identities and Autism and KCS/VAST. Within these communities, there is a greater likelihood of asexuality and aromanticism. Not all ND people desire sex or romance. At the same time, many ND people are very much sexual beings and may identify as gay, lesbian, bisexual, pansexual, demisexual, or sapiosexual, or use other language to describe their sexual orientation. Polyamory is also common, with an understanding that one person likely cannot meet all of a person's needs. BDSM including bondage, discipline, dominance, submission, sadism, and masochism, along with kink, are also more common. These can offer much more diversity to the sensory component of sexuality.

The theory behind these intersections that makes the most sense to me is Dr. Nick Walker's. He coined the term *neuroqueer* and says that just as cis-heteronormativity is a social construct, so too is neurotypicality. It is not innate, but rather, something we perform in a sense. For some people, it takes little to no effort to perform cis-heteronormativity or neurotypicality. Who they are aligns very closely with these social constructs, so there isn't necessarily any dissonance. For ND folx, who are naturally outside-the-box thinkers and exist outside of the norms of neurotypicality, it would make sense that they would also think outside the box as it relates to gender norms and sexual orientation. If one doesn't apply, why should the other, and vice versa?

I want to be so clear here, especially in a political climate that is seeking to erase transgender people: Autism does not cause transness, just as transness does not cause autism. Autistic people are completely capable of understanding their gender identity and gender expression, and in *no way* does one's neurotype negate their gender. That idea is absolutely false and profoundly harmful. It is devastating that many states are pushing for legislation that denies access to gender-affirming care for Autistic people, citing autism as a preexisting condition or some other bs. It is a ridiculous and deeply unjust effort to maintain the so-called status quo of white supremacy, colonization, cis-heteronormativity, neurotypicality, capitalism, and Christian patriarchy, a status quo rooted in fear and power.

Oof, I feel my fire! Clearly, this is another passionate topic of mine that lives in me viscerally. As fire continues to be breathed through me as it wishes to, let's return to the whole notion of neuroqueer or neuroqueering. One does not need to be LGBTQIA2S+ or ND to neuroqueer. We are all capable of disrupting the norms of all of these social constructs. Some of us just have a more innate drive around it because it is the very nature of our lived experience.

As I reflect on the last paragraph, it makes me think of the words freedom and liberation. Getting to disrupt norms and be more authentic to who we actually are can be very freeing and liberating. I also want to make another point. There's a very real way that coming into understanding and having language to describe one's neurotype opens the door to other forms of liberation, too. Sometimes, people come into their Autistic and/or KCS/VAST identity and it puts them in touch with other previously shunned, disowned, or invisible identities such as their sexual orientation and gender. The same is true in reverse. Liberation of one identity can support liberation of other identities. Woo-hoo!

There's one more term on this topic that I want to introduce: *autigender*. It is used to describe the interwovenness of one's gender identity and Autistic identity. They are intimately linked and in deep relationship with one another. For Autistic people seeking language options to better understand their gender, too, this could be a word that feels like a good fit for them.

We've reached the end of Chapter 3 and are preparing for our next transition. Please tend to yourself, including your body, yourself as a learner, yourself as a counselor, and your humanity in whatever ways you need, want, or have access to. When you are ready, I look forward to meeting you in the preface for Part II, where I will introduce you to the model that informs the remainder of this book.

Recap: The Intersections Between Queerness, Transness, and Neurodivergence

- Yes! There is a strong correlation between LGBTQIA2S+ identities and Autism and KCS/VAST.
- Dr. Nick Walker's term neuroqueer is a great theory for this: both neuronormativity and cis-heteronormativity are social constructs; subverting one paves the way to subvert the others.
- Autism does not cause transness, just as transness does not cause autism.
- Autigender: a gender identity that encapsulates the intersections of Autistic identity and gender identity.

PART II

PREFACE TO PART II
An Introduction to Neurodivergent Somatics, the model that will inform the rest of this book

With the foundation set for us, I'm going to introduce the three-part model that I created that I believe informs best practice for working with Autistic and KCS/VAST clients. It is called Neurodivergent Somatics or ND Somatics. What I appreciate about it is that it can be interwoven with other modalities that you use. This is not the be all, end all of ND-affirming therapy, but it is a map for how we can do therapy well. We can use this map as a pathway for distilling out the ableism inherent within most modalities, and we can be as creative or eclectic as we choose.

This model is just as much about working with our clients as it is about working with ourselves as therapists. It forms the basis of what I believe are the primary responsibilities of a therapist when working with Autistic and KCS/VAST clients. Given that this model is deeply relational, as well as rooted in anti-ableism and anti-oppression, it is essential that we as therapists are embodying this work. We then model this to our clients, allowing for resonance and congruence with our words and actions. This congruence is what clients' nervous systems need in order to take us and themselves seriously, to experience a sense of safety with another human, and to heal from trauma. This congruence is how clients build trust. It is the essence of what I believe is good therapy.

The rest of this book will go in depth into each of the three tenets of the model and how to apply them, both with and for our clients and also with and for ourselves as counselors. For now, I will share a brief overview of them.

- Pleasure/Neutrality
- Client as Self-Expert
- Global Permission

Pleasure/Neutrality recognizes that many Autistic and KCS/VAST people live in a state of heightened sympathetic arousal and have much less autonomous access to their parasympathetic nervous system than neurotypical people. One of the greatest gifts we can give clients is to help them feel good, and if or when good is too much for them, then neutral. I'm grateful to Kaden Walsh (they/them) white queer, trans, body-centered psychotherapist for introducing me to the importance of neutrality. Not only is this tenet a pathway for healing, growth, and resilience, but it also allows for tapping into the inherent capacity for wild delight of which Autistic and KCS/VAST people are capable. Their sensitivity isn't just about causing them harm or pain; it is also a pathway to sheer delight, creativity, wonder, and oh, so much pleasure! There is the possibility for so much more to the ND lived experience than suffering alone.

As so aptly stated by a client of mine, therapy for Autistic and KCS/VAST clients isn't about learning to be uncomfortable, which therapy for NT clients typically is. That discomfort is the everyday experience for many, and they don't need more practice with it! They certainly don't need to pay for more practice at it either; life gives plenty of free practice. ND Somatics is filled with sensory delight, psychoeducation about the nervous system and why more parasympathetic input is needed, and opportunities to practice feeling pleasure and neutrality. Sometimes pleasure can be overwhelming, and the absence of any input can be wildly novel; that's when we opt for neutrality.

As we practice applying this tenet with clients, we also get to practice what it means to play with our own attention and focus. We get to exist as humans with needs while simultaneously existing in our role as counselor. We also get to grow our own capacity for orienting toward pleasure, not to dismiss or minimize our challenges, struggles, and/or impacts of systemic oppression, but to provide more access to our wholeness. In addition to supporting our well-being, embodying this tenet can also help reduce burnout.

Client as Self-Expert centers the idea that nobody knows anyone better than they know themselves, including us therapists. While I may have unique insight or knowledge that can help my clients, only they have the lived experience of what it is like to inhabit their exact bodymind. They've known this bodymind since they were born; who are we to think that we know better? Client as Self-Expert is the epitome of anti-ableist, anti-oppressive care. I do not pretend to be the expert on someone else's life. If I did, that would be incredibly offensive and harmful. Unfortunately, by the time clients reach our office, they have likely endured this harm for a very long time. They might even expect us to tell them what they think, feel, believe, want, or need. If therapy is a game, right here, right now, we are changing the game.

There are two key components to this tenet: consent and dismantling ableism. Until we know for sure that our clients are able to say "no" to us, we have no way of knowing whether or not their "yes" is genuine or a fawn/appeaser response. Therapy is about disrupting threat responses, *not* perpetuating them.

No matter our neurotype, whether we are Autistic and/or KCS/VAST, questioning our neurotype, or are NT, the U.S. dominant culture is steeped in ableism and we need to be doing our own work of dismantling it. We embody this tenet by challenging our perceptions of what makes for a so-called "good" client and a "good" therapist. It also means that we do not have an agenda to force clients to unmask or to stop camouflaging their ND traits. While we recognize that mental health outcomes tend to improve with unmasking, we also recognize that these are coping strategies that have been necessary for survival. For some, that survival is about acceptance and belonging. For others it's about keeping jobs, maintaining housing, or not losing custody of children. And for Black, Indigenous, and Latinx ND people, it could mean not getting killed by police.

Hello, fire! Big breath in and out happening in me at the moment. We support our clients to unmask by creating a safe enough relationship and environment for them, and then just maybe, with time and trust, they may feel brave enough to express more of their authentic self with us. And as they grow that sense of safety and trust with us, they may then feel brave enough to practice with people, places, and situations outside of the therapy space.

Global Permission is about lathering clients in permission to be radically themselves, as they are, with what they need, and with who they desire to become. We embody this tenet by taking time to build rapport with clients. We show them that they matter and that what is important to them matters. We express curiosity and genuine interest in knowing them. We offer validation, celebrate their boundaries, and appreciate them for showing up for themselves. We are attentive and listen with our whole bodymind. We encourage stimming, we neuroqueer the counseling space and relationship, and we recognize that sometimes our role is that of executive function coach and cheerleader. We support them to discover what accommodations they need to exist and be well, and then we try to help them get these needs met. Finally, we recognize that both clients and therapists are humans having a human experience, doing the best job we can at navigating a wildly complex existence.

In the name of honoring this transition, I encourage you to check in with yourself. You may want to notice how you are doing, what you are needing, and what will support your integration for this jam-packed first part of the book. Whenever you are ready, whether that be today or another day, I look forward to being with you in Chapter 4 as we explore the tenet of Pleasure/Neutrality and how to apply it.

CHAPTER 4
Pleasure/Neutrality: Prioritizing Parasympathetic States

The first tenet of ND Somatics is Pleasure/Neutrality. Autistic and/or KCS/VAST people are prone toward frequent sympathetic nervous system activation, some might even say an overactive threat response. This is due to a combination of innate biological differences, environmental factors, and systemic oppression. Research on synaptic pruning shows that the Autistic and KCS/VAST neurotypes exhibit low synaptic pruning, causing an overabundance of input registering in any given moment (Chao Xie et al., 2023). The amygdala cannot tell the difference between what is an actual threat versus a perceived threat. While this is true for all neurotypes, for ND folx, a greater frequency of input registers as threat. In addition, challenges with emotion regulation are common, along with having to navigate social, sensory, or energetic input at any given moment; sometimes there is too much input, other times, not enough. Both understimulation and overstimulation can instigate body discomfort or distress, which can activate or exacerbate a threat response. Add to this systemic and institutional oppression and the impacts of micro- and macroaggressions. Autism and KCS/VAST are marginalized neurotypes in the United States, and many ND folx have multiple marginalized identities. The sources of threat are vast and deep.

While this certainly presents ND folx with unique challenges, I want to be careful not to insinuate that this very active protective sympathetic nervous system is a bad thing. In fact, no matter what your neurotype, that you are reading this book at this very moment is evidence that your threat response has done its job well: it has kept you alive! Your sympathetic nervous system has protected you from danger and given you access to fight back, flee, play dead, or appease as needed. You have survived!

Let's take a breath together. Or if that suggestion makes you want to shout "Nyck, *do not* tell me to breathe," then please don't! Instead, perhaps we can take a pause or connect with sensory delight. I share this caveat very intentionally. I've worked with clients over the years who were told "just breathe!" as an inadvertent weapon of invalidation or minimization for their very real present-moment struggle. For them, the idea of breathing as a relaxing strategy makes utterly *no sense* to them and in fact can be harmful.

Yes, we have survived, and for ND folx, not without a cost. Oppression is exhausting and ongoing. That is real. And sometimes, the challenge is that the ND amygdala is too good at its job; it frequently confuses neutral input for threatening input. While there may be a link between a too good amygdala and enhanced creativity, this takes a toll on Autistic and KCS/VAST people physically, mentally, and emotionally.

This makes me think of Atlas, my 10-month-old puppy, who is passionate about his role as protector of the family. He put himself in charge of window patrol, and he loves to lie on the couch, look out the window, and alert us when there is danger outside. In alignment with his instinct to guard his territory, he barks at dogs passing by that he doesn't know. This is fitting. On garbage day, however, the sight of a plastic bag at the curb blowing in the wind is just as alarming for him; he wants to make sure his family doesn't get attacked by that plastic bag! And so, he will bark and bark to ensure our survival. While we appreciate his efforts, the overestimate of danger causes both us and him extra stress.

For the Autistic and KCS/VAST sensory system, there are a seemingly infinite number of plastic bags blowing in the wind that are threatening. This unwanted sensory input can be lights that are too bright, sounds that are the wrong tone or pitch, too many people in a crowded space, the wrong scent, too much stillness, a chair that is too hard, and so much more.

Confusing social input can be a raised eyebrow, a change in intonation, not knowing what to say, unknowns such as "Was that a joke?" "Am I supposed to laugh now?" All these cues are hard to interpret as quickly as a typical social interaction may expect.

Then there's the discomfort of being in a body that may be prone to chronic pain, be it joint or muscular, migraines, chronic fatigue, GI issues, hypermobility, and more.

Heightened sensitivity to energetic shifts is yet another element that they may or may not be able to articulate. Whether it's a subtle cue that a person's words and feelings seem incongruent, a disconnect between a person's vibe and words, or something happens too quickly to process in the moment and before they know it, they are disconnected from themself and dissociated.

Any one of these inputs could send off internal alarms, alerting clients to potential danger. That danger could be rejection, overwhelm, sensory overload, or the feeling of getting it wrong. Add to this the potential triggers of past traumas, and they are flooded with a full-body mobilization to ensure safety. Safety is not just in the context of survival, but belonging, being accepted, staying regulated, or sometimes, passing as NT.

I want to be careful not to make this seem like just a ND wiring problem. It is not. Autistic and KCS/VAST people face very real threats from systemic ableism. This is exhausting and is a source of trauma. Particularly for racialized ND folx and queer and trans ND folx, the added oppression from their intersecting marginalized identities is real and impactful. This perpetuates an ongoing and necessary heightened awareness of danger and can make it that much more difficult to figure out which stimuli are neutral, safe, or dangerous. The need for vigilance, often hypervigilance, is real. For folx who have access to hiding their Autistic and/or KCS/VAST traits, this can mean a near constant assessment of where their body is in space, how it's moving and what it's doing (or not doing). "How much of myself can I be in this moment without getting hurt, harmed, or even killed?"

Oof...I feel the heartbreak. I also feel the ways that my white body protects me from some of this. While being trans means that I am quite vigilant when I'm out in the world, being white means that I can take a walk in my mostly white neighborhood wearing a hoodie with the hood up and sunglasses on without fear of being harassed or harmed. Feeling covered up and kind of hidden while outside can be nourishing to my sensory needs. I am well aware that if I were Black and walking in that same neighborhood, it wouldn't matter how cozy or comfy my hood was; I'd be focused on not *appearing* as a threat to others so that I could make it home safely.

This is real. And it sucks. I notice my shoulders round a bit and my chest cave inward. My breath gets a bit shallower, and I feel energy behind my eyes. I associate these sensations as indicators of grief over systemic injustice. I wonder what you are noticing in yourself in this moment? I'm going to honor my impulse to move my body. As if on cue, my hips started wiggling in my chair, and I'm allowing my body to rock from side to side, with the movement originating from my seat. I feel my body's push be supported by the seat of the chair and the floor beneath my feet.

I can feel the energy flowing, and my posture is a bit straighter. I encourage you to honor your own impulses in this moment as you are able to and/or choose to.

✶ ✶ ✶ ✶

All of this is why we help our clients to prioritize parasympathetic states. Autistic and KCS/VAST people do not need more practice in responding to threats. They are already experts at this. Instead, they need the opposite. They need ample practice with intentionally providing their nervous system with input that evokes a sense of being safe enough, or even relaxation, calm, connection, pleasure, or neutrality. This is the essence of trauma and healing work. This is what it means to reorient default patterns and tendencies. Not to eliminate the instinct and brilliance of their sympathetic nervous system, nor to invalidate the ongoing threats they have to deal with, but to have greater access to safety, autonomy, and peace within their bodies at will.

While I knew this to be intuitively true, I'm grateful for the reassurance and encouragement I received from Katie Asmus around these ideas. Katie (she/her) is a white, nature and somatic-based therapist and educator who teaches a course called *Somatic Soul-Based Trauma Training*. It was in this course that I gained the confidence to take myself more seriously, and came to embody pleasure and neutrality as the essence of good trauma work.

Imagine having choice over how you respond in a given moment, rather than that all-too-familiar experience for ND folx of suddenly feeling knocked over by a giant wave without your consent.

It's not that the unwanted input, be it sensory, social, or even a micro- or macroaggression won't still bother or harm them, but their broader repertoire of responses may help them feel more equipped to deal with what is hard or harmful.

Let's try this out so that you can get a felt sense of it for yourself. Knowing that I am centering your autonomy and consent, please choose whether you want to accept, reject, or modify this invitation. Feel free to try this as I envisioned it, or make it your own. This will be an opportunity to have a kinesthetic experience of what I just talked about.

- Step 1: If you haven't already, please gather one or more sensory delights to take with you on this experience. Examples include fidgets, food, beverages, scents, textures, toys, music, beautiful objects, and more. Movement counts, too, so it doesn't need to be a tangible object.
- Step 2: If you choose to, go ahead and pick something to track within yourself. Here are some examples of what you may choose to notice: your internal speed (could

be your heart rate; smart watches can be so helpful for this), internal volume (could be how loud or quiet your thoughts are), quality of breath, body sensation, focus and attention, or imagery. Notice what is interesting to you at this moment or what you are feeling curious about. For simplicity's sake, choose one thing to track for now. Feel free to close your eyes or keep them open, and with a curious mind, notice what you notice.

Depending on what you are tracking, here are some examples of what you may notice: heart rate is slow, eye movements are fast, breath is contracted, volume in your head is quiet, focus is scattered, shoulders are relaxed, or an image of your favorite tree appears. These are just possibilities; there is no right or wrong way to do this. Stay with noticing what you are tracking for as short or long as you choose. My go-to is 1–3 minutes.

- **Step 3:** Shift your attention to your sensory delight. Indulge in it! Notice what you notice. Depending on what you chose, you may be aware of its temperature, speed, taste, smell, rhythm, texture, size, shape, and so on. If your delight is an object, feel free to graze or caress it over different parts of your body, like your cheek or your arm. Allow yourself to get enthralled, curious, even playful. Take as much or as little time as you choose here. Again, my go-to is 1–3 minutes.
- **Step 4:** Shift your attention and awareness back to what you were tracking a few moments ago. What's present now? Is it similar or different from before? Feel free to hold dual awareness and shift your attention back and forth between your sensory delight and what you are tracking. Again, there's no right or wrong, just noticing.
- **Step 5:** If it's helpful for you to take notes, jot down what you chose to track, what you noticed, and what your delight was. Were you surprised at all by what you experienced? As we go throughout this chapter, I'm going

to invite you to check back in with yourself, coming back to what you are tracking and inserting sensory delight at will. This is particularly important when you notice something that bothers you, challenges you, distracts you, engages you, excites you, bores you, or confuses you. Honor your pacing and either slow down or speed up as you need or want to.
- **Step 6**: Prepare to shift your attention back to this chapter. When you feel ready, continue reading.

Now that you have had a chance to try this out for yourself, I want to reaffirm my belief that it is our primary responsibility as therapists and humans to learn how to feel good, if not neutral. White supremacy and neurotypicality teach us that our primary responsibility is to *be* good. To do good anti-ableist work, we subvert these dominant systems of oppression and practice *feeling* good or neutral. I realize that this perspective of prioritizing feeling good or neutral may seem radical, even with better understanding as to the "Why."

- What do you notice arises within you when I say this?

I invite you to stay connected with yourself, with what you're tracking, and/or your delight as I pose some more questions.

- What happens in your own body or present-moment awareness when you imagine getting to lead therapy in such a way that does not perpetually retraumatize you and your clients?
- What happens in your own body or present-moment awareness when you imagine getting to center pleasure, neutrality, and parasympathetic states for yourself and for your clients? This does not mean there are not still

hard moments, but that we're not persistently centering our attention around the threat itself.

*** * * ***

When you're ready, we're going to go over some concepts and definitions here from the field of somatic psychology that are an important part of this theoretical orientation. These concepts are paramount to Pleasure/Neutrality, and you will also notice them resurface in later chapters. Some of this may be review for you. Please note that I am applying these concepts through a specific neurodivergent-affirming, anti-ableist, anti-oppressive lens. Be aware that unless that specific approach is taken, every modality has the potential to be ableist and oppressive.

> **DEFINITIONS**
>
> Please note that I will use language like "we" and "us" here, as these definitions are part of how we as counselors learn to or practice embodying Pleasure/Neutrality. These definitions are applicable to all of us, no matter what our neurotype.
> - **Resourcing:** Resourcing is the act of using something pleasant or neutral to evoke a sense of present-moment awareness, safety, calm, and/or pleasure. Examples of resources include sensory delights, stimming, invoking sensory awareness of the present moment, movement, fidgeting, laughter, and rest. Depending on the individual, something may be resourcing to one person and activating or triggering to another.
> - **Pendulation:** In its simplest and most literal form, it means to go back and forth. If it's helpful, allow

yourself to imagine or look up an image of a pendulum. It sways from one side to the other, back and forth.
- **Oscillation of attention:** This is a form of pendulation. It is the process or act of shifting attention from one focus to another, back and forth. It can be from an area of discomfort to an area of comfort within the body. It can be from processing something difficult to shifting attention to a resource. It can be from inside of me to outside of me, or from me to you and back again.
- **Titration:** Doing a little bit at a time. Pendulation helps us to titrate. For example, when we are processing something challenging, rather than process the whole challenge all at once or endlessly, we do a little bit at a time.
- **Tracking nervous system states:** We use pendulation, oscillation of attention, and titration to help us track our nervous system state. We ask, "Am I on alert?" (i.e., sympathetic arousal) or "Am I feeling relaxed?" (i.e., parasympathetic arousal). We notice what's happening for us in the present moment. We may feel a sense of danger or a sense of safety. Sometimes it can be hard to distinguish which it is, or maybe even both are present simultaneously! From an anti-oppressive lens, I must point out that what evokes a sense of danger in one person may evoke a sense of safety in another; these are not absolutes. The more marginalized identities a person holds, the more sources of danger there likely are.
- **Window of tolerance:** This term was coined by Dr. Dan Siegel, a white, male neuropsychiatrist, educator, and prolific author. Window of tolerance refers to the zone in which we feel okay. Said another way, how much we can tolerate or deal with. I like to imagine (or you can look up an image of) a window; the amount of life I can

handle is the amount the window is open. In times of overwhelm, distress, big grief, or burnout, the window may be only open a little or barely open at all. In times of being well-resourced, having our needs met, and having ample access to parasympathetic states, the window may be open wide(r). This is not a fixed state. Therapy is intended to help us increase our window of tolerance, or the amount of life, sensation, and/or aliveness we can handle. When our window's opening is small, it can make even pleasurable things feel hard to deal with. Pendulation, oscillation of attention, and titration are all intended to support our window of tolerance. Please note: our worth or morality, despite what the U.S. dominant culture may tell us, *is not dependent on the size of our window's opening.* This is also directly influenced or impacted by systemic oppression and access (or lack of access) to support needs.

- **Self-Regulation:** Our mood, emotions, and body are all in sync and using the support of me, myself, and I to achieve this state of being in sync. I can bring myself back from a state of being out of sync to back in sync. For example, when I am really excited and the energy feels too big in my body, I may feel out of control or overwhelmed. In response, I can go for a run, take deep breaths, or make lots of sounds to help me handle the amount of excitement that's present.
- **Co-Regulation:** Using the support of another to help return to a state of being in sync. "Another" could be a therapist, another human, a pet, ancestors, or nature. Co-regulation is the process of receiving the support of something outside of ourselves to help us be okay. ND people may have been told contradicting messages such as "you spend too much time alone and ought to be able to be soothed by others" (i.e., co-regulate)

> or "you ought to not be so dependent on others and should be able to soothe yourself" (i.e., self-regulate). Some people may tend more toward one or the other or access both equally. *One is not better than the other*, though many who have developmental trauma may tend toward self-regulation since humans have been the source of harm.

You may notice that this is a good opportunity to check back in with yourself. If you choose to, come back to what you are tracking and insert sensory delight(s). When you feel ready, you can shift your attention to the next definition.

> **Pacing:** The speed within which we exist or operate. In the capitalist, ableist, white supremacist dominant culture that we exist in, there is constant pressure to be fast, do, achieve, and go-go-go. That is the opposite pace that many ND folx actually need to stay in connection with themselves, to be in the present moment, and to be able to track their nervous system. One of the dominant features of an ableist culture is an inability to keep up. Whether it be sensory input, social input, societal expectations and pressures, communication differences, and more, much of life can feel as if it happens too fast. Permission to slow down, to pause, to take more time before responding, to honor processing speed, to digest the incoming information, request, or demand and then filter it through their own needs, wants, or boundaries so that they can offer actual informed consent . . . what a luxury! Let's also remember that some people tend toward understimulation and may find faster paces deeply satisfying. There is no one right pace.

Whatever your preferred pace, below are some more opportunities for inquiry and integration of this content and process. If you feel up for it, you can take a pause here and notice or perhaps come back to this another time.

- What does it feel like or what do you notice when you imagine being able to live (some or most of) life at your pace?
- Is your pace slower or faster than the pace you are often expected to keep up with?
- At what pace is it easier to access a feeling of safe enough, relaxation, calm, pleasure, or neutrality?
- Would you feel more at ease in your role as therapist if you knew you were allowed, even encouraged, to go at your own pace?
- Would you feel more permission to be yourself when you could go at a pace more closely aligned to your authentic pace?

Shifting from pacing, I want to bring our awareness to the notion of comfort and discomfort. Neurodivergent-affirming therapy isn't about learning to tolerate more discomfort. This is a huge shift in perspective for many providers, and it can make therapy much more sustainable for their clients (and likely themselves too). Most counseling programs teach us that therapy is about learning how to be uncomfortable. As I've learned from my clients and my own experience as a client in therapy, ND people don't need *more* practice at being uncomfortable (just like we don't need *more* practice with being in sympathetic states). Autistic and KCS/VAST people are *experts* at being uncomfortable. For many, it's their baseline. Be it from trauma, ableism, colonization, capitalism, racism, homophobia, transphobia, classism, patriarchy, overwhelm, burnout, chronic illness or chronic pain, and more, there is an overabundance of discomfort. How novel to focus efforts and energy on practicing actually being comfortable, or having an absence of input at all, hence neutrality!

I'm going to offer another few questions for you to ponder, journal about, explore, or be curious about.

- What if being a therapist didn't mean having to hold space for client after client, all the while having their and our own nervous system blown out?
  We know that doesn't work, that it burdens both of us, overwhelms, exhausts, depletes, or makes us dread therapy.
- What if we didn't have to do it like that anymore?
- What if we could actually implement an orientation and model to our work that made us like what we do (more) and made our clients look forward to therapy?

As a therapist who works exclusively with Autistic and KCS/VAST people, most of my adult clients have come to me after having been harmed by previous therapists. We can stop that cycle. Prioritizing Pleasure/Neutrality is a key element to creating a healing and reparative experience of therapy for ND clients. While our ND clients especially need this, all of our clients, no matter their neurotype, benefit from this being the orientation to therapy. We are rewriting the narrative that says good therapy is grueling and tear-filled.

What a moment for a breath or a pause to digest these words and honor your processing speed. A transition is approaching... we are going to spend the next section focusing on applying this concept and approach to our work with clients. Feel free to check back in with yourself and what you are tracking, insert sensory delight, and notice what's present. When you feel ready, the next section is ready to greet you. I hope you can sense my warm, welcoming smile!

Recap: An Overview of Pleasure/Neutrality

- Supporting clients to access feeling good, pleasurable, or neutral is the foundation of this work.
- ND clients have heightened threat responses and need practice learning to turn on parasympathetic states at will.
- This work isn't about making the sympathetic nervous system bad or wrong; it's about bringing more access and balance to the system.
- ND-affirming, anti-ableist counseling is not about teaching clients to be uncomfortable.
- We reviewed several definitions that relate to somatic psychology.

WORKING WITH CLIENTS

We're going to spend this next section exploring how to apply these concepts we just talked about. Theory can be great, but without taking it to the next step of implementation, it won't get us very far. For ND clients, there are two key parts to implementation: psychoeducation and kinesthetic learning opportunities—that is, practicing the thing. The psychoeducation piece happened in the first several pages of this chapter. In this section, we will focus on applying it, that is, kinesthetic learning.

Depending on who the client is, their age, their needs, or what is most relevant to them, I may introduce this as: an embodied activation-deactivation scale, a confidence scale, an anxiety scale, or something else. The name itself isn't that important for me, but it is important that it is something accessible and tangible for my clients. The process is about helping clients have more access to or awareness of what signals parasympathetic and sympathetic states. It is about empowering them to be able to shift from sympathetic states to parasympathetic states at will. Easier said than done, I know! But this is exactly why we practice, practice, practice.

Important things to consider as we get to it.

> Be creative!
> Trust your clients and what resonates for them.
> Keep it simple.
> Alleviate the pressure of getting it right.
> Lead with and continue with consent.

Okay, all that said, off we go!

Step 1: Psychoeducation

We start with explaining the *why* to clients. We both might wonder, why would they pay me to help them feel good?

"But I thought therapy was about me doing *hard work*," they may challenge. (See more on dismantling the internalized rules clients and therapists hold about what it means to be a "good" therapist or a "good" client in Chapter 6.)

I explain, as clearly and as simply or as in depth as my client may need or want. I'm going to share how I speak about this with clients. I encourage your individuality and am not suggesting that you recite my exact words, unless this feels like the perfect script that you've been waiting for, and I just made your life easier. That would be delightful!

"You don't need any more practice at suffering or feeling threatened. You get enough of that just by living and existing each day. What you likely don't have enough support, practice, or experience with is feeling safe, good, at ease, or neutral. Your sensitive system tends to notice threat very easily, and there likely are things that register as threat that aren't *actual* threats, but our amygdala, the part of our brain that activates the alarm bells, can't tell the difference. A fire alarm signaling a smoky building would be considered an actual threat, or being harassed at work or bullied at school. But sometimes we also *perceive* things as threat, like trying a new food, giving a presentation, or hearing a sound in the environment that we don't recognize. All of this helps to keep us safe and alive. This is our sympathetic nervous system and causes us to fight, flee/run away, freeze/play dead, or fawn/people please. We don't want to get rid of this, but we can add in more access to parasympathetic states, the rest-and-digest nervous system that helps us feel safer. This can help bring about more balance in the system and support us through the hard."

I also might add, "When our trauma is activated, it can feel like it is happening again in the present moment. Learning to access parasympathetic states, such as pleasure and neutrality, helps communicate to ourselves that 'Yes, that happened (or is still happening), and it sucked.' Absolutely. And in this moment, here with me in this space (be it an office setting, out in nature, in your own home), that thing isn't happening. This is the essence of trauma work: helping your system to differentiate between the past (or for ongoing trauma, outside of the therapy space) and the present moment here with me. This way we don't keep retraumatizing you. Instead, we boost your sense of being okay or safety."[6]

---

[6] I am making the assumption that the client is not being actively traumatized by their therapist. Unfortunately, all too often, trauma does get enacted in the counseling space from the therapist to the ND client. This can make it that much more confusing and harmful when the person who is expected to be safe enough is actually causing more harm. It reminds me of disorganized attachment, when the caregiver both helps the young one to get their needs met and is also a source of harm, threat, danger, and/or abuse. If you are working with clients who have been harmed by mental health practitioners, please be especially alert to how you speak about trauma and how you show up for your client.

Step 2: Consent

Because ND-affirming, anti-ableist care means *consent is centered* (more on this in Chapter 5, Client as Self-Expert: Boundaries as a Form of Differentiation), I would then ask my client: "There's a way that we can play with this. We can make a very 'you' type of scale that could help you to notice what's happening and the nervous system state you might be in. Would you like to try it out?"

Once an invitation is offered, the client then has the opportunity to say "yes," "no," or "maybe."

"Maybe" could mean they need more information or context. "Maybe" they are interested in the idea, but not right now. Or "'Maybe' I don't yet know how to say no to my therapist, so I'll go with the word that is safer to me and hope my therapist is on point enough to know that I'm not giving my consent." The response of "Maybe" is an indicator to check in around pacing; the client may need for us to slow down. It is also an inquiry for us to consider what additional support or explanation might be needed, and an opportunity to lean into the client's autonomy.

When humans have been the predominant source of danger and oppression has been rampant, rest assured that your client's autonomy has been sacrificed, lost, or stolen. Their hesitation is a gift they are giving you (it may be ripe with information about the person's history, needs, and wounding) and a beautiful invitation for you to meet them *better, more gently, more slowly*.

In other words, here is where you get to show them that you are invested in repairing the harm that has been caused to them by the mental health field and by humans across other domains and settings. Instead of bypassing their needs or boundaries, judging them for not being an automatic "yes," or forcing your will onto them, you can honor, even *celebrate*, their autonomy. You can trust that *they know what is best for them*. In other words, *scaffolding* might be necessary in order for the client to begin to have more access to their parasympathetic nervous system, particularly in the presence of another human.

I feel my deep exhale. This might be a moment to check back

in with what you are tracking, inserting sensory delight, taking a break, journaling, or connecting with yourself in whatever way might be most supportive.

Because these are real life actual humans we are in relationship with, it's also possible that a client may say "no" to your invitation to create a scale. Honor that. Respect their "no." I like to express direct appreciation when my clients tell me "no." Particularly for those who are historic fawners, this is another gift they are giving me. It is an indicator that we are building safety and trust, and that some part(s) of them believes that they can set a boundary with me, and I won't disappear, reject, abandon, or otherwise harm them. Dr. Carla Sherrell teaches exploration of how these dynamics can be similar for racialized clients. Systemic racism can mean that saying "no" to a white person could have dangerous consequences, especially "no" to a white person with the positional power of counselor. It is my responsibility to help them access and trust their "no" in our relationship. When a client offers a "no" to this type of suggestion, I may ask (after appreciating them), "would it be okay if I were to ask you about this again in a future session, and again you can still say 'no' if it's something you don't want to do?"

Clients who are grappling with intense internalized ableism may have also internalized a rule that says something along the lines of "I'm not allowed to feel good" or "I don't know how to feel good, and I can't risk getting it wrong." I notice a sinking sensation in the center of my chest as I write that. It evokes a feeling of such sadness. I feel the visceral experience of those words, those self-punishing words that can get so embedded in a person through years and decades of ableism, oppression, and relational trauma. This is another invitation to slow down and perhaps begin with neutrality rather than pleasure.

This trauma is most certainly *not* all they are as ND people, but this is the very truth of what many have endured and still do. And to truly support them, see them, and know them, their therapists need to recognize that their clients' pain is valid and deep. This validation of clients' needs is essential and necessary. We are not sidestepping this truth. We respond compassionately. We give our clients permission to feel good and to reclaim what was once natural for their body to engage with, such as: permission to have loud hands, stomp their feet, twirl their hair, look away while they talk, walk on their toes, rock back and forth, and so much more. We deeply honor and respect when our clients don't equate feeling good with being safe. Feeling good may be wrapped up in danger, rather than liberation.

For me, breath is a valuable resource that I've come to rely heavily on over the years. As I finished that last paragraph, I found myself noticing a deep breath, in and out, flow through my body. It was satisfying, and reminded me to be intentional about inviting you into another moment of respite. Please take the time you need or want, and when you are ready, we'll go to Step 3.

Step 3: (If Consent Is Given) Offer Possibilities of Indicators for Them to Track

Hello again! In honoring all the feels that are arising within me as I write, I can now turn my attention to the giddiness I'm noticing. I feel giddy that I now get to share what happens next when a client gives their consent and offers the green light to go forward with this exploration. For some reason, this evokes an image of being on a ride at an amusement park, clicking my seat belt into place, and readying myself for the ride to begin!

All these words later from me, let's get into how we might go about co-creating this embodied scale with our clients. Some people respond best to quantitative measures, while others will prefer a more qualitative style. For clients who do not rely on spoken communication, using pictures or images for the different steps of the scale could be very helpful. Whatever indicator the client chooses to track or pay attention to can then be accessed quantitatively, qualitatively, or with pictures. I'm going to provide a list of examples of possible indicators to track (this may seem familiar from when we tried this out together earlier in the chapter).

In true, circuitous ND-communication fashion, *before* I get to that list, there's one more thing to mention. (I can hear a loved one's voice jokingly saying, "One more thing." Whenever we're trying to leave the house, there's inevitably always *one more thing* I just have to do before we can exit! Anywho, I digress.) I'd like to remind us that to be somatic, to include the body in the therapy process, *does not* mean that it must be a body sensation. For clients with less access to interoception or even alexithymia (a lot of difficulty in knowing how one feels), inner body sensation may not ever be what they choose to track. ND-affirming somatic indicators are about present-moment awareness, not "I can tell you exactly what's happening in my big toe right now." Unfortunately, much of western somatic psychology is steeped in white supremacy and ableism, making it not just inaccessible, but harmful for Autistic and KCS/VAST clients. I am being very intentional to integrate anti-ableism with somatic practices.

Now that we have that named and out of the way, we can finally move on (or leave the house!). Here's a list that I've come up with:

> **POSSIBLE INDICATORS TO TRACK**
>
> **Internal speed:** This could be helpful for clients across the interoception spectrum. Some people may be easily clued into how fast or slow they feel on the inside; others may use the support of an external device that measures this for them. The gift of smart watches is that they can track heart rate and report back to the person wearing the watch what is happening quantitatively in their body. Speed could also relate to the pace of one's thoughts.

Internal volume: Like all of these indicators, they are variable depending on the person using them. For some, when their head feels loud, like there are many voices talking at once (which are often outside voices that have been internalized), this could indicate distress. For others, when their inner volume gets really quiet it could indicate distress.

Focus and attention: The biggest attribute to this one is "What am I paying attention to?" Is it on what's happening in the present moment, what happened in the past, or what might happen in the future? Do I feel scattered or spacey, or do I feel present, focused, or engaged in what's happening right now? Is my body here, but are my thoughts somewhere else?

Body sensation: Are there areas of the body that respond to my mood or emotional state? Some people might hold their stress in their neck, shoulders, jaw, or abdomen (these are only a few examples). When distress arises, there may be tightening, clenching, or gripping. In times of greater ease, there may be an absence of sensation in that area of the body or even a quality of relaxation.

Energy: How awake or tired am I? As with all of these, this one is particularly interesting to me because of how many different ways there are to interpret energy level depending on the person. Tired and sleepy could be an indicator that the client is relaxed and at ease. Maybe they are yawning a lot as an indicator of "Ahhh, I can finally relax and let go." For others, that could signal dissociation, overwhelm, or even shutdown. In a similar but different way, someone feeling really awake could be in a state of hypervigilance and distress, while someone else might feel safe and at ease.

Imagery: For those who are visual thinkers (in case you didn't know this, some people don't have access to mental pictures; this is called aphantasia), there may be particular imagery that arises that indicates how they are feeling. Is the lake in their mind's eye calm and still, or are there a lot of ripples, almost to the point of waves on the surface of the water? The state of the water could be correlated with nervous system state. Again, there may be some people who associate a calm lake with a freeze state, while others might associate it with a parasympathetic state.

Rhythm or speed of stims: Some people may engage in consistent leg tapping, finger tapping, or other rhythmic or repetitive movement. When distress happens, the speed of that movement or the flow of the rhythm may change. For some, it may be that a speeding up or a more seemingly erratic rhythm is an indicator of sympathetic arousal. For others, their movement may slow, even slow to a halt in the presence of a freeze or other threat response. There is likely a baseline steady pace during times of neutrality or pleasure.

Color: This may be particularly useful for clients with synesthesia, when two or more senses are connected, like someone who smells colors or tastes textures. There may be a color associated with particular feelings or a state of being. For example, when a person is aware of light blue, this may be an indicator of feeling relaxed and at ease. When they are aware of red, it could mean distress. As with all of these indicators, the color that is relaxing or soothing for some may be distressing to others.

Scent: Somewhat similar to color, there may be a particular scent that is associated with sympathetic or parasympathetic states. Perhaps the fragrance of lilacs is associated with a feeling of sweetness, but the smell of cigarette smoke signals distress. I know I'm being repetitive, but I will emphasize (one more time!) that what indicates threat to one person may indicate safety to another. Be vigilant of your assumptions or biases.

While I tried to be as thorough as I could in writing this list, given how diverse our community is, I'm sure there are others that I did not mention. I know how easy it can be to discount our own wisdom when someone doesn't directly affirm our own thoughts or experiences. Please know that if there are indicators not on this list and they have been helpful, they are just as valid as any on this list.

As I prepare to transition to the next step, I notice myself chuckle at how thorough I was in sharing that list of indicators. I will add this to my ongoing check list of "yep, definitely Autistic." This may also be a helpful moment to pause, check in, notice what has your attention, and allow this to percolate before moving on. When you feel ready, here's the next step.

Step 4: Have Clients Choose an Indicator and Spend Time Noticing It, Both in Distress and in Their Version of Ease

Clients will choose an indicator for this playful exploration, being reminded that they can adjust or change it at any time. I recommend offering a few quiet moments for them to notice what draws their attention to help them choose. Once they choose, invite them to explore a little bit further and notice what they notice about their indicator in the present moment. This may be when they choose whether it will be a quantitative or qualitative scale. It can often be easier for clients to notice indicators in times of distress, so invite them to notice what happens when they feel, sense, and/or imagine feeling anxious, overwhelmed, triggered, threatened, and/or like something is too much, and so on (choose whatever words seem most applicable to that client). Continuing with this present-moment awareness, have them notice what happens to that same indicator when they feel, imagine, or sense they are relaxed, safe, at ease, or even joyful.

Depending on the client, they may need to recall both a difficult and a pleasurable moment in order to connect present-moment awareness with their indicator and their nervous system state. For some clients, this process will seem really intuitive, easy, and interesting. For others, it may seem a bit strange or weird. They may need more support and reassurance from you that there is no way to get it wrong and that this can very much be unique to them. And again, your collaborative creativity is encouraged!

Step 5: Create the Actual Scale by Choosing the Type of Scale and Selecting Measurements

Now it's time to create the actual scale. I'll use some examples to hopefully make it easier to follow.

"When my anxiety goes up, my jaw tightens and my palms get sweaty. When I'm less anxious, I don't notice anything in my jaw and my hands feel normal."

"When I'm relaxed, I'm lavender. When I get overwhelmed, I'm green."

"When my anxiety is at a 3 out of 10, I'm at my baseline. At a 9, I'm heading toward a panic attack."

"When I'm relaxed and engaged, I can hear the words you are saying really well, and I feel attentive. When I'm distressed, I feel scattered, and I stop making out your words. They become just one continuous sound."

"When I'm having a hard time, it's like a pinball machine that just keeps clacking and clacking; there's loud music and bright flashing lights. When I'm soothed or at baseline, the pinball machine is powered down."

Step 6: Determine When to Pause

There is so much room for creativity, individuality, and autonomy. There truly is no right or wrong way to do this. Now here's where our client may need us to lean in a bit more. Once the indicator and measurements have been determined, it's time to choose what number or quality will indicate that it's time for a break or pause. The pause calls attention to evidence of sympathetic arousal and invites us to shift our awareness to what evokes parasympathetic states. In other words, when a client starts to get activated, we take a break. We signal to their body that there is some degree of safety in this present moment together. We communicate to their nervous system that the threat or danger is not actively happening in this very moment.

Given the dominant culture of white supremacy, neurotypicality, colonization, capitalism, and other systems of power that oppress people, many clients will overestimate when to press "Pause." Here's an example of what I mean:

"My baseline anxiety is a 3 out of 10. Let's take a break when I'm at an 8."

While I honor their autonomy and investment in their therapeutic work, here's where I would lovingly and gently insert myself:

"Hmm, I wonder if 8 is actually too high? I know we are so conditioned to working hard, sucking it up, or just dealing with it, but I'd love for us to try something else. In the name of strengthening the "On" switch for your parasympathetic nervous system, what if we were to make 6 the pause? This way you're not having to feel quite so bad before we take a break. Would that be okay with you if we tried that just to see what it's like?" I feel my gratitude to Katie Asmus here. Even though her course wasn't specifically designed to be ND-affirming, her approach encouraged permission and gentleness, both for therapists and for our clients. Her teachings, integrated with my anti-ableist, anti-oppressive lens, influenced how I approach pauses with clients.

As a general rule in my counseling practice, I aim for clients to not exceed a 6 or 7 (or qualitative equivalent) during our sessions. Above a 7 is likely reactivating trauma and perpetuating sympathetic states rather than helping to bring balance to an overwhelmed system. This is not about censoring clients or inhibiting big feelings; it's about providing containment and practicing something new. I know it is not always so cut and dry, and we won't always be successful. This is my intention, though. I am actively working with clients to increase their window of tolerance by expanding the amount of time spent in states of Pleasure/Neutrality, or said another way, parasympathetic states.

Step 7: Client Chooses Sensory Delight or Stim to Pendulate To

We have an agreed upon an indicator, measures of baseline, neutrality and/or pleasure, distress (which I'm using as a catchall phrase right now for symptoms of sympathetic arousal), and a pause. Then we have the next little chat with our client. We invite them to track their indicator and let us know what they are noticing, particularly when they are at the number or quality that indicates a pause. We also seek consent. We let our client know that when learning something new, it can take time and a lot of trial and error. We ask if we can help them out:

"As you're practicing this, it might be tricky at first to notice when you need a break. I wonder if it would be okay with you for me to interrupt if I notice a shift in you?"

Please note that for PDA clients (persistent drive for autonomy), the act of being witnessed, seen, or known by another can be particularly distressing. While our intention may be to communicate attunement and care, it could register as threatening to the client. It could be a good idea to ask them about how to best approach this with them before outright suggesting it. Naming our intentions, being explicit about not wanting to cause harm, and seeking their input for how we can be most supportive will go a long way.

It is vulnerable to learn something new, and in times of distress, we are less likely to implement a new strategy that we are still learning. I lead with consent to center client autonomy, acknowledge their bravery at trying something that may seem strange or radical, and take the pressure off. Most times, when I ask for permission to interrupt, clients generally say "yes."

I make it clear that there is no such thing as getting it wrong; we're just playing with something new.

At the same time, I will not only interrupt when I see, sense, or hear distress levels rising, but every so often I may pause us to check in and see where they are on their scale. Just as I invite you, the reader, to check in with yourself every so often, I offer similar invitations to my clients. When clients are invested in external processing or sharing their story that they so deeply want to be heard in, they may be less connected to their present-moment experience simultaneously. They could miss cues that more support is needed. And there are certainly times when no extra support is needed!

As you may notice, this is a profoundly co-creative process. I am supporting the client to access their own inner wisdom, creativity, and autonomy. I'm also gently and lovingly guiding them in the process, in support of them being more gentle with themself than they are probably used to being. Now that we have gotten this far, we take the next step and choose what resource they will pendulate to during their pause. Again, resources are sensory delights and stims that evoke pleasure and/or neutrality.

Step 8: Client Engages With Sensory Delight or Stim

I notice myself giggle as I realize it's time for another list! Here's where the sensitivity of the ND bodymind is such a beautiful gift. The possibilities are endless for what brings delight, joy, squeals, happy hands, relaxation, or calm. I couldn't possibly list them all, but I will offer some suggestions (more on this in Chapter 10, Pleasure/Neutrality: Joy!). You and your clients may have other ideas. *Just a reminder: your other ideas are good and valid!* Remember, resourcing is all about feeling good, neutral, or less uncomfortable to evoke parasympathetic states. What is resourcing to one person may be distressing or aversive to someone else. It's also important to keep in mind that some resources that are safe and accessible for clients in the counseling space may not be safe or accessible in other environments, largely due to ableism and other forms of oppression. I've generated this list with an awareness of different settings for client work (e.g., in an office, at the client's home, outside) and across ages. No matter the setting, it's essential that we're ensuring client safety with any of the following suggestions.

> **SENSORY DELIGHTS AND STIMS (ANYTHING THAT INVOLVES THE EIGHT SENSES AND MORE)**
>
> **Yummy smells:** Essential oils, candles, flowers, food, etc.
> **Eating a snack:** Some clients may find delight in crunchy, salty, sweet, bitter, smooth, or creamy texture or flavor, or a combination of textures and flavors.
> **Having something to drink:** Think about texture, flavor, temperature, etc. For example, I love seltzer (bubbly water), but I will always fondly remember someone I knew who dubbed seltzer "angry water" and wanted nothing to do with it.
> **Proprioceptive input:** This can be any movement or object that engages body weight or resistance, such as: weighted blanket, weighted stuffies, books, any heavy(ish) objects that are available, including "unconventional weighted objects" like: holding potted plants, moving furniture, rolling up in a blanket or yoga mat, perhaps even using touch to apply pressure to a client (only with express consent!), wall pushes, being squeezed by either self, fabric, a person, or a pet, push-ups, plank pose, cart-wheels, handstands, pedaling a bike, climbing a tree, etc.
> **Vestibular input:** Rocking, swinging, bouncing on an exercise ball or trampoline, swaying, playing on a tire swing, lying or sitting in a hammock, spinning, flapping, etc.
> **Balancing:** Walking a tightrope or balance beam.
> **Contact with Earth:** Bare feet on the grass or outside

ground, lying down on the ground (again, some will love this and some will hate this).

Temperature regulation: Holding ice cubes, a cold drink, a cold compress on head or neck, using a space heater, covering up with a blanket, adding or removing layers of clothing, going outside or coming back inside, etc.

Fidgets: Such endless possibilities! Rocks, crystals, squishy things, sand, things that click, things that are smooth, things that open/close, zippers, bubble wrap, snow globes, jewelry, stuffies, etc.

Pleasurable sounds: Listening to music, water feature, running water, echolalia (repeating sounds, words, or sentences), etc.

Making music/sound: Drumming, singing, beatboxing,[7] playing an instrument, stomping, etc.

Reducing sound: Noise-cancelling headphones, earplugs, loop earplugs, hands or pillows over ears, eliminating as many sounds in the environment as possible, etc.

Dancing: Free-form movement, structured dance moves, twerking[6]

Connecting with nature, plants, animals: Whether inside or outside, access to nature objects like plants, flowers, shells, rocks, dirt, sand, water, gardening, or images of nature, plants, animals, etc.

Pets: So key for so many clients! If working virtually, explicitly invite client's pet(s) into the session. If possible, pets could be invited to in-person sessions or maybe you have a therapy animal.

Taking a "bio break": A chance to use the bathroom, eat,

---

7 When I attended the Autism in Black conference run by Maria Davis-Pierre, a Black Autistic therapist and parent, I learned more about the ways that Black culture shows up in Black people's stims. It's important to notice and be curious about the intersections between culture and stims.

drink, etc. This supports clients who may need cues about body needs due to their interoception.

Taking a "human-free zone" break: I came up with this term because sometimes, being in the presence of another nervous system is just too much for clients (especially for PDA clients). Co-create this with clients. Here are some options: if working virtually, you could both turn cameras and microphones off for a set amount of time or until the client feels ready to reengage outwardly. If in person, either client or therapist could agree to leave the room or go into a different space for a set amount of time or until the client is ready to return.

Rest: Lie down, close eyes, take a short nap, etc.

Art: Doodle, draw, paint, sculpt, color, build things out of Lego or other building blocks, etc. (I've been informed that whether Lego is referred to in the singular or plural form, it is always and only to be referred to as "Lego"; i.e., "I built that out of Lego"; as I said earlier, I learn *so* much from my clients!)

Body sensation: Perhaps there is a sensation in the body that serves as an anchor, is grounding, pleasurable, neutral, or satisfying in some way. Focusing on that sensation could be soothing.

Imagery: Could exist in the imagination or be a memory of a pleasurable experience or favorite place, item, or person.

Engage in an interest/infodump: Client could tell therapist about their passion or perhaps engage in their passion in the moment.

Playing a game: Board game, cards, trading card, online game, phone games, video games, foam sword battles, etc.

Blowing bubbles

Cubing: Playing with or solving cubes; for a long time, I only knew it as "Rubik's cubes," but I've since learned it

is also called "cubing." Whether the client knows how to solve it or just likes playing with it, both are equally valid.
Breathing: I have clients who love me to lead them in square breaths (e.g., count in for 4, hold for 4, out for 4, hold for 4). By me counting for them, my voice and nervous system act as a co-regulator. Others prefer to lead themselves. Sometimes just taking slow, deep breaths can be satisfying. Others like to have a longer exhale than inhale to support regulation (for me that often has the opposite of the desired effect!). There are so many options that clients can explore to find something that may work well for them.
Any rhythmic or repetitive movement or sound
Spiritual: Prayer, chanting, reading or reciting scripture or poetry, using a mala, using a rosary, meditation, etc.
And more: Especially exploring culture-specific stims that would be satisfying for clients.

Wow, that was really fun and satisfying! So much of the time, trauma is the focus when we are talking about marginalized identities. While trauma may certainly be present, there is also a whole world of glimmers (the opposite of triggers) and delights that can bring about sheer delight for Autistic and KCS/VAST folx (more on this in Chapter 10). The term *glimmers* was introduced by Deb Dana, a white clinician, consultant, author, and educator who is well known for making Polyvagal Theory accessible to the public and to mental health professionals. I've seen some incredible memes from Autistic folx about their take on ND glimmers. It feels like my own parasympathetic state got amplified through writing this list.

So soothing...how about for you? What you are noticing may be very different from what is present for me! What might you be needing right now or how might you want to tend to yourself at the moment?

When you're ready, we'll move onto Step 9.

Step 9: Client Determines When They Have Returned to a State of Neutrality, Pleasure, and/or Greater Safety and Chooses What Happens Next

Clients will choose one or more resources to insert and pendulate to. This is an opportunity for them to *revel, be enthralled by, play, or rest*. Some clients will value more or less structure to their resourcing breaks. It might be 5 square breaths, 3 minutes of stimming, 5 minutes of human-free zone, etc. For others, simply engaging at will until they feel done, notice a desire to stop, or feel relaxed once again will be preferred. Again, as co-creators of this process with them, collaborate to find out what they prefer and how you can support them. You can make an agreement that at a certain point you will check in with them to see how they are doing. More consent!

Once a client is back at or near their baseline, or reports feeling some degree of Pleasure/Neutrality, relaxation, soothing, ease, or safety, we arrive at another choice point of collaboration and consent. Here are the three options as I see them:

1. Pendulate back to the topic that the client was engaging in before they took a pause.
2. Keep taking a break.
3. Take a break from the topic for the rest of the session.

We may need to offer encouragement to our clients to keep taking a break or to take a break from the topic for the remainder of the session. Similar to taking a pause in the first place, clients will likely have internalized ideas about being "good" in session (more on this in Chapter 6 on dismantling ableism) and believe they need to be "pushing themselves," "working hard," or that "therapy is supposed to be grueling." Offer reassurance and validation that taking a break is good! Remind them that this is all about repatterning tendencies, and so if taking a break would mean they are engaging in a new pattern, encourage that. They may worry that they would disappoint you or let you down by taking an extended break. Honor, encourage, and celebrate their boundaries and self-advocacy!

If you're feeling worried that you would hold judgment about a client choosing not to "work hard" in session, rest assured that in Chapter 6, we'll look at these possible internalized rules in support of dismantling our ableism or internalized ableism. In the meantime, a gentle reminder: keep coming back to the notion of "Client as Self-Expert."

Before we wrap up this section, I want to offer a couple of different ways this scale can be used in real time. For clients who experience constant anxiety, this can be very helpful. We might call it an *anxiety scale*. Before our work together, clients may or may not notice their indicators that anxiety is present. This scale offers them more awareness of and autonomy for how they respond to their anxiety. Rather than anxiety always having power over them, they can notice when their anxiety is rising, pause, and insert something resourcing at will. As they practice this in the session, they may be able to then practice this on their own in their daily life.

I've also used this scale as a way to measure when a client is resourced enough to talk about something hard. For instance, imagine a client who wants support with interpersonal relating, but feels very insecure about relationships. Before processing a recent social interaction that felt bad to them, we would make sure that they were feeling confident in themselves, another manifestation of parasympathetic states. Perhaps this person's scale is a *confidence scale* and resourcing happens first! Once they have reached their "confidence threshold" on the scale, if they choose to, we could engage around the difficult social interaction. In this case, we might have an agreement that we wouldn't address the hard topic until they were at least a 6 or

7 out of 10 in confidence level. This way of relating can then be shared with loved ones, including parents when working with youth, as a way for them to be more mindful of how and when they give feedback.

A final note before the section recap. In my sharing of this scale idea with you, it may seem formal and lengthy. When you play with implementing this with clients, it can be as brief or lengthy as most fits the moment, your personalities, and your needs. If your brain tends toward "I have to do this exactly how Nyck described it," I want to offer explicit permission that you don't have to! Of course, you are welcome to if that's helpful, but I encourage as much of your own autonomy and originality as you desire.

We're getting ready to transition now to the last section of this chapter, which is about applying this to ourselves. Here's another invitation for you to insert a pause and check back in with yourself. You may want to consider what you are noticing, what you may be needing, and what delight or pace might best support you right now.

Recap: The Embodied Activation/Deactivation Scale

- **Step 1:** Start with psychoeducation.
- **Step 2:** Ask for consent to play with this.
- **Step 3 (if consent is given):** Offer possibilities of indicators for them to track (see Possible Indicators to Track list).
- **Step 4:** Have them choose one indicator and spend some time noticing or tracking it, both in distress and at ease/neutrality or pleasure.
- **Step 5:** Determine whether it is a quantitative, qualitative scale, or a picture-based scale, and choose measurements for baseline experience, neutrality/pleasure, and for the client's version of distress, overwhelm, too much, increased anxiety, etc.
- **Step 6:** Check in around the measurement for a pause,

encourage them to lower it if it's higher than a 6 or 7 (or qualitative equivalent). Ask for consent to interrupt.
- **Step 7:** Have client choose what sensory delight or stim to pendulate to (see Sensory Delights and Stims list).
- **Step 8:** Have client engage with their sensory delight or stim.
- **Step 9:** Help client identify when they have returned to a state of neutrality, pleasure, or feeling safer. Remind them of their options: pendulate back to the original topic, keep taking a break, change the topic altogether, or do something else

Whew! And there you have it.

WORKING WITH OURSELVES

I want to check in around how you are doing with my suggestion that the foundation of our work with clients is to support them to feel good.

In my work with therapists over the years, people are generally either:

- relieved, excited, maybe even validated that they can practice this way;
- hesitant, need more time to process, learn, practice, and integrate;
- or this feels so radical to them that they are doubtful they could do good therapeutic work with their clients.

I want to respect wherever you may find yourself along this continuum. You don't need to agree with everything I'm suggesting, *and* I'd really love for you to take time to explore it, play with it, and consider it. As we address dismantling ableism and internalized ableism in Chapter 6, that might also offer some more insight, clarity, and support around all this.

- ♦ If you find yourself struggling a bit, I want to invite you to jot down what you notice arising in you, including thoughts, feelings, images, etc.
- ♦ If you find yourself excited or hesitant, I invite you to do the same if you wish.

To accept radical ideas means to examine the old ideas we have previously held and hold curiosity about where they came from, who they are intended for, and what is their purpose. When it comes to anti-ableist and anti-oppression work, most often the resistance to these ideas stems from systems of power and dominance such as white supremacy, patriarchy, cis-heteronormativity, neurotypicality, colonization, and capitalism. Please be gentle with yourself as you bravely hold this inquiry. I know it can be intense.

Take your time as you need to here. When you feel ready, I'm going to offer some ways you can play with these concepts with yourself as a therapist. I truly believe that we can only teach something as well as we have practiced embodying it within ourselves first. To support that process, I'm going to engage us in inquiry.

- ♦ Do you ever wish that your needs mattered in a therapy session? That, while the focus is on tending to, showing up for, and supporting your client, your humanness was also valid?
- ♦ How can we truly expect our clients, who hold such marginalized identities in this dominant culture, to really take us seriously if we say one thing but then do another for ourselves? The power we hold in modeling for our clients what is possible is immense and not to be underemphasized.

I notice myself take a long, slow, deep breath. Ah, that felt nice. Perhaps you would like to take a deep breath—or your own equivalent resourcing moment—for yourself...

✼ ✼ ✼ ✼

As therapists who are also human beings, with our own histories, trauma, lived experiences, strengths, and challenges, we have our own support needs around staying engaged in our sessions. Let's be honest. As much as we might cherish and adore our clients and our work, sometimes we'd rather be off duty. Sometimes we get bored, distracted, overwhelmed, or triggered. We are not perfect, nor are we supposed to be (despite what we may have been taught). I want to normalize our own humanness and offer a tool that can help support your very real needs as they arise throughout your work.

Pendulation is a valuable tool that can also be used by us. For clients, we emphasized pendulating between what is distressing to what is resourcing and back and forth as needed. For us, we can pendulate from awareness of our client to awareness of ourselves. We track our client, we track ourself, back and forth, over and over. It's a way of checking in, of quietly asking, "Where is my focus right now?" "What do I need to stay engaged?" "Is what's showing up in me right now mine, theirs, or both?" These are all really valuable questions to be holding. While this will be further explored through the theme of boundaries as a form of differentiation that we will get to in Chapter 5, pendulation can help.

We notice our client. We track their body language, words, tone, movement patterns, and what and how they are expressing. Then we shift our focus and notice ourself. We notice our own attention, energy, body language, perhaps inner body sensation, temperature... all of those indicators we talked about in the previous section (you may want to refer back to the Possible Indicators to Track list in the previous section). Here's where you are encouraged to choose one or two to track in each session to help you stay in connection with your own nervous system state and needs. In the same vein, choose one or more resources to insert in response (you may want to refer back to the Sensory Delights and Stims list in the previous section). I'll offer some examples of how I play with this:

Example 1

A client is talking about their day, and I notice my mind start to wander. (Normally I'm deeply engaged and present with my clients; it's one of my favorite things about being in session: when the present moment is all that exists.) In response, I draw my attention to my foot fidget and add some more input through the sole of my foot. I take a few sips of the beverage I have with me (oftentimes I have two, one that is hot, one that is cold, or one that is simple and one that is flavorful). I may pay more attention to what I am doing with my hands. Are they occupied with a fidget, or do they need more or less stimulation? I may notice that I'm sleepy, and in order for me to stay engaged, I need more stimulation.

Example 2

Here's another one. A client is sharing about a difficult relational experience they had, and it reminds me of a conflict I had with someone in my own life recently or a relationship matter in my own life that is unresolved. I shift my attention back onto myself, and I might notice I feel a bit antsy. Maybe there's a sense of urgency or increased speed in my body. I take a few deep breaths, acknowledge to myself that I resonate with what they are saying, and I use my own sensory support to slow my internal pace, thereby slowing my external pace. In the slowing down, I have a moment to notice whether or not this is an opportunity for self-disclosure.

If the answer is "no," I might jot a quick note on the notepad on my desk so I can come back to this later for myself in my own processing, therapy, or supervision.

If the answer is "yes," I might say something like, "wow, I really resonate with what you are saying. It sounds so hard. I know how hard that type of thing is for me."

Depending on my relationship with the client, I may even ask them a question: "I can really relate to what you are saying, and I know how isolating this can be. Would it be helpful to hear from me about how I'm navigating a similar situation in my own life?"

Or I might say something like, "oof, this is so hard. I'm still trying to figure out how to handle this type of situation for myself. It's so complex!"

There are a few things happening in my response. I am aware that countertransference is taking place. I am offering self-disclosure in support of normalizing the client's experience, reducing the power differential between us, reducing isolation, honoring their boundaries and consent, and validating what they are going through. I am showing them that I believe them and am taking them seriously.

As surprising as it may be, it may be profoundly novel for a client to be believed, taken seriously, validated, *and* to have this happen on *their* terms.

If I weren't tracking myself, I might have missed the countertransference and an opportunity to slow down. Instead, I might have accelerated, gone into fix-it mode, and infringed upon my client's autonomy. At worst, I might have projected myself onto them and left them feeling shut down or steamrolled. At best, they might have felt confused, annoyed, or not sure of what just happened.

In addition to using pendulation to help us track countertransference, we will come back to this with additional tools as we explore boundaries as a form of differentiation in the next chapter.

While it can be tricky to focus on myself, still be aware of my client, and not miss anything important, it has gotten a lot easier with practice. The reality is that sometimes I do miss something. When that happens, I get to practice being human yet again and role model for my clients. I might say something like, "I'm so sorry, I was processing what you were saying, and I think I missed something. Could you repeat that?" Or depending on my relationship with the client, I may say, "I noticed a lot come up in me as you were sharing. Would you mind if we pause for a moment so I can process that?"

Moral of the story: pauses aren't just for our clients; we can initiate them for ourselves, too. In my experience, most of the times I have requested a pause, it was actually perfectly timed for the client to pause and process as well. Tracking myself helps me to better track my clients. Whether through mirror synesthesia (a scientific explanation for why I feel in me what someone else is feeling), somatic resonance, or being empathic, sometimes I feel in myself what my clients are experiencing within themselves. Then it becomes yet another opportunity to check in.

Here's an example: "Wow, I notice a spaciousness through my center as you share that. I wonder if you notice anything like that, too?" Or I might say, "I notice I just got really hot all of a sudden. I'm not sure if that's a me thing, or if you noticed anything similar in you?" This can be a way we practice and express attunement.

I want to emphasize that we get to be human, role models, mistake makers, and repairers. It's all part of the process.

Now that we've covered the overview of this tenet, how to apply it to clients, and how to apply it for ourselves, we've reached the end of this chapter. I realize that I am offering you a lot to digest, and I honor that we all have different processing speeds and paces. As you check in with yourself and notice what is present, you may find that you'd like to take a break before continuing onto the next chapter. Or you might be ready to continue right now. Either way, I look forward to greeting you in Chapter 5, Client as Self-Expert: Boundaries as a Form of Differentiation.

Recap: Why Pendulation Is So Beneficial for Us in Our Role as Therapist

- To support our focus, attention, and engagement. Do I need more or less stimulation?
- To be aware of countertransference

Pleasure/Neutrality: Prioritizing Parasympathetic States

- o To help bring awareness to what our client may be experiencing in the present moment
- o To honor our own humanity
- o To help us be a role model for our clients
- o By embodying the concepts of Pleasure/Neutrality and pendulation, we can better support our clients with these same concepts

CHAPTER 5
Client as Self-Expert: Boundaries as a Form of Differentiation

While the word boundary is often associated with "Keep out," "No!", and conflict, as it relates to ND Somatics, I am defining it as simply a demarcation of beginning and ending, a source of differentiation. Due to oppression, trauma, sensory issues, and/or hiding Autistic and KCS/VAST traits for safety and belonging, clients knowing where they end and the air, environment, or others begin is not innate. In other words, for many of our clients, knowing "I am me and you are you" can be a great challenge. This can make it extremely difficult for them to know what they need and want, what they don't need and want, who they are, and who they aren't. In this chapter, we will explore different contexts that influence differentiation and play with practical tools to help support this differentiation, both for our clients and for ourselves. This differentiation is an essential part of supporting wholeness, accessing consent, reducing harm, and getting to exist.

I'm going to offer a few more descriptions of this idea of boundary as I am relating to it. When I think of skin as a body boundary, it differentiates the inside of the body—tissues, bones, fluids, organs—from the outside world. It keeps everything on the inside intact and contained and still allows us to deeply engage with the world (and everything in it).

This next example is a direct expression of how much I learn from my clients. That is how I came to better understand that a boundary in this differentiation context is also a form of energetic proprioception. As we talked about in Chapter 3, proprioception is about knowing where we are in space. Said another way, it helps us to feel "Here I am!" In a similar way, when other people express a boundary, it provides an opportunity to feel "Here I am!" There is something metaphoric or energetic to push up against, and in the pushing, we can better feel ourselves. We can feel that there are two beings, not just our never-ending, spilling-out self who has no access to containment. In fact, boundaries of this nature actually support a sense of safety. It's a way of expressing, "I know where the edges are. I won't fall off the cliff. There is a ledge to stop me."

This also makes me think about parenting, especially with teenagers. In my work with teens for a number of years, I had lots of opportunities to think about this and to support parents. As Dr. Carla Sherrell teaches, when parents set a boundary with their teen, in essence, it can be an expression of care and love. It's a way of saying, "I know you, and I also know that your prefrontal cortex isn't fully developed yet, so I'm here to help as you might need it." It provides something for teens to push up against (and they will and do!). In doing so, it helps them to know themselves better. It helps them to learn more about who they are, what they need, what they value, and who they want to be. Boundaries, in essence, are not a form of punishment or asserting control (though they can be misused that way); they are a means of increasing safety and containment, and a reminder that someone cares.

Boundaries and Oppression

A boundary, at its core, acknowledges "you are you, and I am me." We may coexist and be interdependent, yet we are also two separate beings. There is a beginning and an ending. As I learned from Dr. Carla Sherrell, we may be vastly alike and also vastly different. And we get to be two distinct beings with *both* similarities and differences. Sharing similarities does not have to negate our differences, nor do our differences have to negate our similarities. She teaches that this is especially important as it relates to intersecting marginalized identities, connecting across identities, and even within identities. For instance, two Autistic women of different races may have some similarities in their lived experience as women and Autistic. A Latina Autistic woman and a white Autistic woman will also have vastly different lived experiences. Anti-oppression work can mean that we acknowledge and respect these differences and similarities. Boundaries allow us to not assume universality, and hence to not negate, minimize, or dismiss the very real impacts of systemic oppression.

Dr. Sherrell also taught me to notice that oppression can divide communities from within, pitting people against one another. Even for two ND people who share the same neurotype, race, gender, sexual orientation, socioeconomic status, culture, and similar age, they will still have differences from one another. Respecting these similarities *and* differences allows each person to exist as they are with their own autonomy. All too often, the impacts of oppression have people constantly wondering, worrying, "Am I x enough?"—be it Autistic *enough*, KCS/VAST *enough*, Indigenous *enough*, queer *enough*, trans *enough*, and so on. Oppression instigates competition among individuals and groups, leaving everyone to feel they have to prove themselves and their worth. This is deeply harmful and hurts people.

When we are allowed to be *both* similar *and* different, we can be our own unique, individuated selves with our own unique support needs, strengths, challenges, capacities, and disabilities. We do not feel the need to speak on behalf of others, assume we know best for others, assume we are the authority for an *entire* community, or marginalize members of our own communities.

Tiffany Hammond comes to mind again. She shares so generously, and sometimes so painfully, about her and her children's lived experience as Black Autistic folx in the United States. She has repeatedly been ostracized by and excluded from Autistic spaces, had her language policed, and been marginalized within already marginalized communities. This happens all too often and generally from white people.

I really feel my heart as I write that and think about what she and so many other racialized Autistic and KCS/VAST people go through. The intersections of racism and ableism are real and cause tremendous harm. I am aware of the ways oppression aims to disembody, which makes it feel even more important to pause and tend to the grief that is present within me.

I encourage you to check in with how you are doing too. If you want to, take a moment to notice what is present for you, how you might be able to best tend to yourself, and notice any adjustments you need to make for yourself.

The work of ND-affirming care is deep, tender, and complex. It is the essence of anti-oppression work. As said by Jen White Johnson, Afro-Latina ADH and disabled artist-educator and parent of an Autistic child, "to be pro-Neurodiversity is to be anti-racist." Heather Clarke, a Black Afro-Caribbean, Autistic abolitionist educator and parent talked about this at the Autism in Black conference in 2024. She shared brutal, yet essential to be known, history about the *DSM* and racism, and she named head on: "ableism is anti-Blackness."

There are many courageous Black, Indigenous, Latinx, Asian American and Pacific Islander, and Southwest Asian and North African ND leaders and advocates who are boldly speaking the hard, needs-to-be-heard, painful truth.

FOR WHITE THERAPISTS

For the moment, I would like to address white therapists specifically. Racialized readers, I invite you to rest, move, play, whatever might be the most nourishing or resourcing for you.

White therapists, we *need* to listen. Dismantling white supremacy is our work to do. We need to remain differentiated so that we can truly hear, know, and hold safer space for our racialized clients and colleagues. They deserve to be safe and to rest.

While I hold plenty of marginalization as a trans, queer, multiply-ND person, I am still white. I also lived for decades as a high-masking, unidentified, speaking Autistic person, meaning that I'm able to pass as NT. What that means is that I have ample privilege, too. And it is my responsibility to keep understanding, unpacking, and dismantling my privilege.

How are you holding and working with your own privilege?

Boundaries as a form of differentiation are essential to the well-being of our racialized clients. We do not, and will not ever, know their lived experience from the inside. We have no right to assume we do, and the harm we are capable of causing (and has been caused for centuries) is vast.

As a white person in the United States, dismantling racism and working with my privilege is a lifelong investment and journey. It is for you too. Yes, it is uncomfortable, and yes, it is *absolutely necessary.* Please refer back to the support and foundation in Chapter 4 as you engage in your anti-racism work.

A final note for the moment: white therapists, no matter what your neurotype, whether you are ND or NT, please put in the effort to avoid projecting your lived experiences onto your racialized clients. It will require diligence and inner work on your part not to do this, *and* it is essential to anti-ableist counseling. Listen, learn, and remember that our clients are self-experts.

Racism and other forms of oppression steal a person's autonomy, access to consent, and boundaries. Reclaiming autonomy, body and other boundaries, and restoring consent are *essential* to anti-ableist, anti-racist, anti-oppression work.

There are several books in the reference list at the end of

> this book that I highly recommend you read as part of your anti-racism work. And please keep listening to and learning from racialized ND folx.

I notice an impulse to take a dance break for myself, to continue to lean into embodiment. A chance to stand up, move my body in gentle ways that feel satisfying, and allow this important and intense work to process and move through me. I wonder what you might be needing or wanting right now? This is an invitation to care for yourself in whatever ways you have access to and do what might feel good, nourishing, or even satisfying. When we come back, I'll share a bit more about the theory behind boundaries as differentiation to finish out this section.

✶ ✶ ✶ ✶

I'm so grateful I took that opportunity to insert resourcing after noticing myself needing a break. I played a couple of songs whose sound deeply resonates for me. Inspired by my 5Rhythms practice (a movement meditation/ecstatic dance practice developed by Gabrielle Roth), I freely and creatively let my body move as it desired. I noticed waves of grief in response to this injustice, and I kept moving through them, the tears right there behind my eyes. The size and intensity of my emotions are just way too big to fit inside of me. Dancing helps me to feel myself expand, to connect with earth, and to give ample space for this energy that is so much bigger than you or me alone. This is collective grief.

When you are ready, we will move onto the next subsection.

Boundaries, Sensitivity, and Permeability

I'm thinking about justice sensitivity and how deeply injustice touches me. My particular flavors of neurodivergence mean that I feel deeply, *all the damn time.* As challenging as it can be, I wouldn't actually change this about myself.

I've heard many other Autistic and KCS/VAST clients offer a similar sentiment about how deeply they feel, their justice sensitivity, and what a potent source of connection with other humans their sensitivity offers them. When I would bring up boundaries in our work, I'd be met with an assumption that boundaries meant an energetic bubble, a form of separation that would cut off their innate empathic beingness. This would follow with a "No!" They helped me to fine tune and better understand boundaries as they relate to differentiation. This is where the imagery that we will get to in the next section originates.

Boundaries as I mean them in this ND-affirming anti-ableist way are about each person getting to wear their own shirt. Rather than two people both trying to squeeze their head and arms through the same holes in the same shirt and being confined to a teeny tiny space that likely inhibits freedom and movement, they each get to wear their own piece of clothing. They get to be as close or apart as they desire. In this way, they can still feel deeply connected to those around them, and they can also feel themselves.

I feel the urge to repeat that. They can feel deeply connected to those around them, *and* they can also feel themselves.

I think it's worth offering it in the first-person tense, too, to really let it digest for ourselves as counselors:

We can be deeply connected to those around us,
***and* we can also feel ourselves.**

This is huge and novel for so many Autistic and KCS/VAST people. Particularly for those who embodied a chameleonlike way of being for much of their lives, they can feel that they are permeable. Getting to be connected yet different is a wild concept. For a lot of reasons relating to how people are socialized, it is especially common for assigned female at birth (AFAB) ND people to be deeply observant of their surroundings, watch how people exist and move through the world, and learn how to mimic others to fit in, blend in, or be accepted. This can also be said for racialized folx navigating predominantly white spaces. While this is an adaptive skill and effective survival strategy, there is a cost. In exchange for greater likelihood of being accepted or safer, the person sacrifices their sense of self. They do not get to have needs, be known in their authentic truth, or take up any more space than the environment expects of them or permits.

Boundaries as differentiation can be like getting to take a deep, nourishing breath. Or coming up for air after being submerged for a long time underwater.

I feel tenderness arise within me as I remember being in my late 20s and being confronted with how all this lived in me. I'm going to share a story, aka therapeutic self-disclosure.

Within a span of a short period of time, two different family friends, unprompted and unexpectedly, both commented on how different I was from my sisters. I was utterly shocked. I literally had no idea that anyone saw us as separate. At the time, I was unknowingly trans (and queer, Autistic, and KCS/VAST) and still living as a cis-het NT passing woman who grew up with three older sisters.

As I reflect on these two moments in time, I can still feel the awe and confusion that I felt then. I remember my reaction. "What do you mean?!" I had no idea that I was my own person, whatever that even means. Interestingly, within the next year or so, I got help for the debilitating chronic pain I was dealing with, found my way out of a deep depression, and made some major changes in my life. While the timing caused a lot of chaos within my family of origin, it wasn't long before I gave my life a complete overhaul. I discovered Naropa University in Boulder, Colorado, quit my job, packed up my car, and moved across the country from New Jersey. While I moved there to study to become a somatic psychotherapist, *another* intention was just as foreground: to differentiate from my siblings and family of origin.

Over a decade later and after a lot of therapeutic support, moving through deep grief, lots of dancing, multiple coming-outs, intense self-growth, and very special chosen family who helped me to learn how to have and practice boundaries, I'm the most differentiated I've been. Even so, it's an ever-evolving, ongoing journey, and I know there is a lot more for me to learn and practice. As I share this tidbit of my life with you, I'm reminded of several key people from my 20s who were instrumental in me getting to where I am right now.

As I take a moment to feel my gratitude for these mentors and loved ones, you may notice that you are feeling reflective or contemplative too. If you are, I invite you to notice what's present for you. Perhaps you want to jot some notes down, move your body, pause, hydrate, feel your own gratitude...whatever you need, I hope you are able to give it to yourself.

It feels good to remember that as alone as I felt during the very difficult decade of my 20s, there *were* people who saw me, believed in me, and wanted what was best for me. Even though none of them had the knowledge of or awareness to be able to say, "Nyck, I wonder if you might be Autistic and KCS/VAST (and queer and trans) and if that is a huge missing piece of understanding the beauty of who you are and also why you struggle the way you do," they feel like lanterns of love put on my path to show me the way forward. As a dear friend likes to say, "Grief and gratitude, they go together." Indeed, it all seems to come back to that: grief *and* gratitude.

Through the art of differentiation, it becomes possible for clients to know themselves better and consider unmasking. They get to feel themselves more acutely, discover who they might be under, behind, or beside their masks. At first, they might feel *more* lost, but with time and quality support, the pathway to greater liberation is made possible.

We have arrived at the end of this section. Coming up next, we'll explore how to *apply* this principle of differentiation. As we transition, please care for yourself however you might need or want, and consider that whatever arises for you is valid and worthy.

Recap: ND-Affirming Boundaries as Differentiation

- Boundaries are "This is where I end, and you begin."
- Boundaries are a form of energetic proprioception.
- Boundaries help us to be honest and real about our similarities *and* differences.
- Ableism is tied to anti-Blackness, as neurodiversity is tied to anti-racism.
- Boundaries help reduce harm, especially across difference.
- Boundaries help offset chameleonlike tendencies and help us to discover our support needs, wants, who we are, and who we want to be.

WORKING WITH CLIENTS

For many ND clients, whether already identified or not yet identified, the notion that they could or are allowed to have boundaries is quite novel. When clients have access to their own differentiated self, they gain greater access to their autonomy and to consent. They are lathered in permission to have needs, wants, "yesses," "nos," "maybes," and to be recognized as the experts on themselves. After all, they are the only ones living inside their body; how could anyone else know that experience better than they do? Hence, boundaries as differentiation is a key principle of the foundational tenet *Client as Self-Expert*.

While this is not true of all Autistic and KCS/VAST clients, many of my clients are visual thinkers or find imagery a valuable means of communicating and processing information. For that reason, I will lead us through a visualization exercise so that we can play with, try out, and get a kinesthetic feel for how we can implement this. By trying it out for yourself, you'll get a felt sense of how to then lead clients through this exercise.

There are two different ways that I offer this to people. One way is the custom, individualized shirt I referenced earlier, and the other is a custom sphere. Some people may blend the two or get inspired to create something different from either of these two suggestions. Creativity and uniqueness are encouraged, and all of your ideas are valid.

If you are someone who does not have access to mental pictures or visualization, also known as aphantasia, I want to support you to make this as concrete as possible. It is likely that the custom shirt that I offer will be the more accessible of the two options. It may be most helpful to relate to the prompts with an awareness of the shirt you are presently wearing (if you are currently shirtless, feel free to put on a favorite shirt or article of clothing for the purpose of this exercise).

BOUNDARY AS CUSTOM SPHERE

I'll start with the custom sphere. For those who may not find visualizations helpful or would rather it be more concrete than that, I've included a blank sphere for you to design.

I intentionally chose a sphere and aim to differentiate it from the notion of an energetic bubble. For me personally, I associate the word bubble with popping. To me and many clients I have worked with, it also signals that whatever exists outside the bubble is potentially bad, harmful, or to be avoided.

As a somatic psychotherapist, I learned about kinespheres in graduate school. I think of a kinesphere as the amount of energetic and/or physical space that we take up. When I am cradled in a fetal position, my kinesphere is small and my end points are all close together. When I am outstretched as far as I can possibly reach in all directions, my kinesphere is at its most expansive. The thing about kinespheres as I understand them, though, is that they can only get as large or small as my body is positioned in space.

When it comes to a boundary sphere, it can be as big as the globe (or bigger!) if that's what is present in the moment. Depending on the moment, the day, the year, and other factors such as energy level, emotional state, and more, the size, style, and design may change. This is not a fixed image, though it may be for some. It is intended to meet who we are and what we need in any particular moment.

Please know that depending on how systemic oppression lives in your particular body, you may notice preset limits to how much space you were taught that you are allowed to take up. I encourage you to be gentle with yourself, to trust your process, and to play with what feels accessible to you. You may notice that the environment you are currently in influences your comfort level or sense of safety for how much space you take up. Your autonomy is centered here, so please remember you can stop at any time.

If it would be helpful, feel free to get into an even more comfortable position, record yourself reading this subsection and then play it back like a guided meditation, or have someone else read it aloud to you. This could also be used as a script with clients if that feels helpful for you. Feel free to gather markers, colored pencils, crayons, paint, glitter pens, stickers, pastels, or anything else of your choosing to play with and design the blank sphere that I've provided.

This is your customized sphere, designed to fit you, to help you to take up the amount of space you would like to exist within, and to know where you end and the world around you begins. As connected as all beings truly are, this sphere is your own little supportive space that allows you to feel *you*.

As you start to let your mind wander to this notion of existing within a sphere of your own creation,

- Notice how big or small you might like it to be. It's okay if it starts out as one size, and then as we go, you notice you would like it to grow or shrink.
- What is the texture and shape of your sphere? Is it translucent, thick, cloudlike, dense, round, blob-like, or something else?
- What color or colors is your sphere? Is the inner lining different from the outer lining?
- What covers the lining? Moss, carpet, fleece, silk, paint, something else? Are there images or words that line the sphere? Maybe even affirmations?
- Is there anything with you inside the sphere? Furniture, plants, animals, nonphysical beings, a swing or hammock? Are there any sounds, perhaps a fountain with the sound of a babbling brook or a favorite song?
- How might you include a drain in your sphere? A drain allows any energy that isn't yours, doesn't belong to you, or that you are ready to let go of to be released from your sphere. This is especially helpful for people who are really energetically and emotionally sensitive.
- How does it feel to exist within your sphere? Do you feel more or less connected to yourself? More grounded or embodied?
- Play with being in your sphere and noticing objects or other beings in your environment. What is that like?

Take as long as you like here. Be as curious, playful, and creative as you like too. This is uniquely yours; there is no right or wrong. Notice your preferences or aversions. Feel free to take what is in your mind, and if you haven't already or would like to, create it on the page to the best of your ability. If the sphere I provided is too small, please feel free to create something bigger!

When you feel complete with this, you can let it go, shake it off, release it, exit it, whatever helps you to put it aside for now while we try out the other option. Take as much time as you need or want before you transition to the next option.

Boundary as Custom Shirt or Article of Clothing

Some clients are so accustomed to their empathic, permeable nature for feeling connected to others that the idea of a sphere feels too alienating. The custom shirt may be a better fit for them. If a shirt feels too limiting, it can be any article of clothing. Personal preference is important with any of these tools, so we'll get to try this one out and notice what it feels like. You may notice preferences, aversions, or your own original ideas. Be curious and honor them. Similar to the custom sphere, feel free to get extra comfy, record this next piece and play it back like a guided meditation, or have someone else read it aloud to you. There is no wrong way to do this. Again, I have provided a blank page for you to draw your shirt if you wish, and this script could be used directly with clients. When you are ready, I will begin.

YOUR CUSTOM SHIRT OR ARTICLE OF CLOTHING

Take a moment to imagine your most favorite shirt. It may be a shirt that you currently have, one that you used to have, one that you dream of having, or a completely made-up piece of clothing. This shirt evokes the essence of you, your personality, your confidence, maybe even gender euphoria. You may feel super comfortable, sexy, casual, formal, anything goes. For those with aphantasia, I encourage you, if possible, to put on a shirt you have that evokes what you desire to experience.

- As you envision or wear this shirt, notice what the material is. Is it soft, stiff, silky, thick, thin, light, heavy?
- Are there sleeves? How short or long are they?
- What about a collar? Notice the neckline.
- Also notice how long the shirt is. Do you tuck it in; is it flowy; does it just fall straight on your body?
- Are there buttons, snaps, zippers, cuffs, or pockets?
- What colors or patterns is it?
- If possible, feel yourself wearing this shirt. If you aren't actually wearing it, imagine it is on your body. What does it feel like? What do you notice?
- See if you can watch yourself at a distance while you wear your shirt. What do you notice, sense, or feel?

Take as long as you like here. There is no such thing as a perfect shirt, and remember that just like the sphere, it can be ever evolving. You are not locked into this as your one and only shirt. Once you feel complete with this, go ahead and imagine taking the shirt off. You can hang it up, fold it, throw it on the floor, hang it on a chair, and so on (either all in your mind's eye or literally).

Processing This With Clients

Once you've led clients through either or both visualizations, you can take some time to process the experience with them. Some clients may wish to describe their imagery; others may prefer to keep it private. Here are some questions or prompts to engage clients with:

- "How was that for you?"
- "What do you notice about your indicator(s) (from Chapter 4's Possible Indicators to Track list) while you are in your shirt or sphere?"
- "How do you feel now? What's present for you now after having done that?"
- "How might this be helpful for you?"
- "I'm curious what you notice about your sense of connection with yourself and your connection with others."
- "I wonder if consent feels any different or easier when you are in your shirt/sphere?"

Particularly for clients who have historically been invalidated in their thoughts, feelings, and experiences, it may feel quite different, novel, or even bizarre to have such permission to take up autonomous space. Be gentle with them and affirm that whatever their reactions or experiences are with this boundary play are valid. You may even make agreements with one another about how to use this tool in session together. It could be interesting for them to play with existing within their custom boundary with you and then without it to notice what might be different. You can also play with both existing within your boundary at the same time and then both existing without it simultaneously. Be aware that both you and your clients are more likely to be aware of your sociocultural differences through this. This is a reminder why doing ND-affirming work means also being invested in anti-racism work, decolonizing, and dismantling cis-heteronormativity.

It could be helpful to ask clients:

- Would they like you to remind them of this tool?
- Would they like for you to encourage using this tool before engaging in anything relational between the two of you?
- Would they like to know about your custom shirt or sphere?

These are just some ideas. Here's another opportunity where your creativity and originality as a therapist are so valuable. At the same time, keep reminding yourself that your client is a self-expert.

As we conclude this section and move onto the next one, we'll get a bit more curious about how to use our shirt or sphere while working with ourselves. For now, I encourage you to jot down any additional notes, images, or wonderings that you may have. Notice any needs that may be arising within you that wish to be tended to, including taking a break. When you feel ready, I'll meet you in the next section, Working With Ourselves.

Recap: Tools to Explore Boundary as Differentiation

- One option is to create a custom sphere to exist in. Design it as simple or detailed as you wish, to include size, texture, imagery, shape, etc.
- Another option is to create a custom shirt or custom article of clothing to wear. Design it as simple or detailed as you wish, to include style, design, material, accessories, etc.
- If visualizing isn't accessible for you or your client, you can make it more concrete by focusing on an actual shirt that you can put on.
- Take some time to process this with clients and validate their experience.

WORKING WITH OURSELVES

My rationale for leading you through this, as I mentioned earlier, is so that you could have a kinesthetic and embodied experience of this concept for yourself. Once it makes sense to you and transcends your cognitive pathways alone, it is much more likely to be of value to your clients.

When it comes to being differentiated from our clients, there are a few main points that I think about:

- Trusting the client as the expert on themself
- Helping us to identify and navigate countertransference
- Reducing enmeshment with our clients and honoring their individuality
- A guidepost for when self-disclosure could be a helpful tool to implement
- Helping us to better understand and relate to our own privileged and marginalized sociocultural locations and identities

I will go ahead and expand on each of the above, offering prompts and things to be curious about, maybe even journal about if that's helpful for you.

Trusting the Client as the Expert on Themself

As you engage in our own exploration of boundaries in your therapeutic role, I invite you to either reenter your sphere, put your shirt back on, or return to whatever custom boundary you created for yourself. I encourage you to be intentional about this.

- Notice what it's like to exist outside of it.
- Then notice what happens when you are in it.

Client as Self-Expert: Boundaries as a Form of Differentiation

- If it's helpful, feel free to enter and exit a few times to help you notice what, if anything, changes.

Go ahead and enter once more.

- What is it like to consider that, as your differentiated therapist self, you are not required to have all the answers?

I feel relief pulsate through me as I write that.

- What do you notice?

You are not expected to solve your clients' problems for them, have their lives all figured out, or always know the perfect thing to say. In fact, you can't. It's impossible (though it sure might leave you feeling like a hero if you could). *It's also not your job.*

Let's be real. We don't have our own lives all figured out either. That's an unreasonable expectation of us as human beings! We have our own share of imperfections and challenges, and we are not supposed to magically transcend these just because we are therapists.

Our role, as ND-affirming, anti-ableist counselors is to show up for our clients and help bring forth *their* wisdom. To help them *trust themselves*. To *take themselves seriously*. We are not fixing, as there is nothing broken in the first place. Remember, Autistic and KCS/VAST people are whole and complete Autistic and KCS/VAST people, *not* broken NT people. They need us to help *amplify their own voice*. We are more like a guide, mentor, coach, or companion.

- If it's helpful, imagine yourself at work in a session with a client. See/feel/sense yourself existing in your sphere or shirt.
- Is it easier to slow down, talk less (or more for those who have a harder time leaning in), insert yourself less (or more), trust the process more?
- Does it support you to take up less space and give your client *more* space to exist within? Not to diminish

yourself, but to level the playing field as much as possible?

Take your time here, linger in your inquiry and curiosity as much as you choose or are able. When you're ready, we'll go on to the next theme.

Identifying and Navigating Countertransference

I have the sense that across the board, there is a general sentiment among therapists that countertransference is a bad thing. I disagree. I think it is net neutral, to be expected, and something to connect with. Given that many therapists who are drawn to working with ND clients are ND themselves, there is going to be *a lot* of countertransference. There is so much we can relate to and resonate with our clients. There are shared human experiences and similarities. Our work is often to maintain our sense of differentiation and not to assume that we know *exactly* what our client is going through. We sure might feel real darn close, though!

I'm a believer that the work of a therapist is also deeply personal. It can be hard to draw a clear and solid line between the professional and personal. After all, we're all just humans doing the best we can to exist and if possible, to thrive. No one has it all figured out!

At the same time, for NT therapists working with ND clients, there is still plenty of room for countertransference, even if it takes on a different flavor. I've worked with a number of seemingly NT therapists over the years, only to discover through their learning about ND-affirming care, that they, too, are Autistic and/or KCS/VAST and just didn't know it yet! This is so common.

For therapists who still identify as NT, even after they learn more about autism and KCS/VAST, there is still plenty of countertransference to be had! It could be more linked to their own ableist ideas or expectations, though. Oftentimes, without closer examination, they might not have even realized they were steeped in ableism.

There seems to be a mystical, unexplainable element about the clients who show up at our proverbial door. They seem to need just what we have to offer, and their growth is often just the teaching we need to propel our own growth journey forward. My clients reflect back to me my own wounds *and* my own healing. This is why my work as a therapist fits me so well: one of my primary passions is self-growth. I am constantly provided with opportunities to learn more about myself and to keep on growing. Inevitably, it also seems that whenever I take the next step in *my* growth journey, my clients soon after seem to take *their* next step, too. We evolve together. We learn together. We teach each other (more on this in Chapter 9 on transitions, ritual, and the Sacred).

This to me is part of the essence of ND-affirming counseling. We are humans sharing in a human experience. The client is the expert on themselves, and I am the expert on me. I also learned a few other things along the way, wink wink. Together, we co-create our sessions and the journeys we take together. They are in the driver's seat; I am in the passenger seat. Or we are meandering through a forested trail together, exploring, being curious, and being present with what arises.

In order for us to do this well, we must be engaged in our own work, whether it's our own therapy, supervision, coaching, peer mentorship, spiritual support, whatever most resonates with you or what's accessible. We are growing just as much as our clients. Our sessions with clients are *not* the place for us to do our own work; that happens outside of the session. While I do believe the therapeutic relationship is everything for our ND clients and that our clients can teach us much about ourselves, I also believe that being in right relationship with them means that they do not carry responsibility for our well-being. In that way, we are not yet another human they have to take care of, appease, or educate. We hold a strong container for *them* to lean into, to be held in, and to feel deeply cared for.

Takeaway: of course we will be impacted by our clients! Please expect this, and take responsibility for how you are impacted by your clients. Please also do your own growth work, so that you can be as clear a conduit and space holder for them as possible.

If you notice a break or insertion of sensory delight might be supportive, now is a great time! Then we'll get into our next theme.

Reducing Enmeshment With Our Clients and Honoring Their Individuality

It seems each theme leads right into the next. Whether the client and therapist share the same or a similar neurotype or have very different neurotypes, it is all too easy to merge with clients, or any humans for that matter. This is why we have to track our countertransference, do our own work, and remember that no matter how similar to our client we might be, we are also different. No two humans on the planet are completely identical in every single way.

For ND therapists, there may be a tendency to overidentify with clients or to compare and contrast yourself with your clients, perhaps unconsciously seeing if you "measure up" in your neurodivergence.

For NT therapists, there may be a tendency to think you have all the answers and that if the client just "did as you said," they would be better, "fixed," or fine.

When I exist within my boundary, and I perceive my client in their boundary, I recognize each of our respective inner wisdoms. I recognize that my clients' growth or seeming stuckness is not an indicator of my failings as a therapist. It could be an indicator that I am missing something, that additional support is needed beyond what I can provide, that their pace is different from what I might have expected, or that we are trying to change something that won't ever change.

When I see my clients as separate autonomous beings who

did fine before me and will be fine after me, I can honor their wholeness and the wisdom of their human journey with greater ease. Ultimately, their healing and growth isn't actually about me. Sure, I may be a big support for them, but they are the ones who do the healing and growth. I don't do it for them, nor could I. When I remember that, it's easier to see them for them and me for me. It's similar to the idea of "I stay in my lane, and they can stay in theirs." I bet we can all relate to moments, whether with clients, partners, loved ones, or whoever, when we feel that impulse to cross over and try to solve whatever is going on in their lane.

Takeaway: having empathy, compassion, and understanding for our clients is not the same thing as merging with them. We honor and center their autonomy and individuality and can better do so through showing up embodied in our sphere or shirt.

Feel free to pause, take a moment to process, jot down some thoughts, move your body, or rest as you need. When you are ready, we will transition into the next theme.

A Guidepost for When Self-Disclosure Could Be a Helpful Tool

Here's another one of those elements of therapy that I think has been dubbed as inherently problematic. Again, I disagree. As I've heard other ND therapists say as well, skillful self-disclosure is a really important facet of the ND-affirming counselor-client relationship.

Much of the lived Autistic and KCS/VAST experience in an NT-dominant culture, even more so for those with multiple marginalized identities, is to feel isolated and alone in how we think, feel, perceive, and experience being human. When there is true resonance or connection with something a client is sharing from their own lived experience, it presents the therapist with an opportunity to lean into connection.

Typically, I like to connect back in with my sphere or shirt first. That can help me to better gauge if my timing is accurate. At the same time, in leading with the Client as Self-Expert and me not having to have it all figured out, I may handle it like this:

"I'm not sure if this would be helpful or not. I notice as I listen to you that I can so relate to what you're saying. Would you want to hear about an experience that I had that reminds me of this?"

This does a few things:

1. Practices consent.
2. Acknowledges that I don't have all the answers.
3. Shows my client that I honor and respect their autonomy.

Sometimes clients will say "no," and that is totally okay! Sometimes clients will say "yes," and that is totally okay!

I feel my belly sink a bit as I recall a moment in my own life when self-disclosure would have potentially saved me a lot of seemingly unnecessary isolation and suffering. It's been a decade since this happened, and there is still some tenderness around it. Since I can't outright ask for your consent, I'm going to go ahead and share this story with you, and of course, you could always choose to skip over it, wink wink.

When I was in my second year of grad school, my mom died. I remember returning to campus after going home for the funeral, and I made a point of meeting with my professors to check in and get some support for my reentry.

I returned to campus feeling like a stranger. That feeling reminds me of lyrics to a song that used to live on repeat in my head. Of course now I can't remember it! So naturally I paused to look it up, and it's Sheryl Crow, "Every Day Is a Winding Road." I *loved* her music. I knew this stranger feeling well from when my dad died and I returned to my undergrad campus after his funeral. It wasn't any more comfortable or bearable the second time around.

I remember being in one of my professors' offices and him saying something like "Others have gone through similar things before," and I didn't believe him. Probably due to my unknowingly Autistic brain, I truly thought I was the only person at my school to have ever gone through this. For the remainder of the semester and throughout the entire next (and last) year of my graduate program, I felt very alone in my grief and experience.

Fast forward to several months after I graduated, and I had the sacred opportunity to participate locally in a grief ritual with Sobonfu Somé of the Dagara Tribe in Burkina Faso, West Africa. At this gathering, there were about five people from the graduate school I went to who were in the cohort a year behind me. All of them had a dead parent. Of the five of them, I think four had parents who died *while they were in grad school.*

I was in complete and utter disbelief. "What?! You were all on campus at the same time as me, in the same program, grieving the death of your parent, and I didn't know?!" I couldn't make sense of how my department never offered the possibility of obtaining consent from these other students to connect us. Neurotypicality, white supremacy, and the rules of the mental health field keep individuals separate and apart. Everyone is expected to figure it all out on their own. This is the antithesis of ND-affirming, anti-ableist care. Instead, we think outside the lines. We ask for consent. We subvert norms (more on this in Chapter 8: Global Permission: Questions to Dismantle Normativity in the Counseling Space). We honor confidentiality, while also exploring how to create bridges. We reduce isolation.

Ten years later, my work synchronistically reconnected me with someone in leadership in my department at the time. I got to tell my story, be heard, and be met with compassion, care, and empathy. I shared what the experience was like for me and what I wish had happened instead. It was a truly reparative experience. The sting didn't dissolve completely, but it reminded me that it is never too late when it comes to repair.

Additionally, it helped me to zoom out from my internal experience and hold more of the big picture, particularly the systemic and institutional lenses. At the time, I wasn't able to hold the complexity of the situation; it felt so personal. As I share this now, I can feel the simultaneous tenderness for myself, gratitude for the allyship and support I did receive, and compassion for what it means to operate from within the complexities of an institution.

Having spent a decade impacted by this experience serves to fuel my passion for skillful self-disclosure. Yes, there absolutely is a skill to it. We try not to just blurt out our own stuff and put that on our clients. But with their consent, absolutely. Sometimes I am uncensored with my clients, and it's very freeing! I've been known to have "spicy thoughts" on occasion, but again, I usually only express them with their consent or when I can't slow myself down fast enough to get consent first! In which case, then I check in afterward about how that was for them, and if necessary, I engage in repair.

I also want to acknowledge how culture plays into self-disclosure. I think we all know how white supremacy squashes it.

- How do you relate to self-disclosure based on your culture and your values?
- What are your thoughts on this?

Take as much time here as you'd like. I'm going to offer our takeaway from this theme and then head into the last theme of this section. When you feel ready, I look forward to having you join me.

✷ ✷ ✷ ✷

Take-away: Self-disclosure can be such a valuable tool for reducing isolation and stigma and supporting connection and community. Some clients may appreciate it more than others. Keep centering their autonomy and consent.

Better Understanding and Relating to Our Own Privileged and Marginalized Sociocultural Locations and Identities

In the introduction part of this chapter, we talked quite a bit about the connection between boundaries and differentiation and how they relate to perpetuating or reducing oppression. This is important to keep coming back to.

When I am actively embodied in my shirt or sphere, I am in more direct connection with my privilege and my marginalization. I take up my space, stay anchored in my seat or pelvic floor, and feel how I am both similar *and* different to my client. When my client and I share multiple identities, I sometimes have to effort *more* to remind myself, "They are them. I am me."

When my clients and I differ in our identities, be it gender, race, sexual orientation, age, culture, religion/spirituality, socioeconomic class, and so on, I also have to effort! Dr. Carla Sherrell taught me a lot about the practice of relating to and supporting clients across differences in social power. This has included staying aware of the varying identities that clients and I each hold and being mindful of who holds what social power. As a therapist, I will always hold power in my role (whether I like it or not), but sometimes I also hold more social power than my clients, as when I work with racialized clients and therapists.

When working with racialized clients and therapists, I practice staying in my differentiated state to help me listen closely, truly hear them, back up (uncensored me so deeply wants to say "back the f*** up") to give them *more* space to take up. I ask for even more consent. I do this in an effort to create a therapeutic space where we are subverting the harmful impacts of racism and white supremacy, creating greater equity, and creating more balanced power dynamics. I strive for them to have a reparative, safe enough, growth-oriented space where they can be their autonomous, authentic selves. This is not about me shrinking, but about avoiding whiteness from interfering.

Through Dr. Sherrell's teaching, I learned that when working with clients who hold more social power than me, I also need to effort to stay in my differentiated self. Despite my power as a therapist, it can be easy to take up less space or quiet my voice in the presence of greater social power. This may not serve the client nor me. By feeling my shirt or sphere, I can stay in greater connection with my pelvic floor and sense of grounded embodiment. I practice taking up space, while still honoring all the rest of my values as a therapist. Knowing how it feels to hold less social power helps me to more skillfully navigate my role when I hold more social power.

If you feel up for engaging in some reflection, here are a few prompts to notice or be curious about.

I say this with love, and a gentle nudge to white therapists: if you notice a desire to get away from this section and avoid thinking any more about this, your response is relevant. Take a break as you need to, but please return to this and keep engaging in your anti-racism work. It is essential to doing good ND-affirming, anti-ableist therapeutic work.

Here are the prompts:

- What's coming up for you as you read and think about boundaries, social power, privilege, and marginalization?
- How do the identities you hold impact you and your work?
- What would you like to keep learning about in particular with this topic?

Please honor your pacing, processing speed and needs, and whatever else is present for you as you engage with these prompts and digest this chapter. We've reached the end of Chapter 5. Whenever you feel ready, we can meet back together in Chapter 6, Client as Self-Expert: Dismantling Ableism.

Recap: Staying Differentiated From Our Clients

- Staying differentiated from our clients helps us to:
  - Trust the client as the expert on themself
  - Identify and navigate countertransference
  - Reduce enmeshment with our clients and honor their individuality
  - Have a guidepost for when self-disclosure could be a helpful tool to implement
  - Better understand and relate to our own privileged and marginalized sociocultural locations and identities

CHAPTER 6

Client as Self-Expert: Dismantling Ableism

As we enter this next chapter together, I am aware that talking openly about ableism and efforts to dismantle it may feel intense. I encourage you to bring along sensory delights, your custom boundary, and ample permission to take breaks to orient toward Pleasure/Neutrality as often as you choose. Depending on your neurotype and your history, this may feel deeply personal; it may evoke a sense of pain, wounding, hurt, anger, and so on within you. It's also okay if it doesn't. Either way, gentleness is encouraged.

My intention is not to retraumatize anyone but to be explicit about so much that has become implied or embedded in the NT, ableist, white supremacist dominant culture within the United States. For that reason, I'm going to name some very common ableist language that our clients have likely heard at some point throughout the course of their lives. (You may know of others that I did not mention; they are equally valid.) While the chapter opens with naming these offensive statements, the journey we are about to go on together will take us to deconstructing these ick statements that often started early in life. Then we will go on to how they may show up in the counseling space and counseling relationship. This heightened awareness is what will support us to better advocate for our clients, to help them notice how internalized oppression lives within them, and to help them better understand themselves through a ND-affirming lens that deeply embraces their wholeness. Naturally, in order to show up for our clients in this way, we will also need to tend to how ableism lives in and through us. And we will do this important work in as gentle a way as possible.

I notice my own solar plexus area recoil a bit as I get ready to type out this list. In Chapter 4, sharing lists of indicators and sensory delights was pleasurable. Sharing a list of words that cut a person down, break their spirit, or shred their self-worth is *not* pleasurable in the least, though it is necessary. This is a reminder for me to be gentle with myself, too, and that even though I am writing these words, they are not being directed at me (at least not in this moment), nor are they being directed at *you*.

Please truly hear me when I say, "I am not talking about you." Your shirt or sphere may be your biggest ally right now.

> **COMMON ABLEIST STATEMENTS**
> **(often said starting in childhood)**
> - "You're lazy."
> - "You're dumb/stupid."
> - "You're manipulative."
> - "You're too emotional/too sensitive."
> - "You're defiant!"
> - "You're selfish. You don't care about anyone else."
> - "Why can't you live up to your potential??"
> - "If you just tried harder . . . "
> - "Suck it up."
> - "What the hell is the matter with you?"
> - ND person says "I feel *x*" (insert sad, scared, a belly ache, sick in some way, anxious, etc.) and parent, caregiver, teacher, and/or other person responds "no, you don't. You're just trying to get attention!"

First, let me acknowledge my ROAAARRR!

Secondly, this may be inappropriate timing, but with two dead parents by age 32, I've earned my right for having inappropriately timed humor, haha. Whenever I see "x" used in a sentence like this, it makes me think of one of my all-time favorite memes. It's a total dad joke; it cracks me up every damn time. Here goes:

"Dear Algebra: Stop asking everyone to find your x. She's not coming back."

Even now, I'm cracking up! I wish I knew who to credit with that brilliance; it is definitely not a Nyck original. I'm not that funny.

Apparently, that was me inserting a resource-humor-in the midst of a challenging and distressing section. I hope the joke was helpful. Eye rolls are okay too.

So where were we? Right, I remember reading somewhere a few years back that by the time KCS/VAST kids reach adolescence, they have been corrected about 20,000 times.

Twenty thousand times!

Maybe you're like, "Yeah, you don't have to tell me, that *was* me." Or, maybe that surprises, shocks, or dismays you. This is one more reason why this book exists in the first place, why ND-affirming, anti-ableist approaches are so necessary. They are necessary not only in the counseling and mental health field, but also in the education system, in the medical system, in the workplace, and in the home. In other words, everywhere humans are, ND-affirming, anti-ableist approaches belong.

Whether this is your lived experience or not, it doesn't take rocket science (uh oh, my uncensored self is making an appearance again) to consider how much ableism harms people. It negates who they are, what they need, what they are good at, what their struggles are, and what kinds of support they need. Add in intersecting marginalized identities like race, gender, sexual orientation, socioeconomic status, and so on and there would be many additional lists to be named. I'll spare us.

I'm about to repeat each of those ableist messages so that I deconstruct them and get to what's really underneath. Before going there, feel free to take a break, check in with what you might need for yourself, add in some resourcing, take some notes, and so on.

I feel fired up for this section. The first part, writing the stand-alone list, sucks. This time, I get to apply my ND-affirming, anti-ableist lens and go deeper. Something to consider as we proceed: many of these messages were said to Autistic and KCS/VAST people, unidentified or identified, when they were children. These words were often spoken by people in power, such as parents, caregivers, family members, teachers, community members, and peers. They may still be spoken by bosses, coworkers, family members, therapists, doctors, and friends to adult ND people. I share this not to shame anyone, but to inform and educate.

Here goes:

- *"You're lazy."*

This is usually an indicator of a need for executive functioning support, specifically with task initiation and transitions. (More on this in Chapter 7, Global Permission: Accommodations and Executive Function Supports; Chapter 9, Global Permission: Transitions, Ritual, and the Sacred). Getting started can be *so hard* for ND folx. It doesn't necessarily happen naturally. Jessica McCabe, a white ADH advocate and author of *How to ADHD*, talks about four key factors for supporting KCS/VAST folx with motivation:

1. Add urgency.
2. Make it interesting.
3. Make it just the right amount of challenge.
4. Add novelty.

Laziness is rarely about a sheer lack of willpower. More often it's about some other invisible obstacle(s) that hasn't yet been addressed. Alternatively, perceived laziness could be an indicator of burnout, an expression of "I just can't," or a signal of lack of interest.

- "You're dumb/stupid."

Many Autistic and KCS/VAST folx also have learning disabilities, motor-planning difficulties, slower processing speed (as compared to NT peers), auditory-processing challenges, diverse forms of communication, and think outside the box. These can be misinterpreted in all sorts of inaccurate and harmful ways, and even more so for nonspeakers. If someone is struggling in school, it could be related to many factors, and it's not because the person isn't smart. The environment may be over- or understimulating; things might be being taught in a way that doesn't support their learning style; or they may be afraid to ask questions or have been bullied and made fun of when they have. There could be language or communication barriers between students and teachers or community members. When these harsh words are spoken, it is usually because the person speaking them feels out of control and doesn't know how to effectively communicate with the ND person.

- "You're manipulative."

This one more often gets applied to AFAB people, though not exclusively. I remember one of my professors in graduate school saying "Kids can't be manipulative. They are just trying to get their needs met and will be as creative as possible in order to do so." I would say that the same is true for most adults. If someone's behavior *seems* manipulative, chances are there are unmet needs that haven't yet been acknowledged. Or when the person has voiced these needs in the past, they were shunned, shut down, punished, ridiculed, and so on. The question to ask instead is "What is the unmet need(s) here, and how can I support?"

- "*You're too emotional/too sensitive.*"

Here's where my shirt comes in handy, because otherwise I might say something like, "You're talking to me?!" I heard this one *a lot* growing up. Our sensitive systems can feel big feels and have a hard time regulating these big feels. What might be neutral to "meh" to a NT person could feel like the end of the world to ND folx. This is not some sort of moral failing or character defect. It is, however, why we are often so invested in justice, righting injustice, being honest, and being kind. When a ND person is having big feels, the best thing would be to assure safety, be as patient as possible, validate, offer containment as needed, and give the person time and space to let the feelings move through. In a counseling session, that might look like a quiet pause, engaging in movement, offering verbal reassurance, and being really patient. How you respond will depend on whether your client is more an internal versus external processor.

- "*You're defiant!*"

While all of these harmful statements are expressed across race, unidentified racialized ND kids, especially Black kids, are most often labeled as defiant or oppositional. Tremendous assumptions are made based on their behavior, and all that gets distilled is "*willful* noncompliance" or a "lack of discipline." Oof, this is so painful and deeply problematic. It can and does happen across race, too. I've heard many stories over the years of parents of Autistic kids being ridiculed at the grocery store for not, so called "disciplining" their child. Maybe the person is overwhelmed or understimulated (though not likely at the grocery store!) and a meltdown is looming. Maybe they are confused and expressing their distress at not understanding what is being asked of them. Maybe they have unmet biological needs that they are trying to express. Seeming defiant could also present as anger, rage, or rebelliousness, especially in adolescence and adulthood. Look beyond the behavior and see the human there who is calling out for compassion, understanding, and a need to be taken seriously. We need to ask ourselves, "What is this person experiencing, and what support might they need?" I cannot emphasize enough: we need to disrupt racist *and* ableist narratives.

- "You're selfish. You don't care about anyone else."

Being Autistic and/or KCS/VAST means that our needs are a bit different from NT people, and the impacts of not having those needs met could be catastrophic for us, like meltdowns, explosions, shutting down, and/or self-harming. This is not always the case when our needs are unmet, but when we are expected to go along with the crowd, dismiss our sensory needs, or pass as NT, it can be misinterpreted by others. A mask that many AFAB people wear is the people pleaser or appeaser. For us, centering ourselves and prioritizing what we want and need can be brave, radical, and misunderstood. This is especially true for folx of all genders from more collectivist cultures and intergenerational communities where excluding oneself from the group, family, or community is seen as disrespectful or perhaps is not tolerated. The question to consider instead is, "What might they be trying to protect or protect themselves from?"

- "Why can't you live up to your potential?"

Oof, what a doozy. Well, let's see: executive function challenges, unmet support needs, sensory overload, too many demands, unrealistic expectations, not enough scaffolding, lack of interest, too much challenge, boredom. I remember the first video I watched of Jessica McCabe, who has a YouTube channel by the same name as her book, *How to ADHD*. She said that a cornerstone of being KCS/VAST is being inconsistent. Between the impacts of sleep or sleep trouble, medication effectiveness, sensory input from the environment, energy level, demands, and so on, we are not the same moment to moment, day to day. I think this is just as true for Autistic folx, too. The questions to ponder here are, "What are the invisible obstacles that this person is facing that cause them to struggle?" "What supports or strategies might be helpful, knowing that some of these struggles can't be solved and may never go away?" "Are my/our expectations realistic for this person?"

In the name of self-disclosure and transparency, I want to own that I remember saying this to one of my siblings. It's a distinct memory of us being out to eat when we were in our 20s. I told her how much potential she had, and she got so mad at me. She felt so offended, and at the time, in my ignorance, I didn't understand why. I thought I was complimenting her. Years later, knowing what I know now, oof. I messed up.

- *"If you just tried harder…"*

This one is so painful and makes ND people feel so invisible in their disability. I could easily just copy and paste what I wrote for the one above about potential; I'll try to be original, though. There's a misnomer that if a person can't do something, it's obviously because they aren't trying hard enough (for those who don't pick up on sarcasm, that was definitely sarcastic). Trying to do something and being able to do something are two completely different things. Again, we need to think about the underlying and invisible obstacles with which a person is struggling. We need to be curious and creative in our inquiry of, "Well, why not… what else could it be other than a lack of effort?" Effort does not equal success, but that does not negate all the effort that is being put forth.

While slightly different, this evokes a memory from my 20s when I volunteered with an art- and movement-based organization for Autistic youth. It was a Saturday morning I believe, and I was the support person to an Autistic adolescent during an art activity. I remember him telling me something that I didn't understand, so he started repeating himself, each time getting louder and louder. I could see and sense his frustration growing. I responded in a gentle, yet clear voice, "I hear you, but I don't understand." He just stopped. The seeming magic of that moment still lives within me. I don't think it ever occurred to him that this could be a me issue, not a him issue. He wasn't doing anything wrong. I wanted to help, but I wasn't able to *yet*. His volume of communication was not the problem; he didn't need to keep trying harder to say the same thing. I needed to do better to understand what he wanted me to know. That moment of connection with him has stayed with me all these years.

- "Suck it up."

I lived by this one for such a long time. Suck it up is the ultimate invalidator, minimizer, and enforcer. It usually is followed by or used in conjunction with "just get over it." This often comes in response to emotional sensitivity, overwhelm, overload, anxiety, tears, or a lack of support for dealing with change, disappointment, or the unexpected. Usually, the person saying the words feels overwhelmed by the ND person's outward expression of struggle and wants to make it stop. Eventually, when an ND person hears this enough, they will likely learn how to internalize their struggle instead. This can manifest as self-harm, self-rejection, self-criticism, perfectionism, not trying anything new, overwhelming fear of failure, and shame. What would be much more effective is to be curious about how the ND person is feeling. "Do they need us to slow down?" "Do they feel overwhelmed?" "What am I missing that they are clearly experiencing?" "How can I support?"

- "What the hell is the matter with you?"

Ouch. This just plain *hurts*. Oftentimes Autistic and KCS/VAST people are accused of lacking what is known as common sense. They may miss details that others notice because they are busy thinking about world peace, solving quadratic equations, discerning what that person's facial expression was trying to convey, or noticing the itchy tag on their shirt. (Let's not forget that there's plenty that is *so* obvious to them that NT folx seem bizarrely perplexed by). They may be clumsy or struggle with hand-eye coordination and fine or gross motor activities. Or they may do all the work for an assignment or project, but forget to turn it in. Let's set the record straight. *Nothing* is wrong with them, and yes, they are *different*. It would be much more helpful to ask, "What about that is challenging for them?" "What am I aware of that they may not be aware of?" "What might they be aware of that I am not privy to?"

- *ND person says "I feel x" (insert sad, scared, a belly ache, sick in some way, anxious, etc.) and parent, caregiver, teacher, or other person responds, "No, you don't. You're just trying to get attention!"*

This one really hurts my heart. As a therapist, I'm the one helping clients to mend their hearts from a lifetime of profound invalidation. This happens for people of all genders, and perhaps even more so for AFAB folx. They get perpetually gaslit by others, especially caregivers and educators. Over time, they internalize this sheer invalidation of self and develop what I call their *internalized gaslighter*. They no longer know what is true for them or not. They question everything they think, feel, say, do, and don't do. They rely heavily on external validation and approval in order to feel a sense of self. The notion of permission that I've been talking about is foreign to them. The trauma runs deep. The questions we ought to be thinking about and asking are: "Can you tell me more?" "I see/hear that you are having a hard time, and I want to help. How can I help you to feel better/safer?" Or we take the initiative to survey the environment and be genuinely curious, looking for possible sensory triggers, social triggers, or other emotional triggers. And then we inquire to gather more information. We listen. We take them seriously.

That bears repeating: *We take them seriously.*

Well, that was intense. Before we finish this section, I invite you to take a pause, check back in with how you are doing, insert a resource, take any notes that might be helpful, move, scream, rest... you do you. I'm going to take some time to tend to myself, and if that is your desire too, I hope you can and will.

✶ ✶ ✶ ✶

I know I said it earlier, but oof, oppression is exhausting! I took some time to be barefoot on the Earth and asked for support in holding all this with me. I could feel my insides start to slow down, relax a bit, and feel my connection with nature. This collective pain and trauma are so deep and vast. There is so much energy to metabolize, and I'm so grateful for the trees, land, and air who are so willing to be in this with me. In tending to this collective energy, I then noticed I was hungry, and I took time to nourish myself with food. Talk about pendulation in action: from the collective, to myself, and back out again and again.

And now, to return to where we left off. These ableist refrains are the foundation for the masks that our clients wear. They form the basis of the mold of *who not to be* in order to avoid hearing those harsh words. Or they tear a person down so much that they eventually live into those expectations. "Well, my effort is never taken seriously, so why bother?" Or "I'm just going to be told I'm lazy anyway, so there's no point in trying." People learn to suppress their emotions, turn inward against themselves, rage outwardly (or inwardly), hide who they are, camouflage to blend in with their environment, or effort at all costs to not be that thing they've been told *all of their damn life*.

As therapists, we look out for these words, phrases, and insinuations, and we interrupt. We lovingly and gently don't let our clients get away with saying such things about themselves, at least not without their awareness that such things are signs of internalized ableism. And, we certainly *do not* say any of those things to them, either.

As we move onto applying this to our work with clients and

to ourselves, we will explore the internalized rules clients have about what makes them a "good" client and what makes us a "good" therapist. Most of this often goes unspoken, so we bring it out into the open, have conversations, and create spaces that reassure clients that they are acceptable as they are. We will also explore the likely hidden rules or expectations we as therapists hold about ourselves and our clients. We will bring them to the foreground, hold inquiry, and dismantle them. You may also notice that through the dismantling, we make way for what we will cover in Chapter 7, Global Permission: Accommodations and Executive Function Supports.

A transition is upon us, which means here is your overt invitation (if it's helpful!) to check back in with yourself, tend to your humanity, and meet yourself in the ways that you most desire to be met in this moment. When you are ready, I'll meet you in the next section, Working With Clients.

Recap: Examining Ableism and How It Gets Expressed and Perpetuated

- Ableism usually starts in childhood with the messages that parents, caregivers, family members, schools, educators, and community members give to ND kids (whether identified as Autistic and/or KCS/VAST yet or not).
- Look out for clients using words like: lazy, selfish, too emotional, too sensitive, manipulative, defiant, stupid, or not trying hard enough. These are indicators of internalized ableism.
- Look deeper at these words to try to understand what the invisible obstacle or unmet needs may be; lead with curiosity; and take them seriously.
- These harmful ableist messages form the foundation of clients' masks and trauma.

WORKING WITH CLIENTS

In the first part of this chapter, I focused on how ableism plays out interpersonally. It's important that we acknowledge that the interpersonal realm is not where ableism originates. I will reference the four I's of oppression. If you are not familiar with this framework, it addresses the ways structural and systemic oppression originate within the *Ideology* of a society. From there, the oppression embeds itself into the society's *Institutions*, such as the medical system, education system, financial institutions, religious institutions, and so on. Then it gets absorbed by the people who exist within this society who enact said ableism *Interpersonally* onto others, be it family of origin, community members, teachers, doctors, coworkers, and so on. Finally, this oppression transcends to the *Internalized* level, or "me with me" level, where it becomes internalized ableism.

As I share this with you, the teachings of Dr. Carla Sherrell are very present with me. As we were ready and able, she encouraged us to courageously and deeply notice the interwoven, multilayered ways that oppression functions in our clients' and our own relationships, and within and across institutions—including counseling. She teaches that such awareness is a crucial step in dismantling ableism and all forms of oppression in support of healing.

The external messages from ideological, institutional, and interpersonal oppression get unknowingly digested and metabolized as an individual's truth. For example, "I've always been told I'm too sensitive, so it must be true." And then the person goes on to harass, judge, police, or even harm themselves whenever emotions arise or something impacts them. This is why, as I've mentioned before, humans are a primary source of trauma for Autistic and KCS/VAST folx. Hopefully you now have more context for why that is so. This puts us as counselors in a very important and deeply sacred role. We have the power to co-create interpersonal relationships with our clients that are reparative, healing, and *potentially even satisfying*.

By centering the interpersonal relationship between us and clients as our primary modality, we can model what our clients deserve. We embody the principle of unconditional positive regard and we live it moment to moment with them. We show up knowing that they are the experts on themselves, we give them respect, we lead with curiosity, we take responsibility for our mistakes, and we let them know that we are human, too. We refrain from judgments, assumptions, and power-over dynamics. We open our hearts and our minds and show up with genuine curiosity, care, and a deep willingness to learn about who this person is and what their needs are.

This is done both implicitly and explicitly. In our efforts to dismantle ableism, we co-create agreements with our clients about our relationship. Just as we've talked about seeking consent in previous chapters, we continue to do so as we make agreements about what is and isn't okay in this therapeutic relationship. Here's an example.

A client has a relationship with linear time such that they are consistently "late" to things, including therapy (I'm choosing to put the word "late" in quotes to bring awareness of and attention to the influence of colonization and white supremacy on linear time). They have a lifetime of being scolded and punished for being "late," both by family members and anyone they've ever had an appointment with. No matter how hard they have tried, being on time in any consistent way has not happened. Ever. It does, however, continue to be a huge source of stress, shame, and guilt for them.

Every time they show up to a session, they profusely apologize for being late. In my own neurodivergence, I know full well how hard linear time is for me, too. It seems to always keep moving! This helps me to have additional compassion, plus I notice a cycle that needs to be interrupted. As great as I am at my job, I know full well that I will *not* be the hero in this person's life who magically solves linear time for them. It's not gonna happen. (And yes, we tried a number of strategies already.)

Fortunately, dismantling ableism means that there are other options available. We get to change the narrative. Instead of, "Your lateness means you're bad, you don't respect me, and you don't care," we can rewrite it. "You struggle with linear time and probably always will. I know you respect me and that your being "late" has nothing to do with me. Could we create a new agreement together?"

Rather than both of us living with the illusion that if they *just tried harder*, they'd start being on time, we can intercept their continuous cycles of shame and guilt. Here's a bold idea: "How about we just accept that you'll be 'late,' and you stop apologizing? What if your respect for me is a given, and you show up when you show up?"

How radical. I'd anticipate that at first, they wouldn't know if they could trust it, but all we would need is a willingness to give it a try. If 15 minutes past the start time is typical for their arrival time, I would mentally block out their session time as starting 15 minutes past the start time I tell them. This would allow for as close to a full 60 minutes with me as possible, while I also honor my own boundaries and needs. When I have enough flexibility on my end and we start more than 15 minutes later, I may offer to end the session later. Otherwise, we will have shorter sessions. I am intentional about when in my day we meet to minimize my stress levels around timing and to be as flexible as I'm able to be.

How exciting when they finally show up to a session and don't apologize! What a victory! This would show me that they were brave enough to take me up on my offer. It may take many sessions for them to trust that they can be "late," and that I won't abandon them. Over time, the client may even get to feel the relief of being taken seriously, of being accepted as they are, and of accommodations being made to honor their needs and the realities of who they are (more on this in Chapter 7).

Being "on time" is one of many internalized rules clients may hold about what it means to be a so-called "good" client. Co-creating explicit relationship agreements means that these internalized rules get brought out into the open to be explored. Together, we get to dismantle how ableism shows up in our relationship by intentionally co-creating a neuro-affirming, anti-ableist foundation as much as possible.

Oftentimes, the messages shared at the beginning of this chapter are intricately connected to who clients perceive they are supposed to be in the therapeutic relationship. For a moment, I'm going to touch back into that ick to make explicit connections between how historical ableist narratives can translate into present-moment internalized rules about their role as client.

> **ICK ABLEIST MESSAGE → POSSIBLE INTERNALIZED RULE AS CLIENT**
>
> "You're lazy." → "I must work hard in therapy."
>
> "You're dumb/stupid." → "I have to act as if I always understand."
>
> "You're manipulative." → "I must not have needs."
>
> "You're too emotional/too sensitive." → "Uh-oh. Don't feel too much."
>
> "You're defiant!" → "Be good! I must comply with whatever my therapist suggests."
>
> "You're selfish. You don't care about anyone else." → "I must put everyone else first, including my therapist."
>
> "Why can't you live up to your potential??" → "I better try to be the best."
>
> "If you just tried harder . . . " → "If it's not grueling and hard, it's not good enough." Or, "Why even bother?"
>
> "Suck it up." → "I don't get to take breaks or have needs."

> "What the hell is the matter with you?" → "How can I prove that I don't suck?"
>
> ND person says "I feel x" (insert sad, scared, a belly ache, sick in some way, anxious, etc.) and parent/caregiver/teacher/other person responds "no, you don't. You're just trying to get attention!" → "If you don't agree with me, then I must be wrong."

In the name of dismantling ableism as a key tenet in ND-affirming, anti-ableist counseling, we're bringing awareness to the ways and moments when ableism is present. We use the skill of pendulation and tracking attention to notice what "I's" of oppression are present. In other words, we focus on the client's internal experience while also zooming out enough to notice the presence of ideological, institutional, and interpersonal ableism and oppression. We name it, call it what it is, question it, and tend to it. All too often, clients are unaware that their internalized ableism does not originate with them or even with their family of origin. They need to be reminded that they've ingested the ideological and institutional oppression that is embedded in the dominant culture. While it deeply affects them and requires support, we can't emphasize enough that this is not a *you* problem, but a structural problem that profoundly impacts you.

In addition to offering this broader perspective, we also meet the client where they are. Depending on the moment and the client, that could mean processing the trauma associated with the ableist narrative; making space for grief, anger, and/or rage; turning toward resourcing; and/or creating new relational agreements that disrupt the old pattern. This will all involve lots of repetition, particularly the relational bit. It will take a lot of new evidence to disrupt old neuro-pathways and relational patterns and to create new ones. The ableist concrete multilane highways in the brain do not disappear easily. But we can create a construction zone with glaring detours that lead to new paths lined with wildflowers and butterflies that are perfect for exploring.

If you would like to support your clients to bridge their cognitive and relational awareness with their somatic awareness, you could invite them to notice what arises for them when these ableist beliefs or internalized rules show up. There may be very obvious cues of sympathetic arousal such as tightening, constriction, an urge to flee, elevated heart rate, the presence of their internal roar, shutting down, or fear of rejection. Memories or images may appear. Proceed slowly, gently, and compassionately. Invite in sensory delight and resourcing. Offer reassurance as needed. Be tender with yourself and with them, and reorient toward parasympathetic states when they are ready. The activation/deactivation scale from Chapter 4 could be really helpful here to offer structure and form for processing, taking breaks, resourcing, and pendulation.

Validation can also go a long way here, along with permission to not process trauma if that is not what the client is up for in that moment. Just as masking is often a trauma response, ableism and oppression are likely the source of the trauma. Not all clients will identify that this is trauma, but it's important that our nervous systems are cued to acknowledge it as such and that we tend to ourselves as such. You may want to invite them to return to their sphere or shirt from Chapter 5 to feel their differentiated self, their essence, as distinct from the external harm. You also may want to enter your boundary to help feel your own differentiation from the client and from the harm.

Your own nervous system may be starting to feel the integration and interwovenness of the individual chapters that make up this model.

In addition to clients having rules about what makes them a "good" client, they are likely showing up with rules about what they think is a "good" therapist. This is another valuable area to be explicit about and then co-create agreements together. Oftentimes, the biggest myth clients hold is that we as therapists "have it all together" or" have it all figured out." Through skillful self-disclosure as we talked about in Chapter 5, this dismantling process can happen both in finite moments and throughout the ongoing relationship over time. It comes back to modeling and showing our clients, not just telling them what we want them to hear and believe.

We also provide their system with new evidence to dispel other myths (or very real experiences they've had with other therapists in the past). Some of these other "good" therapist rules/myths that clients may hold could relate to internal confusion or distress around paying for someone to care. Sometimes it can be hard for a client to digest and integrate how deeply their counselor cares for them, knowing there is a money exchange. As in, "I pay you to care about me." It can be so important to communicate to clients, both explicitly and implicitly, that they pay for our time, not our genuine, heartfelt care. Clients who access equity pricing, sliding scale rates, or free counseling could worry that the counselor could stop working with them for their being "difficult" or "asking for too much." Because of the influences of colonization and capitalism, clients may worry that if they are not paying the market rate, their humanity and needs may not be taken as seriously. I feel my heart sink as I write this, and I am reminded of how deeply brave and vulnerable it is to receive support in this dominant, oppressive culture.

Another "good" therapist myth is that we don't make mistakes. Oof, how inaccurate that is! And disrupting this notion is key to co-creating a reparative human-to-human, counselor-to-client relationship. Again, both explicitly and implicitly, we communicate to our clients that we are indeed fallible beings; we demonstrate this by admitting our mistakes when they happen, taking ownership, and engaging in repair.

For example, by pendulating to ourselves and tracking our own internal experience, we may notice cues that something we said or did, or didn't say or didn't do, had a potentially negative impact on our client. This could sound like, "I noticed my chest get tight after I said what I said a moment ago. I think my words might have been hurtful for you, and I'm so sorry about that. Could we check in about what happened and what that was like for you?" Depending on the client and their history with people pleasing, they may not feel safe enough to disclose if they felt harmed. If that's the case, we can offer another apology and let them know that we are open to feedback at any point, even if it's not now. That also honors their processing speed and acknowledges that they might not actually know yet how they were or weren't impacted. If the client genuinely didn't feel harmed or bothered by it, it's another relational opportunity. We get to acknowledge our own humanity. If we ever do say something that feels bad to them, we invite them to let us know so we can repair and make it right.

We can also be intentional or preventative about our inherently human, well-intentioned, yet fallible beingness by offering a *feedback ritual*. At a particular structured time in the session, the client is invited to share what worked well for them, what didn't work for them, and what they would like to be different in the next or future sessions. This can be a spoken ritual or a written ritual, whatever is most accessible for the client. For those whose processing speed means that they might not know until after the session is over, being explicit that this feedback is welcome anytime is important.

A final "good" therapist rule I'll offer, though there are certainly more that exist, is "my therapist is always right." I feel my gut clenching and closing in as I say that. What a profound expression of white supremacy, colonization, and neurotypicality. Gross. Every element of our therapeutic relationship needs to dismantle this grossness. It is why I offer everything to my clients as an invitation. "I have an idea of how we could explore this, would you like to hear it?" If, and only if I get a yes, will I share the idea. And I am explicit that my idea is an invitation, meaning they can say "yes," "no" or "modify it." Sometimes, when I've known a client for a long time, they may tell me that I don't have to ask permission to share my thoughts, input, or ideas anymore; only then will I shift my style of communication around this, but I will continue to make it easy for them to say "no" to me.

Both explicitly and implicitly, I continually communicate to my clients that they are self-experts, and I could not possibly know them better than they know themselves. For many high-masking, later identified, AFAB Autistic folx like myself, this commitment to clients being the experts on themselves, that I do not have all the answers, and that I am continually learning and growing, too, comes from a deeply personal history of experiencing the opposite.

A final note as we wrap up this section. There is a delicate balance for us as counselors between humility and holding a safe enough, strong enough therapeutic container. On one extreme is acting ignorant and like "I know nothing; the client knows everything." Not helpful. On the other extreme is "I have all the answers for my client, and my client has none." So not helpful. The art of ND-affirming, anti-oppressive care is "You have a lot of wisdom, and I have a lot of wisdom. May we collaboratively and co-creatively share this wisdom in a way that honors your autonomy, communicates respect, supports your self-trust, and helps you to get your needs met."

We have reached the end of this section and are approaching a transition. Each section offers much to explore and digest. Please take all the time and space you need, and when you feel ready, I'll meet you in the final section of this chapter, Working With Ourselves.

Recap: Helping Clients Notice and Dismantle the Ways Ableism Shows Up for Them

- The client–therapist relationship is the most important and fundamental "modality" of this ND-affirming therapeutic model.

- We can co-create a reparative relationship that actively engages in dismantling ableism together through relational agreements.
- Internalized ableism from earlier in life often forms the basis of internalized rules about what makes for a "good" client or therapist. For example, "You're manipulative" could translate into a client believing "I must not have needs."
- Using resourcing (Chapter 4) and boundaries as differentiation (Chapter 5), you can support clients to process and be cared for in this dismantling process.

WORKING WITH OURSELVES

In her teachings, Dr. Carla Sherrell often invites reflection on how oppression is in the air we breathe. She encourages us to think about this as we consider our own and others' varied identities. In a similar way that the air we breathe is steeped in white supremacy, racism, and colonization, that same air is steeped in neuronormativity and ableism. The same is true for cis-heteronormativity, homophobia, transphobia, sexism, and classism. I've already mentioned about the prevalence of queerness and gender expansiveness among Autistic and KCS/VAST folx. I know I keep saying this in one form or another, but all of these forms of oppression are interwoven, and all stem from assertions of dominance. This is why, no matter what your neurotype, dismantling ableism is necessary, though it can't be done in isolation from the other forms of oppression. I say this not to overwhelm or dissuade you from doing your own work, but to be real about the gravity and depth of all of this.

There are some variations in how we approach this based on the neurotype of the therapist. Let's start with Autistic and KCS/VAST therapists, including those who are in the questioning stage of their neurotype.

Addressing ND Therapists

- How were you impacted by all the ableist messages shared in the opening part of this chapter, and then again in Working With Clients?
- Did you feel like I was talking to you at one or more points as I was laying out ableist messages and then dismantling them?
- What are you noticing in the present moment as I invite you to shift your awareness to what you've been noticing in yourself throughout this chapter?

Feel free to notice body sensation, imagery, colors, emotions, or anything else that may be present. Stay connected to your sensory delights as you desire too!

For those of us who are ND therapists, the work of ND-affirming therapy is deeply personal as much as it is professional. Our nervous system is one of our greatest instruments as a therapist, and we need to tend to it as such. That means not minimizing our own pain or trauma, thinking we don't need support because "we are a therapist after all," or avoiding the very real countertransference that shows up with our clients. We are absolutely growing right alongside our clients, and it is imperative that we are engaged in our own healing work.

We are only as effective as we are able to model and embody what we share with and teach our clients.

That is why I often think about how brave it is to be a therapist! In my theoretical orientation, being a therapist means that I am invested in my own growth, and for as long as I am alive this will not ever be complete. Though thankfully I've learned how to pendulate and take a lot more breaks as I get older. At this point, my growth journey looks a lot like an interweaving of processing trauma and what is hard alongside discovering just how much pleasure I can tolerate and allow.

- That said, what supports do you have in place to process the ways ableism has impacted and continues to impact you?
- Do you have your own therapist, coach, or practitioner? Or perhaps do you have a trusted colleague, friend, peer, or loved one you can share openly with, be emotionally held in your vulnerability, and create new relational agreements with, who has little tolerance for unchecked ableism?

Just as your clients need and deserve this support, so do you. I hear so often from other therapists about how much easier it is to show up for our clients than it is for ourselves. I can relate to that too. And I want us to keep investing in a new culture that doesn't encourage that type of double standard, but instead one that holds a standard of us caring as deeply, compassionately, and sensitively for ourselves as much as we do for our clients.

I notice myself take a few deep breaths as I finish writing that last paragraph. I feel really present to the ways that double standard lives in me. It evokes sadness, tenderness, and heaviness in my heart. I wish it was as easy for me to accommodate myself as it is for me to care for and accommodate my clients. I am definitely a work in progress. This reminds me of how important this upcoming section is where we will look at what rules we have internalized about what makes us "good" therapists and what we believe makes for "good" clients. Even though we ND folx are known for our rules (and we love them!), people of all neurotypes have their share of rules too. Before we get there, though, I want to address NT therapists.

Addressing NT Therapists

- How were you impacted by all the ableist messages shared in the opening part of this chapter, and then again in the "Working With Clients" section?

- Did you recall yourself saying those messages to people in your life at one point or another (this is not about shaming you, just brave curiosity)?
- What are you noticing in the present moment as I invite you to shift your awareness to what you've been noticing in yourself throughout this chapter?

Feel free to notice body sensation, imagery, colors, emotions, or anything else that may be present. Stay connected to your sensory delights as you desire too!

You may find that you are less personally and viscerally impacted by the content of this chapter; however, you may have clients, family or friends, or other community members who know this content viscerally. Nobody is immune to being impacted; some just have the privilege to not feel it in the moments they choose not to. I aim to meet us all with compassion and gentleness, whether or not we share the same lived experience. Being a therapist is a brave role no matter what our neurotype!

If you're holding any uncertainty, one way to tell whether you hold NT privilege is to ask yourself this question:

- Did you feel shocked by any of the ableist messages shared earlier in the chapter?
- Did you find yourself wanting to push back at me or tell me why that wasn't ableist?

I notice some belly churning in response to those questions. I think it's a mild form of jealousy that there are actually plenty of humans who haven't experienced that type of harm. I'm glad they haven't! And I also feel sad that I and so many others have. It reminds me of when Trump was elected president of the United States in 2016. I remember racialized folx sharing a similar sentiment about white folx being shocked by the results of the election. They know all too well that this nation is founded on white supremacy; they live it every day. Seeing it played out publicly was far from shocking to them, however disappointed, enraged, and betrayed they might have felt.

I want to own the complexity of being in a marginalized location sharing with those in a privileged location. It's vulnerable and tender. I don't wish for you to have a different neurotype, nor do I wish for my neurotype to change. But I do recognize the differences in our lived experience and the risk I am taking by sharing openly about mine and others like me. It is from this place of heart and tenderness that I implore you to invest in your own work around dismantling ableism and other forms of oppression.

- Who in your life can you talk openly and honestly with about how ableism lives in you?
- Do you have a peer group, therapist, practitioner, supervisor, and/or consultant you can process with?
- Are you connected with other NT-identifying therapists you could read and process this book together with, holding each other lovingly accountable?

Again, it's in the air we breathe. There is no shame or blame here, just an openhearted invitation to use your power and privilege to create the change necessary that could create more safety and access to well-being for ND folx. I know you don't technically have to, that's what privilege is all about. And I deeply, profoundly thank you for being invested in co-creating a more just, accessible world for all us to coexist in together.

Addressing All Neurotypes

All right, let's regroup now. As I say that, I simultaneously feel really connected to my heart. This truly is work of the heart. This is a deep calling, a soul-driven calling that knows greater harmony is possible. It holds the vision of people of all neurotypes thriving together, each contributing and being supported in their own unique ways. I think this is what Dr. Nick Walker means with the term *neurocosmopolitan*. While it likely won't happen in my lifetime, I dream of a future where every person's creativity, expression of genius and wonder, needs and desires are welcomed, cared for, and tended to with love and respect, and no one is left out or relegated to the margins. Where there is no such thing as a "supreme" race, neurotype, gender, sexual orientation, religion, culture, ability, or ethnicity. Where right relationship with nature, land, water, and the Earth is the norm.

While that last paragraph could be considered a digression, wink-wink, I think it's important to be holding the big picture in mind as we shift back to internalized rules about "good" clients and therapists. Actually, I think this is a great moment for us to take a pause, and then we'll get right to it (I know, "One more thing, Nyck!"). I notice an impulse to move and stretch a bit, and perhaps there is something you would also like to allow for? Perhaps your own creative form of integration or a break? See you in a moment, or whenever you are ready to return.

✹ ✹ ✹ ✹

I hope that was as satisfying for you as it was for me. I'm returning with deep gratitude and restoration. With the help of India. Arie's brilliant music and a stunning nature backdrop, I danced and then did some yoga poses. My body was deeply receptive and my heart feels nourished.

Thinking about, journaling about, and talking about the rules we hold as therapists about who makes for "good" clients and "good" therapists isn't exactly something I'm "excited" about, however necessary it may be. So having taken a break, I now want to encourage you to keep your sensory delights nearby or engage with them as we engage in some reflection. No matter what your neurotype(s), please really take this in when I say, this isn't about shaming or judging ourselves. It's about humility and willingness to examine the air we breathe, rather than take it for granted. If you've already been on a journey of looking at and dismantling these rules, I applaud you. If this is a new concept for you, I applaud you. Western psychology is rooted in white supremacy and ableism, so I think it's accurate to say that none of us left graduate school without some ableist rules in tow.

Please be gentle with yourself as you engage in curiosity. Let's begin with clients. Depending on what is most useful for you with the following prompts, feel free to think about them, journal about them, talk about them with a peer, dance with them, be in nature with them, meditate on them, make art about them, and so on. Other prompts may come up for you as you engage, and please know that they are just as valid and worth exploring!

When you think about what makes for a "good" client, what comes to mind?

Some things to consider are:
- How frequently do they come to therapy?
- What are they like in session?
- What is their "work ethic" or "level of engagement" like?
- What do you notice about their focus and attention?
- What about their sense of timeliness?
- Do they ever miss a session, whether advance cancellation or no-show?
- Do they communicate with you between sessions?
- Do they ever say "no" to you?
- What is their communication like?

There's no right or wrong with this, just noticing and then engaging in inquiry. As you reflect on what you've come up with, consider exploring:

- Where does this idea or rule come from?
- How does it help or hurt my clients?
- Do I notice any neurotypical expectations embedded in these ideas/rules?

Take as much or as little time as you choose to here. I bet it would be really interesting to chat with a peer about this if you haven't already. When you feel complete for now with this, knowing that you can revisit it at any point, I encourage you to take a break. Perhaps use movement, a mindful pause, a chance to disengage, sensory delight, or stim. When you're ready, we'll move on to exploring our rules about what makes for a "good" therapist.

Similar to the invitation from the "good" client section, feel free to engage with this question and these prompts in the way that is most accessible, interesting, or creative for you. Allow whatever else comes up that may not be a direct prompt from me. I trust your wisdom and insight.

- When you think about what makes for a "good" therapist, what comes to mind?

You may find it easiest to think about your rules for yourself, or if you prefer, think about your rules for therapists in general. For accessibility sake, I'll write these in the third person.
Some things to consider are:

- How frequently do they meet with clients?
- What are they like in session?
- What is their "work ethic" or "level of engagement" like?
- What do you notice about their focus and attention?
- What about their sense of timeliness?
- Do they ever miss a session, whether advance cancellation or no-show?
- Do they communicate with clients between sessions?
- Do they ever say "no" to their clients?
- What is their communication like?

There's no right or wrong with this, just noticing and then engaging in inquiry. As you reflect on what you've come up with, consider exploring how these directly apply to you:

Client as Self-Expert: Dismantling Ableism

- Where does this idea or rule come from?
- How does it help or hurt me?
- What is the impact on my clients?
- Do I notice any neurotypical expectations embedded in these ideas/rules?
- Are my rules different for me than they are for my clients?

Take as much or as little time as you feel inspired to here. I strongly encourage you not to skip this altogether, but if you need a break right now, please prioritize returning to it when you are able.

Welcome back. I wonder, what was that like for you? This inquiry can often generate some discomfort. How might you be able to or choose to support yourself right now? If you notice a desire to connect with another, who could you reach out to?

I mentioned earlier that it is brave to be a therapist. I wonder if you are feeling brave in this moment? Examining the stuff that we may or may not be aware of, that could possibly be causing us or others harm, is brave. Thanks for being brave with me! I'm reminded of what I shared earlier in the chapter, that the most common theme I hear from therapists after exploring these prompts is their double standards for themselves and for their clients. Did you notice something similar? Again, there's no right or wrong.

It can be tricky to distill out what is ableist and what are helpful boundaries that support clients to feel safe enough, contained enough, and that they matter. It's possible that the answer might be different depending on the client. It's important for us to remember that modeling having needs, mattering, and getting our needs met is vital to showing clients that they, too, get to have needs, matter, and get to have their needs met. Yes, we are therapists, yes, we have unique relationships with our clients, and yes, we are also human, all at the same time.

As we near the end of this chapter, I want to encourage you to let these prompts integrate over time. You may have been pleasantly surprised by what you discovered; you may feel neutral about it; or you may feel disturbed by what you discovered. All reactions are valid. If you feel disturbed, it might be useful to get support from a colleague, therapist, or supervisor. It may also be supportive to pick one or two from each list and engage with them further. I say one or two so as not to overwhelm yourself and unrealistically expect drastic changes immediately (unless you notice that without drastic immediate changes, you will actively cause harm to others, in which case I definitely recommend supervision or consultation with an ND-affirming supervisor).

Here are some thoughts about how you could engage with this further. Given that white supremacy and neurotypicality thrive by isolating humans and keeping us separate, similar to how shame works, I think the most important next step would be to engage with others around this. Be it peers, colleagues, your own therapeutic support, or community members, invite people you trust into a conversation/exploration. Share openly about what showed up for you when you made your lists. Be curious, seek feedback, admit your humility, and honor your boundaries.

If it feels like too much or too soon to engage externally with others about this, I encourage you to explore how else you could engage. Dance, movement practice, nature, journaling, and music all come to mind. How could you be in relationship with this material and give it form through your body, voice, or words? How could the trees, rhythm, instruments, or the helping spirits support you to process and be with what lives in you?

While I deeply honor your process, your way of engaging, and your uniqueness, please resist the urge to remain in isolation about this content. As Dr. Carla Sherrell says, "Oppression teaches us that we must remain isolated." Please remember, to be human is to be fallible. There is no shame in that. May we continue to be brave, honest, curious, and gentle with ourselves.

Thank you, again, for being on this courageous journey with me. I know that was a lot. I encourage you to rest, relax, take a break, nourish yourself in whatever ways you are drawn to and able to. When you feel ready, we'll transition into Chapter 7, Global Permission: Accommodations and Executive Function Supports. Now that we have created more internal space and gotten clearer on possible unmet needs or invisible obstacles, we will tangibly explore the question asked many times throughout this chapter: "How can I support you?"

Recap: Dismantling Ableism in Our Counseling Practice

- ND therapists need to do their own work around the ways the trauma of ableism likely lives actively within them.
- NT therapists need to do their own work around recognizing the harm that neurotypicality causes ND folx.
- Therapists of all neurotypes come away from graduate school with rules about what makes for a "good" client and therapist. Western psychology is rooted in white supremacy and ableism, so it's nearly impossible not to.
- These rules are a pathway to greater awareness about possible ableism and lay a foundation for dismantling this ableism.
- Using a list of prompts to guide our inquiry, we reflected on and answered these two questions:
  1. When you think about what makes for a "good" client, what comes to mind?
  2. When you think about what makes for a "good" therapist, what comes to mind?

CHAPTER 7
Global Permission: Accommodations and Executive Function Supports

Welcome to the world of identifying support needs and finding creative solutions for how to get those needs met! Autistic and KCS/VAST people tend to have challenges relating to executive functions (EF). This is sometimes referred to as executive dysfunction, but I avoid that language. Executive functions are vast and relate to the many things that our prefrontal cortex helps us to do, such as planning, organizing, adapting, task initiation and completion, socializing, emotion regulation, self-advocacy, repairing interpersonal conflict, impulse control, and so much more. For grown-ups, it's often associated with what we think of as "adulting." For kids and teens, it's more obvious as it relates to things like schoolwork and organization, like keeping their room clean. For people of all ages, executive function very much relates to being flexible or adaptable in the midst of unexpected or unwanted changes, dealing with emotion regulation, having impulse control, and being social.

EFs are already tricky for these two neurotypes, and then to make it more challenging, when there are big feelings or a threat response is present, it only gets harder. When emotions are high or a threat response is activated, which happens in the amygdala of the midbrain and is helped by the lizard brain, the prefrontal cortex is less accessible. In simplest terms, it's like the midbrain says "I've got this!" and powers down the prefrontal cortex, but amps up the lizard brain. From a physiological perspective, this is quite brilliant. The prefrontal cortex is where complex thinking and problem solving take place. If we're suddenly being chased by a predator, there's no time to analyze and do complex problem solving (unless maybe you're MacGyver). The body needs to mobilize immediately and either start running to safety, fighting for safety, or freezing and playing dead. If the predator is a human, then fawning to appease them could also be a viable option. When the threat is solving quadratic equations, however, these responses aren't so helpful.

Supporting people with executive function challenges requires the following:

- Support emotion regulation first.
- Expect that some of these may be lifelong challenges that need ongoing support or reinforcement.
- Set realistic expectations.
- Get creative.
- Play with strategies that are unique and apt for the specific client.
- Be willing to change the strategies and try new ones.

As we mentioned in Chapter 2, Autistic people tend to crave routines and schedules, while KCS/VAST people tend to thrive on novelty and a sense of urgency. In both cases, whatever strategies are played with, they need to be interesting and the right amount of challenge. If it's not interesting, it's likely a waste of time even trying. This is why it's essential to be creative and come up with strategies unique to the individual. If it's too challenging, it will likely lead to overwhelm, frustration, panic, or some other form of distress. If it's too easy, it will likely lead to boredom, understimulation, and checking out. Finding the right amount of challenge is key, especially in order to feel a sense of success versus additional perceived struggle or failure.

When identifying and supporting EF challenges, it's essential to approach from an anti-ableist lens. This reminds me of an example I shared in Chapter 6 about a client who struggles with linear time. Our anti-ableist approach was to accept that they will be late to session! Not to try to change or fix them, or try more strategies that were doomed to fail, but to accommodate who this person is and isn't. Accommodations are specific types of support that allow people to access their life in ways that work for them. Think about all the people who might be able to access counseling when we are able to accommodate their relationship to time. Accessing accommodations is a form of self-acceptance and self-compassion.

If only it were as simple as "if I'm kind and loving to myself, then I will have all the support I need to exist and be well." Unfortunately, it's not. There are many situations where people's very real struggles with executive function and capacity are known, and there is an awareness of the accommodations that would be helpful, but they are too expensive, unavailable, or otherwise inaccessible.

Let's use some examples here. I'm going to default to they/them pronouns to allow for this to be someone of any and all genders.

Example 1

An Autistic parent is parenting two children, each with their own unique support needs and requiring ample time and attention. Having a relatively clean and decluttered home is ideal for the parent's mental well-being and sense of order, both in terms of being able to find things in the home and feeling calm enough to focus on parenting. Yet no matter how hard the parent tries, it's impossible for them to keep up with the needs of the house. It is clear to them that hiring a cleaning service and possibly a personal assistant are accommodations that would resolve their persistent struggles as it relates to the home. However, their full-time parenting demands mean that they do not generate income and cannot afford to hire such help; nor do they have community support that is able to come over and help out with cleaning.

While there is awareness of what accommodations are needed, there are financial and other barriers to accessing that support need. Unfortunately, this is all too common for ND folx, particularly those with multiple marginalized identities. As therapists, it is our job to be creative *and* realistic. It would be utterly inappropriate to insist that a client who may be just getting by financially should hire additional help. As therapists, we also need to know about the resources available within communities that our clients can access. Sometimes, our role is about validating how real the struggles are, and how painful it is that sometimes they are unresolvable. This is what it means to be Autistic and/or KCS/VAST in a dominant culture that does not care well for its disabled community.

In the dominant, ableist, capitalist culture of the United States, to be Autistic and/or KCS/VAST is a form of disability. I am referring to the social model of disability that puts the onus on the environment, not on the individual. When people are forced to choose between their mental health *or* physical health, between them *or* their children, between their well-being *or* getting a paycheck, between buying groceries *or* going to the doctor, there is no question that the environment is problematic.

This is one of those moments where I feel myself being bold and direct, and I notice myself sit up taller in my chair! I'm taking this as a cue to pause, check in, and notice. I invite you to do the same. You may find yourself nodding along in agreement, feeling your own sense of fire flowing forth. Perhaps you feel constriction in your body, annoyance with me, or an urge to disagree or argue with me. Or maybe you don't feel anything. There's no right or wrong way to respond here, just another opportunity to notice what is present for you. I hope you can be gentle and soft with yourself in your noticing.

I'd like to offer another example of accommodations and how privilege is directly related to access.

Example 2

A KCS/VAST person works at a company that has cubicles. This person is deeply creative and good at their job; however, being forced to be contained in a small area without windows or access to the outside feels very restrictive, does not provide enough stimulation for them, and inhibits their creativity. They just know that if they had more freedom of movement and access to more stimulation while they worked, they would be more resourced, regulated, creative, and therefore, more productive. They have already talked to their supervisors about accommodation possibilities, and there were none. Everybody at the company, except for upper management, works in cubicles.

This person is partnered and their partner has a high-paying job that more than covers the cost of living without a second income. After assessing their options, they choose to leave the job, take some time off, and then go find something that's a better fit. Privilege has allowed them the freedom to assert their will and prioritize their autonomy over having an income.

Now imagine a different scenario. The same person is single and has no access to financial resources outside of their paycheck. There are no other jobs in this person's field that are available and pay as much. Given the rising cost of living, they cannot afford a pay cut; nor can they afford to be fired. They need the structure that comes with being employed by someone else, along with the social opportunities of having coworkers, so working for themself is not an option. Some might say, "Well, just quit and get a new job." In this situation, that is not an option. Instead, they are forced to do the best they can with the situation at hand, coming up with creative ways to fidget as they are able to, take breaks to go outside when they can, and otherwise, deal with it.

Notice how privilege plays into the options available in this scenario. The only identity we named is their neurodivergence. Statistically speaking, white, Asian Americans, and Pacific Islanders make more money than Black, Latinx, and Indigenous folx, cis-men make more money than cis-women, and cis people make more money than LGBTQIA2S+ folx. There is a lot to think about here, especially as it relates to the intersections of identities and who does and does not get to have their needs met.

You may be thinking of clients you know who are in similar situations to the ones I described. This is the impact of ableism and capitalism and the harm that it can and does cause ND people. I'm not trying to be grim or bleak, but I do want to be realistic about the limitations to accommodations and accessing the array of very real support needs that people have. It is essential that we as therapists *do not* engage in toxic positivity or spiritual bypassing as we support clients with very real obstacles to accessing their needs. I'll be really explicit. Avoid saying things like "it's not that bad!" or "you just have to believe!" or "everything always has a way of working out!" Even creativity has its limits at times, especially in the face of racism, homophobia, transphobia, colonization, classism, and capitalism. This is when listening with our full bodymind is essential, so that our clients feel heard and understood in the ups and downs of their life. As much as I'm a believer in win-win situations, oppression has a different agenda.

Oof, isn't that the truth! *Oppression has a different agenda.*

As we continue in the rest of this chapter, we will talk more explicitly about specific types of accommodations and support needs that clients may have, both as they relate to accessing therapy and for the rest of their day-to-day life. We will then explore what supports we may need for ourselves and how we might be able to better access that support.

Before we recap, let's check in. Are there any sensory delights that you would like to access if you aren't already? Is there anything else you may need before continuing on?

Recap: The Reality of Executive Function Challenges and Support Needs

- Autistic and KCS/VAST clients tend to have executive function (EF) challenges.
- These challenges are exacerbated by emotional overwhelm.
- When supporting clients with executive function, accept what won't change, be creative, make it interesting, make it the right amount of challenge, approach it with strategies that are unique to who the client is, and be willing to try new things.
- Accessing accommodations is a expression of self-acceptance and self-compassion.
- Privilege is directly tied to who can or cannot access certain accommodations.

WORKING WITH CLIENTS

On my way to sitting down to write this section, I took a serendipitous detour that led me to reread some of my original blog posts. In them, I shared openly about how much I struggled for so much of my life, about the self-hate, the harshness I felt toward myself for being different, and not understanding why. Unfortunately, but not surprisingly, I had some therapists/mentors along the way who didn't understand my depth of feeling and left me feeling judged and shamed.

While I never had a therapist ask me, "Nyck, have you ever considered that you're Autistic and KCS/VAST?", I'm grateful that I also found quality support along the way that honored my sensitivity, depth, pain, and capacity for joy. With a lot of various forms of support, some internal, some external, along with the privilege I hold, I found my way through the toughest parts of my journey thus far. I found my way to a place of greater internal stability, more self-love, more self-acceptance, wholeness, and a greater capacity for joy and pleasure. It did not come easy, it was not cheap, and it was not by accident; it was really hard work that I could not have done alone. While some of it happened pre-identification, some of it couldn't happen until I found language and context to understand myself through the Autistic and KCS/VAST lenses (as well as queer and trans lenses).

I invite us to take a moment here to be with the following questions:

- My point is that identification can make a world of difference, *and* what if having a label for our neurotype(s) isn't a prerequisite to getting our needs met?
- What if, by virtue of being human, we are allowed to have needs, no matter how unique to us they may seem?
- And then what if, with acknowledgment of those needs, came all sorts of creative or not-so-creative options for how to get those needs met?

I think this is one of the reasons why I never liked the term *special needs* to describe disabled people. There aren't good needs or bad needs; there are needs, and we all have them. Yes, absolutely, some of us have different needs from the majority and our survival depends on getting those needs met.

To me, this is the essence of the neurodiversity paradigm and how ND-affirming, anti-ableist care supports humans of *all* neurotypes. While some of us depend on this type of support for our survival, others may be less dependent on it to be okay. As we move into a variety of types of challenges and possible accommodations, I want to encourage all of us to rethink what it means to have needs and to get our needs met. May we decolonize our bodyminds and transcend what white supremacy, capitalism, cis-heteronormativity, neuronormativity, classism, and patriarchy have taught us about who is allowed to have needs, who isn't, and how those needs are allowed or not allowed to get met.

I did that thing again where I noticed myself pause, sit taller in my chair, and take a deeper breath. There's my cue, hehe. Here's your invitation from me to check in with yourself and notice. Perhaps you notice your breath, what's happening in your body, what thoughts you are thinking, or any impulses that may be present. I encourage you to take a moment to tend to you, and then I'll be here when you are ready to continue.

✷ ✷ ✷ ✷

We'll begin with accommodations clients may need relating to accessing therapy. This list also gets us thinking about all the possible obstacles involved with accessing care in the first place:

- **Financial access:**
  - Do they have insurance that covers therapy, and if so, are they able to find a therapist who takes their insurance?
  - Can they afford therapy that is self-pay or out-of-pocket?
  - How much can they afford to pay per session (with or without insurance, since most insurances also have copays and/or deductibles)?
- **Time:**
  - Are they able to find a therapist who is available on the day of the week or the time of day they need?
  - Do they have choice in how long the sessions are; are they too short, too long, or just right?
  - What do they need in terms of reminders about their sessions to support their attendance?
- **Location, in person:**
  - Let's consider the myriad of things to navigate or account for when meeting in person:
    - Chronic health challenges
    - Health/COVID precautions
    - Transportation/parking

- Finding the office
- Accessibility of the building in terms of mobility (including ramps, elevators, accessible bathrooms, etc.)
    - Does your office have a gender-neutral or all-gender bathroom for gender-expansive folx to safely and comfortably use?
    - Are they able to manage time well enough to plan for all of these logistics and arrive for their session more or less on time?
    - What possible sensory considerations will they have to navigate in your office: noises, lights, smells, furniture, personal space, or other?
    - Can they opt to meet outside versus inside?
- **Location, telehealth:**
    - Do they have the option of meeting virtually, whether via secure video conferencing platform or telephone?
    - Do they have access to the internet and a secure, reliable device?
    - Do they have a quiet, private space to be in during the session that allows for confidentiality?
    - What agreements might they need to make with people they cohabitate with in order to support their privacy?
    - What potential barriers or obstacles does telehealth remove or add as compared to in-person sessions?
- **Communication:**
    - Do they have the option to communicate in the ways most accessible to them on any given day?
    - Do they communicate in the same language as you, or is an interpreter needed?
    - Can they opt for in-person *or* virtual sessions, to be on *or* off camera, to speak *or* use the chat feature, to talk *or* engage in art, movement, or parallel play?

- I'm using either/or inquiries, but there may be third, fourth, even fifth options for each of these.
- **Compatibility:**
  - Can they find a therapist whose impact on their nervous system is gentle and maybe even promotes greater ease, rather than more frazzled, guarded, or survival mode reactions?
  - Are they able to find a therapist with any shared identities?
  - Does the therapist inherently respect who the client is as a person, including the client's neurotype(s), ability/disability, race, ethnicity, culture, gender, sexual orientation, class, and religious or spiritual orientation?

Getting to therapy can be a feat in itself, without ever doing any so-called therapeutic work! Not only is it brave for us to be therapists, but it's inherently brave to be a client. Having our own therapist or practitioner is a great reminder of this. When I've outgrown a particular therapist or practitioner and needed to find a new one, starting the process with a new person reminds me just how brave it is to ask for support, receive support, and create a brand new, emotionally intimate, therapeutic relationship with *a stranger*. It helps me to have even more awareness, empathy, and sensitivity for my clients, and ultimately helps me to be more skillful. This is one of many reasons why as therapists we need to engage in our own therapeutic work with a therapist, coach, or practitioner.

My body is letting me know that it's ready for a pause to get up, stretch or move about, and hydrate. How about you? Please listen to or notice what's present for you and tend as you are able.

✱ ✱ ✱ ✱

Well, that was insightful, nourishing, and very apropos to this whole chapter on executive function, accommodations, and accessing our support needs. What I thought would be a quickish

10-minute or less break turned into (*obviously*, insert loving eye roll here) a truly Autistic/KCS/VAST experience. I drank a cup of water, then noticed I needed to go to the bathroom, so I did, and then I did some stretches.

"Ah, that was satisfying...oh, wait, I think I'm hungry."

Internal dialogue ensued that ended with "yep, I need to eat some lunch" (it's 3 p.m., so a bit late for traditional lunch, but it was my second meal of the day).

I stopped to heat up some food, eat, and then I had to go to the bathroom again. Thinking I'm finally ready to transition back to writing, now it turns out I'm sleepy! I'm making the choice to have some coffee rather than go lie down because I'm really invested in more writing today. Honestly though, coffee this late in the day is only an option because I know I can have a CBD gummy later to make me sleepy when it's time to go to bed. Otherwise, my choice to caffeinate and continue writing could mean I won't be able to fall asleep tonight, which would make tomorrow a much more challenging day, especially because I have to be up and out early. All things to consider!

I share all of this because taking breaks and all the associated obstacles are a huge part of life for us ND folx. That whole time, I was reflecting on how this writing is a deeply embodied experience for me, which is keeping me connected to my interoceptive input. For a lot of people, especially once they are in a monotropic vortex of attention, connection with their physical needs is lost. And for people with limited or low interoception (I wish there was a nonhierarchical way of expressing that better), it becomes especially difficult because the internal cues aren't available in the first place. This is the reason why some people set timers to remind them to pause, check in, eliminate, eat, hydrate, stretch, rest, and so on to a schedule, *or* they may avoid taking breaks altogether. This second option is generally for one or both of these two reasons: either the thing they are focusing on is a lot more interesting than physiological needs and/or they fear/know that once they stop, they are unlikely to get started again.

This struggle is so real! I've heard my Pops, who is Autistic and KCS/VAST, talk about this many times. When he's working on an outdoor project, he will rarely stop to eat lunch or get a drink because he knows that if he does, he'll realize he is tired and then a nap will take precedence over finishing the project. The anticapitalist in me loves to encourage him to stop and care for himself, and the Autistic/KCS/VAST in me really gets it. Starting and stopping can be so hard!

In addition to starting—also known as task initiation—and stopping, clients may also have a hard time continuing once they do start, especially if there isn't a prebuilt structure for them to follow. Many Autistic and KCS/VAST brains don't automatically insert steps B through Y. They may know how to start, and if they're lucky, they may know where the end is. But the whole middle can be elusive and overwhelming.

"What am I supposed to doooo...?!"

As therapists, we can help our clients figure out what the steps are of any particular project at hand. It could be feeding themselves, specific work- or academic-related projects, dealing with health issues, cleaning the home, scheduling and showing up to appointments, sleep, and so much more.

To an unaware outsider, it could seem like "well, duh, just do the thing!" However unintentional, yes, that would absolutely be ableism.

For ND folx, there can be a myriad of possible obstacles to doing "the thing." I'll use an example related to feeding ourselves. This is especially relevant because both of these neurotypes have higher prevalence of eating disorders than the rest of the population (think sensory issues, diet culture, belonging, body image, rigidity, gender presentation, interoception differences, oppression, and more). Feeding ourselves has so many steps involved and can be very complex. And it's something we do multiple times a day, every darn day (unless we are food insecure and forced to skip meals). As an Autistic/KCS/VAST human who's also a client, I'm going to talk in the "we" tense.

First, there's figuring out what we think we want to eat. This can be a huge obstacle in and of itself. Many of us like to food plan, which means we are also trying to figure out what we will not only want to eat in a few days from now, but what our bodies will allow us to eat (hence the idea of safe foods for the Autistic and KCS/VAST communities). Once we figure out the "What," then we can make a grocery list and gather the ingredients or items that we want. For some people, getting beyond this step can be a monumental feat.

Next comes the shopping. The volume of items, options, and choices in many traditional big box grocery stores in the United States can be overwhelming, plus you might have to interact with humans in the store, and there will likely be fluorescent lights, possibly crowded and cramped aisles, smells from other humans and food items, and so on. Nowadays, being able to order groceries online has been a lifesaver for some people. Others find strategies like going at off-peak hours or to alternative places to shop. Some communities have farm stores or smaller stores that can be less overstimulating and more in touch with where the food is grown or produced.

While shopping, we have to consider the KCS/VAST tax. If we're buying fruits and vegetables, for instance, do we buy the more expensive already washed, cut up, and ready-to-eat items, knowing that we are most likely to eat them before they go bad and have to get composted or thrown away? Or do we save money initially and buy the ones that require us to clean, cut, and/or otherwise prepare before we can eat them? All the while, knowing full well that we may or may not have the motivation, time, or energy required for this task when the time comes, and the food may go bad before we get to it, rendering all the food and money wasted? Alternatively (or in addition), there are so many enticing shiny objects at the grocery store that the budget gets blown because (a) we didn't have a list, or (b) we went shopping while hungry and bought the whole store (not literally, just a lot more than we might have planned on buying).

And then let's not forget all the people with food allergies or sensitivities, like gluten, dairy, nuts, eggs, soy, and so on. This requires even more choices and planning, and generally, more money. While many places have a lot more options available these days to accommodate these restrictions, the options are almost always more expensive.

We also live in a diet culture that has all kinds of rules about what our bodies are "supposed to" look like, what we are "supposed to" feed them, and what constitutes "nourishment." For a lot of us, this can translate into food anxiety and food rules, sensory sensitivities aside. "Is it really okay to eat frozen pizza *again?*" "Okay, I'll buy cookies again, but I'm not allowed to buy cookies *and* ice cream, *am I?*" For people who have a few safe foods and tend to stick with those, there can be a plethora of internalized shaming messages about not having enough so-called diversity in how we eat.

Assuming we answered all of those questions, made all the choices, and secured the groceries, now they need to either be put away for later use or be prepared in some way. This includes some sort of system for where in the kitchen things go. For food that needs to be prepared, it also includes recipes, whether impromptu, made up, or researched. And then all the steps involved in making said recipe, which may include measuring ingredients, which means staying focused enough to measure accurately (i.e., 1 teaspoon, not 1 tablespoon!) and track the right count. It also means staying on task through completion, not getting distracted and possibly burning the food. On top of all that, there is a high likelihood of creating a lot of dirty dishes, pots and pans, and utensils that eventually will need to be dealt with.

Finally, food may be available to consume. One can only hope it's the right texture, flavor, and temperature. This might be a satisfying or pleasurable sensory experience, but sometimes food is just food. Other times, when food is finally ready to be consumed, it can't be eaten. Anxiety or another distress response has shown up, and the presence of sympathetic arousal means no access to the parasympathetic, rest-digest nervous system. In response, we can't physically get ourselves to eat. Oof.

In the event that we are now fed, we hopefully got the calories we need. I'm being very choosy in my language here so as to not in any way reinforce or contribute to ableism and diet culture (which I, and so many others, have been directly harmed by). Now the kitchen is either a mess or at least *something* likely needs to be washed, cleaned, put away, and/or thrown away. We may or may not have any energy left over at the moment to handle any more food- and kitchen-related tasks. Maybe our executive function has been all used up, or we only had enough energy or pain threshold to prepare and eat the food, not to clean up. Or, the sensory ick of washing dishes is more than we can handle by that point, so the dishes stay dirty.

At least we are fed. We'll call that good enough for now. Until it's the next time to eat…

Some people, if they can afford it, will opt for prepared or prepackaged foods, get takeout, or go out to eat; it eliminates so many of the above steps. This can also get expensive and generates more waste. When weighing this expense, many ND folx have to entertain this question: Do I prioritize caloric intake or nutritional value? Whether it's due to financial strain, living in a food desert, sensory issues, or other reasons, they may only be able to eat fast food or processed food. What matters most is that they are consuming calories, and calories are what they need to live. Diet culture and ableism are not welcome here.

I notice myself pendulate back to my internal experience, and it feels important to name this. I'm aware of both self-compassion and a sense of ugh. I'm very present to the harm I have inadvertently caused when I was unaware of how steeped in diet culture I was, and the ways whiteness, colonization, ableism, classism, cis-heteronormativity, patriarchy, and diet culture go hand in hand. Several years back, I couldn't have written this section with as much awareness, inclusion, and nonjudgment. Oof, what a testament to the phrase "when we know better, we do better."

I'm grateful that I have more access to being gentle with myself these days; otherwise, it would be really easy to get lost in shame and harshness. This gentleness helps me to be in touch with the grief that's present, both for the ways I've been harmed by diet culture, and the ways that I then (unknowingly at the time) passed on that harm. I realize that I'm likely not the only one who is impacted on some level by this section. While I tend to my grief—grief that I can sense is both mine and of the collective—I invite you to pause, too. Food and all things food related can be very complex for folx for all sorts of reasons. Would you like to check in with yourself, take any notes, reflect, tend to bio needs, or something else? May you tend gently and sweetly to whatever is arising within you.

After engaging in quite a process, I'm ready to return. I stepped away from the computer, and immediately tears started flowing. Several memories throughout my lifespan showed up, and I could feel viscerally how the intersections of food, oppression, and a desire for belonging are woven into my body's history. What a reminder of the ways the personal is professional and vice versa.

Supporting clients with executive function and accommodations isn't separate from honoring and supporting their wholeness, their history, their trauma, their intersecting identities, and how oppression lives in and through them. As I mentioned already, when big, painful feels are present, executive functioning becomes much less accessible. We can't tend to one without tending to the other. Let's transition back now.

This whole example of food and executive function is precisely why some version of the following has been said by many clients over the years, myself included: "Ugh, I have to eat again?! It's so much effort! If only there was some sort of meal replacement pill I could take instead." Even for those of us who love to eat and find sensory delight from food, the whole process can be so arduous, repetitive, and mundane.

I'm exhausted just writing all of this out! But it's validating at the same time. It's rarely ever just one thing. It's usually 10, 20, or more small steps that comprise the so called "one thing": in this case, feeding ourselves. These are referred to as activities of daily living, and there are many that are expected of us on a daily basis. Think about getting ready for school or work, being at work or school, and getting ready for bed. Each of those has many steps involved. This is precisely why as therapists we need to be so curious with clients, look at all the steps, and uncover wherein the obstacles lie. It also means having honest, anti-ableist conversations about what is *actually necessary* and what can be adapted, changed, or modified in some way. It is essential that we are helping our clients to question the so-called norms society has placed upon us, especially as they relate to the notions of hygiene and daily living.

In addition to activities of daily living, some other general topic areas that clients may want accommodations support with include:

- All things related to education or employment
- Relationships
- How to care for their home (to include cleaning, laundry, dealing with mail, and possibly yard work)
- For those who are parents, parenting!

As you explore these with clients in response to their distress or request for support, remember to keep an open mind, be curious, and help them identify the obstacles that are present. Because of ableism and other forms of oppression, without further exploration, the obstacles can *seem* invisible. These obstacles form the basis for creating and implementing accommodations.

Next, I'm going to offer a list of possible supports. While it is impossible for me to make this a totally exhaustive list, I hope it feels thorough enough. These are both specific and somewhat general accommodations that clients could advocate for both in the therapy space and in the rest of their lives.

> **EXECUTIVE FUNCTION SUPPORT AND ACCOMMODATIONS**
>
> - **Body doubling:** Such a weird name for this, but it means that the presence of another human, whether in person or virtually, can help us to do the thing! Their nervous system can support our nervous system to get started, to continue, and even to finish the task at hand. What we might not be able to do by ourselves can become a lot easier in the presence of another. There are apps and platforms that offer this service. We can do this with our clients in session, and they can recruit friends, family, peers, or colleagues to body double with.
> - **Support swapping:** As we talked about in Chapter 3, how can two or more people help one another in getting their needs met? This is a great way to play upon each other's strengths. We can help our clients with appointment reminders, check in about things on their to-do list, and help them identify who in their life they could swap support with.
> - **Working from home or asynchronous learning:** As with many things, for some this is super helpful; for others it makes things worse. Some people love the freedom and flexibility. They can work at their own pace and be in their own environment. Others find that the self-pacing, lack of external structure or oversight,

or lack of human interaction (e.g., peers or coworkers) increases their executive function challenges.
- **Apps:** This is very broad! There are apps for most things these days, including scheduling, organizing, tending to bio/physiological needs (including reminders to hydrate), tracking heart rate or other rhythms, making friends, dating, turning appliances and lights on and off, and more. These can be individually specific in terms of accessibility. Some people love digitizing their lives; others not so much.
- **Explicit communication and regular feedback:** Whether in the employment sector, parenting, education, or therapy space, clear, direct, and explicit expectations and directions can go a long way. Be literal and take out the subtext; don't leave people guessing what you *might* mean. Mentorship in academic and employment settings can also be helpful for ND folx. When offering feedback, be sensitive to possible rejection sensitivity dysphoria and make sure to focus on the positives, too. Clients can specifically ask this of their supervisors, mentors, or educators.
- **Breaks:** Whether before, during, or after class, at any point in the workday, with interpersonal relating, or in a therapy session, clients may need to take a break to decompress, integrate, tend to bio needs, engage in movement, rest, and so on. This is a valid need and deserves to be met.
- **Opportunities for kinesthetic learning:** Especially for KCS/VAST people, kinesthetic learning is key. For Autistic people who do well with things that are literal/concrete, getting to be hands on, trying things out, and acting as if can be instrumental to learning and succeeding. It can reduce boredom and

increase comprehension. It also is an essential way of supporting bodymind as an integrated whole.

- **Extra time or flexible schedule:** This comes up a lot with people in school dealing with test taking, navigating between classes, or due dates for assignments and projects. This is also true in the workplace and at home. Instead of needing to report to a 9 a.m.–5 p.m. job, a client may be able to adjust their hours to when their energy level is most optimized, which could be 12 p.m.–8 p.m. or something totally different. Or instead of a set schedule, a client may just have a due date for the project and can get it done in whatever time frame works best for them.

- **Ways to reduce overstimulation or increase sensory input:** There's a plethora of possibilities for this one. Instead of an overhead light, use lamps instead. Instead of a sitting desk, use a ball, standing, treadmill, or cycling desk. Go outside or come inside. Use noise-canceling headphones, wear sunglasses, close the shades or open them, play music while doing things, use headphones for the TV or to play music so that the environment is quiet for others, avoid scented products, or use scented products. This is a great one to be really creative with. It's important to be aware that when living with people with conflicting or competing sensory needs, this can get really challenging!

- **Reduced demands:** This one is key, not just for PDAers, but anyone experiencing signs of burnout or distress. Consider what is absolutely necessary to happen or get done, and what isn't actually necessary, even though it might *seem* important. How can we do less? Consider less pressure, fewer expectations, fewer responsibilities, and less scheduled time. And how can we increase autonomy? Amplify self-agency, choice, freedom, and flexibility within whatever structure is needed or wanted. Perfectionism can make this one tricky, so there may be a need for gentleness.

- **Extra time for transitions:** While we all transition at different paces and in different ways, given monotropism, most ND people need more time than our NT counterparts to shift our attention from one state of focus to another. This could mean clients giving themselves extra time between when their session with you ends and what's next on their schedule. Or they can tell themselves that the time they have to leave is 15 or 30 minutes earlier than the actual time, so that when focus shifts and they do several rounds of "one more thing!" they can still leave relatively on time. Often, there is not enough spaciousness between activities, meetings, or plans to allow the nervous system the time it needs to transition and acclimate.
- **Able to go at their own pace:** This is as true in the therapy space as it is for everywhere else in life. For me and a lot of other Autistic people, our natural pace and rhythm is much slower than it is for the dominant culture, whether it is due to variations in our processing speed, the amount of input we are navigating at any given moment, our sensitivity, the depth to which we experience things, our attention to detail, or more. On the other hand, many KCS/VAST people tend to thrive at a faster pace and frequently seek to increase the amount of input they receive in any given moment. This is all person specific, even within and across neurotypes.
- **Honor communication style/format:** As I've said earlier, all forms of communication are valid and worthy. Some

people are nonspeakers entirely, while others do well with less speaking or need opportunities to be nonspeaking. Some people speak a lot and want to be heard. Some communicate with their hands or other body language; some don't. Allow people to be direct, blunt, and explicit. Don't tone police! Be flexible with when and how someone chooses to communicate and express themself. If you're not sure what someone means, just ask! This is as true for the therapy space as it is elsewhere.
- **Medication or supplement support:** With the support of a medication provider, nutritionist, or holistic health practitioner, some people find tremendous value from physiological support. Whether stimulant based or non-stimulant based, SSRI, herbal, and so on, medication and/or supplements can be a game changer when taken under professional supervision.
- **Increased autonomy and creativity:** Allow people to be self-directed and to let their own inspiration guide them. Let them be in charge of their body and their life as much as possible. Let them be the outside-the-box thinkers that they may naturally be.
- **Provide structure**: Structure can be a form of energetic proprioception that reduces anxiety and creates more presence. Many people crave it and need it to feel secure, to know what to expect, and to do well. Structure doesn't have to be rigid, though some people will like it to be. For those who prefer their structure not to be rigid, I love to say "fluid structure," meaning that it can shift and change in how it gets implemented.

Hopefully this list leaves you feeling more prepared for how you can help clients not just in the therapeutic relationship, but also to advocate for what they need in the rest of their lives. You likely may have ideas that didn't make it to this list; here's a loving reminder that your ideas are good and valid! It seems like a great time for a pause or break before we move on to how we might want to accommodate ourselves as therapists. You do you and I'll be here when you're ready to continue. There's no rush!

Recap: Supporting Clients With Executive Function and Support Needs in the Everyday

- When it comes to the therapy space, there are many things to take into account that relate to clients being able to access care: finances, location, time, compatibility, and communication.
- Supporting clients with their executive function challenges and identifying accommodations has a lot to do with identifying the obstacles that are present that could seem invisible due to ableism and oppression.
- Activities of daily living such as feeding ourselves and hygiene have many steps involved in the overall task. Look at each of these individual steps to help identify the obstacles.
- It's important to tend to the emotional and historical aspects of support needs, in addition to concrete strategies.
- Also consider areas of life such as school or work, home, relationships, and parenting (if applicable).
- There is a vast array of types of accommodations for which clients can advocate (and for which you can advocate on their behalf). These include: body doubling, support swapping, working from home or asynchronous learning, apps, explicit communication or direct and regular feedback, breaks, opportunities for kinesthetic learning, extra time or a flexible schedule, ways to reduce overstimulation or increase sensory input, reduced demands, extra time for transitions, being able to go at one's own pace, honoring communication style or format,

medication or supplement support, increasing autonomy and creativity, and providing structure.

WORKING WITH OURSELVES

If you are an Autistic and/or KCS/VAST or questioning therapist, you may have found the previous section applies well to you. Even if you identify as NT, you may have been surprised to notice that the section felt more applicable to you or to loved ones than you may have anticipated. No matter what your neurotype(s), I'm going to introduce a few key areas within our work for which we may need support or accommodations. We will address scheduling, documentation, administrative tasks, and meeting our physiological needs throughout the workday. In Chapter 8, Global Permission: Questions to Dismantle Normativity in the Counseling Office, we will delve further into things like time off, how long our sessions are, time between sessions, and our physical space or office.

In support of kinesthetic learning and integration, I'll ask a number of questions. Feel free to engage with them in whatever ways feels useful, valuable, and/or accessible.

Scheduling
This has multiple parts.

- First, *how* do you schedule your appointments?
- Do you use an online scheduler that allows clients to schedule autonomously and then you keep track of your availability and when you are scheduled?
- Do you do your own scheduling via email, text, or phone call?
- Do you have an assistant who handles scheduling for you, or are you responsible for scheduling your own appointments?

Some people have a really hard time with the scheduling aspect of being a therapist. For that reason, they may intentionally work at an agency, group practice, or other employment setting where someone else manages all of the scheduling for them. Another solution some people in private practice have found useful is to hire an assistant. While that may be a viable option for some, it also involves paying another person and training/overseeing them. Some also use online schedulers.

No matter how it gets done, scheduling requires a great deal of executive function. This is why many therapists resort to a set schedule with allotted appointment times on each day. Perhaps the structure of their day changes day to day throughout the week, or perhaps it is identical each day.

A final thought for now is:

- How many sessions are you scheduling per day?

There can be such complexity to this. For those working in agencies, hospitals, institutions, or other group settings, there may be policies in place that require you to meet with a certain number of clients per day and per week.

- Is that number sustainable for you?

If you are in private practice:

- Have you found a daily and weekly number of clients that works well for you, honors the wholeness of who you are, and generates enough income to live?

The unfortunate reality for folx in the United States is that frequently people's capacity does not line up with the dictates of capitalism. While we'll address money and how much we charge for our sessions in the next chapter, I want to at least acknowledge how interwoven capacity, capitalism, cost of living, and our rate all is.

The idea of "number" was a source of shame and hiding for me for a long time, especially before I had language to understand my neurotypes. I felt like I was perpetually on the edge of burnout, and even when I was working the most I was able to, the number of clients I met with was always less than my fellow NT full-time therapist colleagues. Some people are able to strike a balance between their "number," capacity, and how much they charge that allows them to support themselves financially and be well physically and emotionally. For others, this is a perpetual and ongoing struggle. Some therapists find their sense of balance by doing part-time therapy and part-time other work that does not involve any emotional labor or space holding.

- When you think about having access to support and accommodations as it relates to all of this, what might you actually need? (Gentleness in the face of your self-honesty is encouraged.)

There is no denying that capitalism is inherently ableist and that we are all doing our best to exist within a broken system. Broken, as in, doing what it was intended to do, which is to enforce systems of oppression and dehumanize people who are not white, wealthy, cisgender, heterosexual, male, and Christian. From the lens of honoring and caring for the well-being of all humans, all creatures, and planet Earth, it is truly a destructive and horrific system.

If you are struggling to exist within the capitalist system, please hear me when I say:

This is not a you problem, and without question, you are absolutely impacted.

On the other hand, there are people who do well with many more clients in a week than I could ever handle. I've heard some Autistic/KCS/VAST therapists express feeling marginalized because they thrive on having a very high number of sessions per day or week, and some people pathologize this. In an ideal world, we would all have the autonomy and permission to center our number in our work, and still reliably generate the income we need to live and have our needs met.

Moving on to the next section. Feel free to join me when you are ready!

Documentation

I don't know about you, but for me, this is my least favorite part of my job. Being in private practice and not taking insurance (more on this in the next chapter), I have a lot of autonomy and flexibility with how I handle my notes. Early on in my practice, I used a spreadsheet for my notes. Over time, I began using practice management software and did my documentation in the software. I found that no matter how hard I tried, I was not able to be consistent. I also found that I wouldn't reference my electronic notes once I input them. Eventually, I came up with what felt like a radical solution for myself that actually works, and works well at that. It certainly is ND-affirming, but it is also rather nontraditional.

Depending on your neurotype(s), your preferences, needs, and tendencies around order, organization, and tracking, you may also find that it takes some trial and error to figure out what works for you. I recognize the privilege I have that allows me to do my notes my way. Especially for Autistic and KCS/VAST people, sometimes we don't know what options are available to us until we hear someone else's ideas. For that purpose, I will describe the system that I created for myself.

I have a big three-ring binder. Inside the binder are many dividers. (Writing this reminded me of being in high school all over again, oy!) Each client has their own tab in the binder. Behind each tab is three-hole punched loose leaf notebook paper. At first I was loving using college-ruled, but then I came to prefer the extra spaciousness of the wide-ruled; I managed to find paper that is recycled, which feels more aligned with my values around environmental sustainability. I hand write my notes on my wide-ruled notebook paper. On the top of the page is my client's first name. Each session gets dated, and I jot down what I deem important.

It includes a summary of the session, important things for me to remember, such as the name of their pet, squishmellow, new stuffie, important people in their life; key takeaways or insights; what to return to next time (if there is something specific that we left off with or that the client requested to start with next time); and when we are meeting next. I use the front and back and fit as many notes on a page as I can. This binder is kept in a secure location that only I have access to.

One of my pre-session rituals that I share more about in Chapter 9, Global Permission: Transitions, Ritual, and the Sacred, is to pull out the current and maybe recent past sheets of paper and look them over before the session starts. My previously impeccable memory has become much less impeccable over time, so reviewing the previous note is really helpful for me to feel caught up and ready to go when the session starts.

How I came to know that this system is effective for me is that I've stuck with it for a long time. It is accessible for me. I am able to follow through with it without much internal complaint. I mean, sometimes I still do complain, but it's not about the system as much as it is not wanting to have to do "one more thing." For me and how my neurotypes collaborate with one another, sticking with a system like this is an indicator that it's working. For others, sticking with something long term is unlikely due to lack of novelty over time and boredom setting in. That is so valid! In that case, more frequent creativity to introduce novelty into the systems at hand will likely be needed.

In the event that my documentation is requested, and it has been, whether from grant funding sources or outside agencies providing specific types of support to my clients, I opt to provide a summary. Not only does this feel more ethical to me in terms of honoring my clients' privacy, but it also works well for my style of note taking in the first place.

- Have you found a system of documentation that works well for you and meets your responsibilities?

By responsibilities I am referring to the requirements of your license/credentials, place of employment, payer sources, and so on. Some places of employment have very set protocols and systems in place for documentation. If that applies to you and it is a good fit for you, great! If that applies to you and it is not a good fit for you, here are some thoughts:

- Is there someone you could body double with to get your notes done?
- Is there a way you can make it more interesting or novel? (For example, during or after your notes, you could have a snack, beverage, or delight of some form that brings pleasure and adds incentive.)
- Does it work better for you to do notes between sessions, at specific times during the day, at the end of the day, or if you have a great memory, at the end of the week or other specified time?
- Does it help to jot down handwritten notes in the moment and then go back at a specified time (could be days or weeks later) and get all your notes done at once?
- How else might you be able to simplify your documentation?
- Are there any other creative ideas you can come up with to take the potential struggle out of doing notes?

Take as much or as little time here as you choose. When you are ready, we'll move on to the next topic.

Administrative Tasks

Depending on the environment you work in, this may or may not apply to you. This is precisely why some people would not ever choose to be self-employed, in private practice, or in management positions. That is so valid!

Responding to Emails

If you are responsible for responding to prospective clients who reach out expressing interest in your services:

- What strategies or systems have you come up with that work well for you?

My email inbox can feel like a sea of demand. People that I don't know, have never met, and may or may not ever meet want something from me. It is the nature of my job that I have to respond. Here are some possibilities:

- Create template emails that you copy and paste when someone reaches out. Having systems in place such as this can cut down on much of the executive function needed and help us move past the very real inertia that can get in the way of reading and responding to emails.
- Choose designated times of day or in the week when you read and respond to email.
- Body double with someone else to help you get over the hump.
- Make a delicious beverage or sensorily delightful snack to bring with you to your phone or computer (a cup of coffee, usually half-caf for my sensitive digestive system, does wonders for me to "get shit done" that I might otherwise avoid).
- Give yourself an incentive to look forward to once you are done.

- Set an automatic email reminder that everyone receives once an email gets sent to you. It confirms you received their email and lets them know when to expect a response, for example: "Thank you for reaching out. I respond to emails Tuesday–Thursday. You can anticipate a response from me during that window." I've also seen auto email responses that include reminders that "I'm not available for 24/7 or crisis support; if you are in crisis, please call (insert hotline here)."
- Include in your email footer when you respond to emails so that people can anticipate when they will hear back from you.
- I get many different types of email in my inbox, things that are work related, social justice advocacy related, and so on. In Gmail, there is the option to star emails as important. To help prevent emails from getting lost in the array of unread or unopened messages, I scan my inbox and star the ones from clients, prospective clients, and work-related specifics so that I know which ones require a response and are more time sensitive than others.

While this section focused on emails, some people may also have complex relationships with returning calls and texts. I encourage you to apply the same principles discussed above. If you are someone who greatly dislikes having to call people back (oh, how I know the feeling!), it is absolutely okay to not list your phone number on any of your marketing sources. You can also specify that you are only available for texting instead.

Bookkeeping and Taxes

I know there are plenty of math- and number-oriented people out there. Probably not many will read this book, though, given that we probably chose a career like counseling because it didn't involve numbers, haha. If you love the unemotional work tasks like dealing with the financial aspects of running your business, I am genuinely happy for you! If you are more of an avoider like me, I see you, wink wink. If this is an ongoing struggle, source of "ugh," or an executive function nemesis, you are so not alone.

I have yet to commit to a system that truly works for me, despite my best intentions. Up until a couple years ago, I and Turbo Tax would bond each March/April and that worked well enough. With enough incentive I could actually enjoy a mental and emotional break from my usual work and get down with some numbers. Now, I have an accountant who manages my quarterly and end-of-year taxes. I still have to provide documentation of income and expenses, and I'd be lying if I said this happened with any set frequency at regular intervals throughout the year. I do my best, though, and I've come to accept that my best will just have to be good enough.

- Have you found software or bookkeeping strategies that work well for you and help you to stay on top of tracking the financials of your business?

A lot of the same strategies for responding to emails apply here as well, like body doubling, having a designated time for financial tracking, adding novelty or making it interesting, and using sensory delights.

And a great question to consider, if you are in a financial situation that allows for this, or have loved ones to help out:

- How might you be able to delegate this task to free up energy for the things you are naturally really good at (e.g., being a therapist!)?

For those who have the gift of being good with numbers and with the creative, emotional aspects of being a therapist, then it may be less about being really good at something, and more about the best use of your time, energy, and natural abilities (and only you can determine this).

I'm going to transition to the next topic now.

Meeting Your Physiological Needs Throughout the Work Day

The irony is not lost on me that just as I was ready to start this subsection, my body's need for hydration and elimination became unavoidable. I felt the internal angst of "but I know me, and if I stop to go do that, I can't be certain that I will be able to come right back and finish this, and I *really* want to finish this." And not surprisingly, when I got to the kitchen, my body was totally like "um, I'm hungry!" We had a brief, very mild confrontation about it. I chose to be a little stubborn and center my autonomy; I compromised by eating a quick snack, knowing I needed more food, but that I was choosing to write now and eat more later.

Here's to the realities of being human and having bodies with a plethora of physiological needs, while also being a therapist! Depending on how your day is structured, this subsection may not even feel necessary for you; maybe you've already got it all figured out and handled. If that's you, then woo-hoo!

And, whether it's because interoception is a tricky thing for you, or you get so passionate and absorbed in your work that you forget to stop or don't want to stop, or your day is so busy that it's genuinely hard to center your needs in the whirlwind of an environment that seems to be needing you in five different directions at any given moment, you are not alone. This last one reminds me of the realities of when I interned at a middle-high school; while that was partly true for me, it was very true for my supervisor.

When I'm referring to physiological needs, I'm thinking about eating, hydrating, toileting, and energy level. I'm going to list each one out, offer some things to consider, and share possible accommodations.

Eating: Getting the Calories You Need to Fuel Your Body Throughout the Day

- Do you have regular breaks for breakfast, lunch, and dinner (acknowledging that we all work different hours and your mealtime may very much be in the midst of your workday)?
- Are there certain foods that are most easily digested, accessible, tasty, sensorially safe, or energizing that are your go-tos?
- Do you do better with snacking/grazing throughout the day or having full meals?
- If you work outside of your home and packing food to take with you isn't an option, what alternatives do you have for getting food?
- Can you do a big shop or food delivery and keep a stash of snacks and nonperishable foods somewhere at work?
- Is eating out an option?
- Does having mealtime or break time with a colleague make it easier for you to stop and feed yourself versus working straight through your day?
- Would it be helpful to use an app or set a timer to remind you to eat?

I know food and food-related stuff can be complex, and I honor whatever support needs you may have around it. I want to remind you that your support needs are valid.

Hydrating

I know not everyone enjoys water, or remembers to drink, or wants to pause and drink. Again, there is no right or wrong here, just a lot of care and compassion from me if this is a hard one for you. Here are some ideas that may help you to stay hydrated throughout the day.

- Bring a beverage (or two!) into each session or meeting. By the time the session or meeting is over, drink the contents of the cup. Drinking is a great stim to engage in while in session.
- Carry a water bottle around with you throughout the day (and drink from it!!).
- Make the beverage more interesting, novel, or delightful: for example, make it bubbly water, add fruit or other flavor to your water, pour in an electrolyte pack (so long as this is not contraindicated with any health issues you may have), or drink herbal tea. All of these contribute to hydration. I'm not here to judge, but just an fyi that caffeinated beverages actually have the effect of dehydrating us, so relying on them alone for hydration might not work so well.
- Set a timer or use an app that reminds you to pause and hydrate.

Toileting

I want to acknowledge, again, that this can have its own complexities for people. Whether it's interoception related, gender related due to a lack of available inclusive bathrooms, public toilet or germ related, or your body doesn't need to eliminate very often, I share all this with sensitivity and gentleness. Sometimes even just acknowledging that this can be hard can be so validating that it opens up a plethora of possibilities, a release of emotion, or a lowering of obstacles.

In Chapter 9, on rituals, I share more about this for myself. For now:

- Are there set times of the day when it is easy enough for you to get to the bathroom? (e.g., between clients, between every several clients)
- Would it help to set a timer or use an app to remind you to go?
- Can you have set times in the day or pair it with another activity where it becomes part of your routine to go to the bathroom? (e.g., after I eat, I go to the bathroom).
- If you are trans, nonbinary, or gender expansive and your workplace doesn't have gender-neutral or all-gender bathrooms, and this is a source of stress or obstacle for you (I feel such solidarity with you, and I'm so sorry this is something that even needs to be written about):
  - Have you noticed any trends when the bathroom seems to be least occupied?
  - Is there a coworker who could go to the bathroom with you?
  - Is there any advocacy being done in your workplace to create gender-inclusive bathrooms?
  - Are there any nearby places or businesses that do have gender-inclusive bathrooms that you could more comfortably use?

If going to the bathroom hasn't ever made you fear for your safety because of your gender identity, please consider using your privilege to advocate for all gender, accessible bathrooms in your workplace.

Honoring Your Energy Level

Some people have the autonomy to structure their schedule in such a way that honors their natural rhythms, including when their energy level is highest and when it is the lowest. I've known therapists who are very intentional about what time of day they schedule their clients who are more challenging to them so that the appointment lines up with when they are the most energized. Or they set the times of day they do and don't work based on their energy rhythms.

- What supports your natural rhythms throughout the day?
  - Would you like the option to have a midday rest?
  - Would you like to start work later in the day and end later, or to start earlier and end earlier?
  - Are these options for you? Is this possible for you?
- What supports you to be present and engaged when you are exhausted but still have to work? (I know caffeine isn't an option for everyone).
  - Is there other sensory input that helps you?
  - Is it okay to just be tired?
  - Would a movement break before the session help?
  - Could you adjust how you sit, like bounce on an exercise ball instead of sit in a chair, or sit on the floor instead of a cozy chair or couch?
- How do you replenish yourself throughout the day?
  - When, how often, and how many breaks do you take throughout your day?
  - Is this working for you, and would you like more or less?
  - What is most nourishing for you on your breaks?

As with all of this, there is no right or wrong answer or way to be. Sometimes we avoid exploring this because it feels as if we will gain insight that we can't actually do anything about. Sometimes this is so real, and it is most likely due to systemic oppression and capitalism. Acknowledging we have needs, noticing what they are, and then attempting to get those needs met is brave work!

We covered so much in this chapter! And now we've reached the end of it. I encourage you to notice what you may need or want in this moment, and if possible, to please give it to yourself. Your needs are so beautifully valid, and I honor them. When you are ready to continue, I'll meet you in Chapter 8: Global Permission: Questions to Dismantle Normativity in the Counseling Office.

Recap: Supporting Ourselves With Executive Function and Support Needs

- There are certain aspects to our work as therapists that require a great deal of executive function. Some of us may need support and accommodations with completing these tasks. I encourage you to find what works best and is accessible for you.
- The areas we explored are:
  - Scheduling
  - Documentation
  - Administrative tasks, including:
    - Responding to email
    - Bookkeeping and taxes
    - Managing our physiological needs throughout the workday including eating, hydrating, toileting, honoring our energy levels
  - While we embody the role of therapist, we are also very much human with our own sets of needs, limitations, challenges, and strengths.

CHAPTER 8
Global Permission: Questions to Dismantle Normativity in the Counseling Office

As we've already discussed, the U.S. dominant culture is rooted in an oppressive tapestry that is woven into and bleeds into everything it touches, starting with ideology and societal narratives all the way down to how we think about, perceive, and relate to ourselves. Given that western psychology and the training that most of us received are embedded in this oppressive tapestry, in this chapter we are going to get curious about office-related aspects of our day-to-day work. It is very likely that ableist ideas and policies may be unknowingly present. We will explore how we can keep making adjustments to better serve our clients and support ourselves. We will have abundant opportunities to ask "Why?" a favorite question of so many Autistic/KCS/VAST people. Unlike the other chapters that are divided into three sections: an overview, working with clients, and working with ourselves, this chapter is structured a bit differently. It's all woven together into my response to each inquiry, commonly asked question, or important consideration for us to ponder.

This chapter is about examining the normativity that perpetuates oppression and challenging it. This inquiry calls us to be curious, to notice our biases, to notice our internal rules that we began exploring in Chapter 6 on dismantling ableism, and to notice what may have previously gone unnoticed. This is not about shaming and judging ourselves. I'll remind us of this as we go through this chapter. These may be things you have already thought about, are already exploring, or haven't yet occurred to you. As I said in Chapter 7, *when we know better, we can do better.* Before we continue, I'd like to address ideas for supporting yourself throughout this chapter.

- Because we are going to be exploring practices and policies that are rooted in the oppressive tapestry, entering your sphere and/or custom shirt may support you to feel your differentiation and wholeness. This will also support your differentiation from me. My fire and passion are very present in this chapter! My care for you hasn't changed, but you may sense that my gentleness is less at the foreground. This is an honoring of my wholeness, which includes being bold, fiery, and fierce (i.e., being unmasked). That said, I still very much want you to be gentle with yourself!
- If you notice yourself getting distracted, contracted, antsy, exhausted, or another indicator of possible sympathetic arousal, I encourage you to pendulate your attention back to yourself, acknowledge what's present, and tend to it as you are able.
- The four I's are embedded in this content. In addition to pendulating to yourself, I encourage you to pendulate out as well, to notice the presence of ideology, institutions, and the interpersonal. While this content is personal in terms of how we do our work, this content stems from systemic factors. This is so much bigger than you or me alone.
- Please honor your pacing and engage with the following questions and prompts in the ways that are most accessible to you (e.g., thinking, writing, making art, moving, resting, connecting with others).
- Sensory delights are encouraged!

WHY IS A THERAPEUTIC HOUR ONLY 50 MINUTES?

This never made any sense to me. An hour, as dictated by the construct of linear time, is 60 minutes. In capitalist, colonized, ableist culture, there are all sorts of external boundaries and expectations that get placed on our work. None of these boundaries or expectations account for Autistic and KCS/VAST nervous systems, processing speeds, transition styles, and so on. This brings up a lot to be curious about.

- Given variations in processing speed and nervous system sensitivity, how realistic is it for clients to settle, process, and integrate in 50 minutes, knowing that when the clock strikes minute 50, they will be asked to leave?
- For those who are external processors, how much time do they really need to be heard, to take up enough space, to get out what they need to get out, and to leave time to hear reflections if they desire them?
- What if someone is in the midst of a beautiful, sacred, intense process and the end of the so-called "therapy hour" is approaching?
  - I get really fiery about this, and recognize the complexities of working within a flawed mental health system. How do you navigate when a client isn't done with their process, but the time scheduled for the session is up?
  - Is it fair to expect clients to pay extra if the spiral-like process of human emotion and experience requires an extra 5, 10, 15 minutes or more than we planned to spend together?

This overarching question and all the associated ones with it, are some of the many inquiries that I wrestle with and lose sleep over. Some additional points of inquiry:

- How long are your sessions? Is it because:
  - the agency or company you work for dictates that?
  - of insurance company reimbursement?
  - that is what you were taught in school?
  - you intentionally chose it?
- How does your nervous system genuinely feel about the current length of time of your sessions?
  - Are you constantly anxious that it's not enough time and that you will be forced to rush at the end and scramble to find containment with the client?
  - Is the length of your sessions just right? Just right could mean just right for you based on how your attention works. Beyond that amount of time you might get really antsy, distracted, or bored. Or you'd have to tap into your reserves, reserves that can quickly get depleted when this happens throughout the day.

If you have the autonomy to do so, and I recognize that there are many barriers to this autonomy:

- What adjustments would be needed in order to schedule your sessions for the amount of time that actually honors who you are, who your client is, and the process they are in? I'll be more specific.
  - For clients who typically need more than your standard allotted time, can you intentionally schedule longer sessions with them?
  - If so, how would that impact your fee or reimbursement?
  - Is there a better time of day for these sessions to be scheduled to honor your energy level and the amount of time you need between sessions?

- Can your own attention sustain consistently longer sessions?
- If you do not have the autonomy to extend the time of your sessions, how might you approach this with clients?

Here's what comes to mind about how I might approach this. "I notice that we often run out of time at the end. I wish there was an option to extend our time, but unfortunately, there isn't. It's important to me that you feel resourced enough to leave the session, knowing that we might not actually be done, even though we have to be 'done' for now. I wonder how we might be able to be creative about this?"

I notice a desire to offer some creative, concrete ideas that you could collaboratively explore. At the same time, I am present to the harmful impacts of colonization and capitalism that prioritize profits and social constructs over well-being and wholeness. It feels challenging to be creative in the midst of anger and justice sensitivity. The reality is that we are working within a harmful system. Many Autistic and KCS/VAST nervous systems orient to a pace that is slower than the dominant culture, but the mental health industry was not created with this in mind. I'm going to honor my impulse to take some deep breaths, get up, and move before continuing.

I gave myself permission to let my body move as it desired. I found myself doing "fast feet" (a throwback to my track days in high school), stomping, pushing up against the wall, and making fiery sounds and growls. The proprioceptive input and sounding helped the Sacred rage (I shared this term from Dr. Jennifer Mullan earlier) to take up space and flow. It helped me to notice how often I'm steeped in ethical dilemmas because I work within a destructive system, but how easy it is to forget that it's the system's fault, not mine. In giving myself permission to meet my rage, it put me in touch with the next layer of my experience: grief. I feel the tears flow down my face. I feel how often I forget that the system is harming people; it's not actually that "I am too sensitive", that "I care too much," or that no matter how hard I may try, "I'm just not enough." How interesting, albeit maybe not surprising, that my internalized ableism showed up. And as I allow that to be here and flow, I'm met with tenderness and a lot of self-compassion.

Maybe you don't feel particularly impacted by issues of not enough time and the intersections of capitalism and colonization, or this isn't relevant to you, in which case, there's no judgment: you get to be you. Maybe you do feel particularly impacted by this, and my sharing of my internal process leaves you feeling validated, seen, heard, and understood. As I've said so many times already, there's no right or wrong way to do this or relate to this.

Now that my system is more at ease again, I'll follow through with my desire to offer some concrete ideas.

For a client who seems to need more time than the amount allotted, but more time isn't an option, perhaps they could be your last client before a longer break or at the end of your day, when it would reduce both of your stress levels if the session went longer. Or perhaps you co-create an agreement that with 5 minutes left in the session, wherever the process is, you agree to interrupt and acknowledge that it's incomplete and time to pause. In that incompleteness, you might make a note of where things got left off so that you can start there next time and engage in a containment visualization or ritual. For example, they can put what they are exploring or processing in a container of their own creation and set it somewhere in the Universe. Or they could actually write something down and put it in a real box that gets puts away and then taken out next session. Then, finish with some resourcing or grounding, whether it be movement, imagery, sound, self-soothing touch, a shared hug (with explicit consent), art, or other.

It is important to name the incompleteness to the client and remind them that they are important. These are just some of my ideas; I encourage you and your client to come up with your own as well. These ideas don't mitigate the flawed system, but they at least help us to tend to the human before us.

As we finish this inquiry, I encourage you to be gentle and sensitive to whatever is, or isn't, arising within you. I'll remind us of what I shared earlier: *this is about curiosity, not shaming and judging ourselves.* Sometimes my passion can be intense. Please take the time you need to be with this, using whatever means or supports to process this that best serve you. If you notice shame arising within you, this could be a good opportunity to pendulate out and connect with the four I's. There may be rage and grief that desire tending. Take as much or as little time as you need, and then I'll meet you in the next topic.

WHY DO WE EXPECT CLIENTS TO USE SPOKEN LANGUAGE WHEN WE DO THERAPY?

Neuronormativity expects and assumes everyone to use spoken words from their mouths to communicate. Intersecting with white supremacy, not only are words expected to be used and spoken, but a particular tone, voice inflection, pacing of words, eye contact, and just the right amount of words are expected too. So-called reciprocal communication is also expected, meaning there is a limit to how much a person can say before they are expected to stop speaking so that another person can speak. This time limit is inferred and is not ever made explicit in NT spaces.

I've often heard parents say to young children in distress, "Use your words." While the parent is likely well intentioned, this expectation is very much rooted in ableism and dismisses how valid non-spoken communication is.

Whether a client has access to a plethora of spoken words, uses spelling to speak, uses an augmentative communication device such as apps on a tablet, or uses pictures to communicate, to be Autistic and/or KCS/VAST means to be inconsistent and to have varying capacity moment to moment, day to day. That includes access to words. I'll say more...

I'm reminded of a deeply inspiring post I read by Tiffany Hammond, who I've mentioned throughout this book. She shared about her family's regularly scheduled nonspeaking days. As a neurodiverse family coexisting in a ND-affirming household, they have dedicated nonspeaking days as an entire family. Even though her son Aidan is the only nonspeaker of the family, they regularly center nonspeaking communication as a way to normalize his communication style and to coexist in solidarity. On their nonspeaking days, they live their lives as they usually would, engaging with the community as they need to or desire to, each family member using their own augmentative and alternative communication (AAC) device.

I was profoundly inspired by this and touched, and I also noticed some grief arise in me. Even though I'm someone with access to spoken language, I hadn't yet fully admitted to myself that I crave and need nonspeaking days. I had found ways to give this to myself over the years, but not with an overt awareness of what I was doing. On top of that, I have yet to access the courage to leave my home on those days and interact with other humans. While I may text friends or loved ones from within my home, I have not yet allowed myself to be nonspeaking in public interactions. I feel big discomfort at noticing the privilege I hold that I get to choose how and when I communicate. And I am acutely aware that for so many within the Autistic community, this will never be a choice.

I think this is a great time for some self-reflection and inquiry. Please engage in your own way and as you choose to.

Circling back to our work with clients:

- ♦ What expectations or assumptions do you hold about how your clients communicate or engage with you in session?

- Do you readily offer the option to be nonspeaking in session, whether that means use of the chat in virtual work or writing, texting, art, or movement for in-person sessions?
- Do you acknowledge that situational mutism is real and valid, and sometimes, particularly in the midst of distress or sympathetic arousal, spoken language may become inaccessible?

If the foundation of our work is to support parasympathetic states for our clients, isn't it important that we keep asking what form or style of communication will best support this client to access that sense of rest and digest? This involves both asking ourselves and staying engaged with this inquiry and also explicitly checking in with the client.

May we continue to invest in creating a safe enough space that our clients feel comfortable enough to tell us how they will be communicating with us in any particular moment throughout the session. We'll shift our attention now from processing these inquiries to some examples of how all this might play out in session. Each of these examples involves speaking clients who have intermittent or variable access to spoken language.

Example 1

A client who is underresourced (e.g., tired, overwhelmed, running on empty) needs ample permission to not effort any more than absolutely necessary. They may tell us, "I'm going to use the chat today." To which I would respond, "Great, thank you so much for telling me! And I love that you told me, not asked me. Would you prefer me to speak or to use the chat too? And do you notice whether you would prefer cameras on or off? We can make adjustments at any point if you notice your desire or need changes."

Example 2

A client has verbal dyspraxia, which can make it difficult for them to formulate thoughts, articulate those thoughts clearly and accurately, and then speak them. They typically feel a lot of pressure in social settings to keep up with conversations and to be quick with their responses, which can often lead to more difficulty with self-expression. As a way to practice alternate forms of communication that are a better fit with who they actually are, we add in nonspeaking communication to our sessions. The client takes the lead on using their preferred communication style and indicates to me whether they prefer me to speak or type my responses. For virtual work, this means using the chat. For in-person work, it could mean texting one another, writing notes back and forth, using an AAC device, or other creative forms of communication.

Example 3

A client has something vulnerable they really want to share, but it is too intense for their nervous system to speak it out loud. They are ready to be brave and to allow me to more deeply know them. Perhaps they tell me it's too scary to say out loud, so I offer other options, like the chat, texting, or writing me a note. Or they may initiate using an alternate form of communication, in response to which I would celebrate and appreciate them for telling me what they need and want! After the vulnerable thing is shared and I respond in their preferred form of communication, we can check back in about what form or style of communication they would like to continue with.

For people who are accustomed to and reliant on spoken communication, it may take some inner work and dismantling of ableism to overcome possible internal barriers to inviting nonspoken communication into your sessions. If you resonate with this, it is essential that you engage in this internal work.

Each of these subsections offers a lot to consider. Please keep checking in with yourself, noticing what you are needing and how you are doing. Feel free to resource, connect back in with your sphere/shirt, or zoom out to awareness of the collective. When you are ready, I'll meet you in the next topic. I encourage you to not bypass what is present for you if possible.

WHY DO WE EXPECT CLIENTS TO FACE US WHEN THEY ARE ENGAGING WITH US?

One of the things I appreciated about learning somatic psychology in graduate school is that part of our foundational counseling skills related to facing, pacing, and spacing. Dr. Christine Caldwell (she/her), a white counselor educator, author, and the founder of the somatic counseling psychology program at Naropa University, is credited with these terms. While they were not created specifically from a ND-affirming lens, they absolutely belong in a ND-affirming, anti-oppressive framework.

- Facing refers to where you and the client are looking or what direction your bodies are in relation to each other in any given moment in the session.
- Pacing refers to the speed of the session.
- Spacing refers to the distance between the client and therapist. In other words, how close or how far are we from one another.

Dr. Carla Sherrell taught me examination and practice with these three through cultural and anti-oppressive perspectives across the wide range of identities for client and counselor inside, and outside, the therapeutic relationship. I've woven that in with my anti-ableist lens. United States dominant culture dictates rules for each of these three qualities. Rooted in oppressive social constructs, we are taught that there absolutely is a so-called right facing, pacing, and spacing. Ugh. It is essential that we recognize how each culture has its own norms for these three attributes, and that the individual nervous system of our client, woven with their culture and lineage, will directly influence these.

I'll offer a few examples of how this might play out in session, and then we'll turn our attention inward for some self-reflection.

Example 1

A client has something vulnerable they want to share, and it feels too brave to face me when they tell me. It would cause too much activation in their nervous system and get in the way of them expressing themself. When they tell me this, I would respond with something like, "Yes! I'm so glad you are advocating for what you need and want. Absolutely, I completely support that. Would it help if I turned this way?" And then I would physically demonstrate how I might shift my position to have my head and body facing away from them. This is simultaneously a moment where the client gets to practice self-advocacy and consent.

Example 2

A client has a much faster natural pace than me. They have often been scolded to slow down and be different from who they are. My processing style means that I can only keep up with that pace and stay present, grounded, and regulated for so long. I will engage with the client around this. It is likely that no one else has approached this topic with them from an ND-affirming, anti-oppressive lens. I might say, "I value your communication style and pace so much. And I notice that sometimes it can be hard for me to keep up because my processing speed is slower than yours. Would it be okay with you if every so often I initiate a pause and reflect back what I am hearing to make sure that I am getting it all and really understanding? I so want you to feel understood by me and feel much permission to be yourself!" And then the client is invited to offer their consent or not. If the impact of my request lands as harmful and not affirming for the client, then this would lead to another inquiry. It could be that the client needs a therapist who is a faster processor than me and has a natural rhythm closer to theirs. I am not going to be the right fit for every client, and this is totally okay.

Example 3

A client has historically been told, both explicitly and implicitly, that they are "too much," and that they need to shrink and take up less space. This is all too common for racialized folx and people assigned female at birth. In session, I notice an impulse to give them so much room! Not too much room that it leaves them feeling that I am withdrawn, checked out, or uninterested, but plenty of space that communicates to them, "Yes! Please! Take up space! This is not about me, but about *you*." This could be physical and/or energetic space. I will wait for what feels like the right moment to be explicit about this, and then I will check in with them about how the space feels for them. "Is it too much, too little, or just right?"

Let's take a moment to turn inward and engage in some curiosity and inquiry.

- What rules, if any, do you notice that you hold about what direction you and your clients ought to be facing in relation to one another?
  - Do you unknowingly hold an expectation that you both need to be facing each other at all times?
  - Does this inadvertently tie in to expectations about eye contact?
- Do you find yourself judging clients, consciously or unconsciously, for the pace at which they go?
  - Do you perceive it as too fast or too slow?
- What pace supports you to be the most present, engaged, and focused?

A few more things to reflect on:

- Have you noticed that you have a sense of the right distance between you and your clients?

- Have you ever explored this with your clients to see if what feels right for you also feels right for them?
- Do you ever notice moments when you feel an impulse to be farther away or to move closer?
  - How have you navigated those moments, and if you haven't previously been explicit with clients in those moments, what might you like to try next time you notice this?

One more piece before we prepare to wrap up this subsection. I am reminded of the value of clients having permission to have their camera off when the sessions are virtual. Sometimes, the visual input is too much for them or it's too vulnerable. At the same time, while that might be deeply supportive for them, possibly that makes it harder for us. Depending on how we embody our neurotype(s), the lack of visual input may mean that we have a harder time staying engaged and focused or that we may miss information when we have to rely on auditory or written input alone. This is okay, and we can be in relationship with clients around this if that would be helpful. Here's how I might approach this: "I really want you to have the autonomy to have your screen off and to take care of yourself in that way. I also know that without getting to see you and your body language, I may miss something. If I miss something, is that okay with you? If you feel like I'm misunderstanding, would you be willing to correct me, knowing that I deeply want to understand?"

- Please take the time to consider your biases and internalized rules about clients being on or off camera as it relates to virtual work. Most likely, these are rooted in ableism, and some dismantling work is needed.

Take as much or as little time as you need here. You may notice a desire to be in contemplation, to connect with a peer, colleague, or support person, to move your body, or to lean into the support of nature or the ancestors. This content is collective; it is not as small as me or you alone. Please take whatever time you need here before moving on to the next section.

WHAT ARE OUR STANDARDS FOR WHAT IT MEANS TO BE ENGAGED?

We just alluded to this at the end of the last subsection, so I'll be brief. Our Autistic/KCS/VAST clients tend to be the most engaged when, by NT standards, they seem the least engaged. Ableism teaches that to be focused and engaged, we are still, quiet, and making eye contact. Gross. For our clients, movement of some form is most likely necessary in order for them to be engaged. When I used to run social communities for Autistic teens, I had some of the most incredible learning opportunities around this. The person who by NT standards seemed the most distracted and not paying attention knew exactly what was going on. They just needed more stimulation and so they were finding ways to get this need met while I or others were speaking.

We all process differently. For someone who doesn't know anything about me or my neurotypes, they could easily misinterpret my processing pauses, looking up and off to the right or left when I'm thinking, constantly spinning in my chair, or looking away when speaking. All of these *support me* to be present and engaged.

Tying in pacing from the last subsection, some clients will thrive on long, spacious pauses throughout the session. Some therapists can find this anxiety provoking and are not sure how to handle this. In the midst of their own discomfort, they may fill the space with their voice or internally judge the client as being disengaged.

This is another one of the many reasons that I love that explicit communication is the essence of Autistic/KCS/VAST-affirming communication. How I navigate this is that I have a conversation with clients about this early on in our work together and then return to it as needed. For example: "We all process at different paces. I want to leave ample space for processing pauses for you. I also know that sometimes pauses can feel awkward for some people. If I'm not sure if it's a processing pause or a desire for me to respond, as in 'Nyck, where are you, I'm waiting for you to say something,' would it be okay if I ask?" And then over the course of our work together, if I'm uncertain about the pause, after some time has passed, I will say something like, "Processing pause, or are you wanting a response from me?" I love that I don't have to have it all figured out, but I can ask and the client can tell me what is happening!

Repetitive, compassionate Nyck wants to remind you, *the intention here is curiosity, not shaming and judging ourselves.* If shame or self-criticism is arising, please notice what systemic pieces might be showing up and how they live in you but do not originate from you. Please honor your process. Journaling, connecting with others, or feeling into what is bigger than you might all be helpful. I truly believe we are all doing our best, and this is a learning process. When you feel ready to join me, I'll meet you in the next inquiry.

WHAT IS OUR CANCELLATION POLICY AND IS IT ND-AFFIRMING?

Most likely, no matter what setting we are working in, we have a cancellation policy that we uphold. It may have been created by us for our private practice, or it may be an agency, group practice or institutional policy that we did not have a role in creating. This is a common topic brought up in ND-affirming spaces. Knowing that Autistic/KCS/VAST people may be navigating executive function challenges, inherent inconsistency, or other co-occurring physical health issues such as chronic pain or chronic illness, cancellation policies can be complex.

How do we honor the strengths and challenges of our clients, honor our own boundaries, and be anti-oppressive in our cancellation policy? Such an important and valid question, one that we are all finding our own answers to. *What matters most is that we are holding inquiry around this.*

As someone in private practice, I have the autonomy to address my policy on a client-by-client basis. My general policy is that if clients cancel within less than 24 hours, they are charged the full fee for their session, unless they are sick or they have an emergency. The night before every session, I send out a reminder, including the link, for our session the next day. Some clients prefer to be texted; others prefer to be emailed. Now I'll share the nuances of how I implement my policy.

- For clients who struggle to remember our session and would like this, I offer to send a reminder about an hour before the session. That has been very successful at supporting them to avoid missing sessions.
- For clients who have chronic health issues that are unpredictable and debilitating, we co-create our own policy. Here are some examples of what that might look like in my practice:
  - Charging my full fee (not offering an equity-pricing option), but not having a cancellation policy. As part of our reparative therapeutic relationship and my efforts to be anti-ableist, they may cancel last minute and will not be charged for the session. In support of my own needs and the unpredictability of whether we will meet or not, when we do meet, I charge my full rate. I also request a text to confirm or cancel (since I don't always check email before sessions), and I make sure to check my phone before the session.
  - Offering a sliding scale rate or equity pricing due to financial need, having a cancellation policy (meaning that I do charge for cancellations with less than 24-hour notice), but a clear agreement that their missed sessions are not a reflection of their investment in our relationship or any sign of disrespect. For clients who have a history of missing appointments and being shamed for it or having it

be misconstrued as a sign of disrespect, offering this explicit validation is so important.

It is actually rare for my practice to have clients cancel with less than 24-hour notice and it not be due to illness or emergency. In that case, generally, clients are very understanding and expect to be charged. I still feel sensitive to this and try to be as relational as possible. There is a great deal of mutual respect. While it is the policy, it is still uncomfortable for me to implement.

Here are some questions to consider or contemplate.

- Do you feel in alignment with your cancellation policy or the policy of your workplace?
- When you contemplate that, who or what does the policy serve: you, the client, an institution or agency, health insurance companies, or capitalism?
- Is it possible to individualize it for clients?
  - What changes may you want to make, or who would you need to talk to about updating the policy to be more ND-affirming and anti-oppressive?

The financial privilege, or lack thereof, of the therapist definitely has a role here. Whether due to the impacts of racism, chronic illness, or other reasons, some therapists can't afford to not get paid when they are expecting to work and a client doesn't show up. It can be complex.

Whatever the policy, it is essential that it is transparent and the client agrees to it at the beginning of your therapeutic relationship.

This is the end of this subsection. Please tend to yourself as you need or want to. We're about halfway through the big questions in this chapter.

✳ ✳ ✳ ✳

WHAT DO WE NEED TO EXPLORE RELATING TO MONEY AND ACCESS TO OUR SERVICES?

I think about this one *a lot*. Knowing full well the harm of colonization, capitalism, white supremacy, classism, ableism, and so on, this weighs on me. Mental health care and support ought to be freely and easily accessible to all people, no matter their income. This is not the reality in the United States in the present moment. People with financial privilege have much greater access, and those with less or without have significantly reduced or no access. *This is not okay.* This is the big picture of this question.

This big picture is why some therapists choose to work in agencies, nonprofits, or be Medicaid providers. Others may be credentialed with a variety of insurance panels, work with companies that act as intermediaries between counselors and insurance companies, or offer equity pricing. And some counselors are not even thinking about this.

The amount we charge per session limits who can access our services. This is reality. It is incredibly challenging to work in a field that is an inherently broken system, and mental health care in the United States is a broken system. For those of us in private practice, it is then up to us to create our own policies and determine what is most aligned with our values and our needs. How do we reconcile this, especially for those of us who are navigating very real limitations and capacity concerns due to our own neurodivergence and other marginalized identities? Our services provide tremendous value for our clients, but we exist in a system that does not value equitable access, nor supports its disabled or otherwise oppressed communities.

As a therapist who only works with ND clients, I charge my full rate to those with financial privilege and access. For racialized clients, I offer equity pricing in acknowledgment of the very real impacts of systemic oppression and as reparations. I am fully aware that colonization and white supremacy have caused rampant intergenerational trauma. It is backwards for racialized folx, especially Black and Indigenous clients, to then have to pay a white therapist to support their healing and return-to-wholeness journey when white people enacted the harm in the first place, and when white therapists continue to benefit from white supremacy. This is what it means to consider the impacts of the four I's.

At present, I do not have set equity rates publicly posted; I co-create the rate with the client based on the realities of their financial situation. For my counselor education trainings that I host through my organization, I offer tiered pricing in support of equity, and each person chooses their tier based on what is most accessible for them. They are inherently more intimate in nature due to smaller group size, which means that the pricing is higher. I also intentionally offer continuing education trainings through companies that are able to set prices much lower due to the large audience nature of the events.

I am also aware that I have made the choice to be out of network with all insurance companies. Again, I feel conflicted about the ways this impacts access to my services, and I also know that I have very real executive function challenges and much lower capacity than NT therapists. This choice is in alignment with my efforts to reduce burnout and increase my autonomy in how I practice, but my justice sensitivity knows that I am working within a destructive system and is plagued by this.

I'm going to shift the focus now to self-reflection.

- What are your financial policies and arrangements?
- How have you determined your rates?
  - Did you choose them, are they set by the agency or organization you work for, or are they set by insurance companies or grant funding?
  - How do your financial policies account for the

impacts of racism, chronic illness, disability, homophobia, transphobia, and so on?
- How do you navigate all of this while still making sure you earn enough to make a living?

A lot to consider and digest, I know! Money is a complex topic for many, largely due to capitalism, racism, and classism. Many of us are taught that we are supposed to be secretive and quiet when it comes to money. A great way to interrupt possible shame cycles relating to money is to connect with a trusted, safe enough other person, and explore being vulnerable with them. So much of dismantling oppressive systems is about bringing out into the open what we were taught to keep quiet and not question. And all of this gets to happen at your own pace.

That's the end of this subsection. I'm going to transition to the next topic now.

WHAT IS OUR INTAKE PAPERWORK LIKE FOR NEW CLIENTS?

Ugh, paperwork, haha. In all seriousness, though, this is an important topic that deserves some attention. There are so many barriers to accessing support, and intake and initial paperwork can be a very real obstacle that prevents people from ever accessing services in the first place. Whether due to executive function challenges, the paperwork being so in depth that it triggers trauma, or the paperwork is just outright not inclusive, the issue of paperwork needs to be addressed.

This may be different depending on your credentials and the state you practice in, but for me as an LPC licensed in the state of Colorado, I am required to have clients complete a disclosure statement that includes details about my practice, how to file a complaint, and consent to services, along with basic demographic information.

No matter what our credentials may be, when a person makes the choice to meet with us for the first time, we are a stranger. It doesn't matter that we went to school for this. We are a stranger to them. Why on earth would we expect someone who has never met us or has no relationship with us to open up and share the most intimate, likely traumatic details of their entire lives, especially before ever meeting us? This doesn't make any sense to me. Even though I may seem intense, this is genuinely about holding curiosity about our policies and procedures.

A therapeutic relationship, like any other relationship between two humans, takes time to grow and to build trust. For us to ask clients for an in-depth history before they even come to their first session or even to their second just does not sit well with me. I don't care that I know I'm trustworthy; the only way my clients will develop trust with me is through time and gathering evidence through experience that shows them that I am trustworthy. It is likely unwise and downright harmful for their nervous system to be expected to share anything with us before their internal autonomy and consent indicate to them that they are ready to share. For some, this may happen quickly; for others, it may take much more time. I feel my passionate fire here!

Whatever forms you or your place of employment uses, it's really important that you take a close look at them and be curious, honest, and critical. I'm now going to shift into questions for you to reflect on this now.

- What do we absolutely need to know about a person before their first session, and what can we ask them when we are with them?
  - What needs to be known at the beginning, and what can be learned over time in an organic way?
- Are the intake forms inclusive?
  - When they ask for name and basic demographic information, do they ask for pronouns? Not preferred pronouns, just pronouns.

- If the form requires a legal name for insurance purposes, does it also ask for a preferred name that the client chooses to be called?

In addition to nicknames, some trans, nonbinary or gender-expansive folx go by a name they haven't legally updated.

◆ Another thing to be curious about: Do you need to ask a person's sex on the form? Asking someone's sex is the same as asking, "What genitalia do you have?" Sometimes, statistics for funding purposes or insurance companies require this information.

It is a good idea to ask about gender identity so that you can be affirming of who they are (and aren't).

It is also a good idea to ask about racial or cultural identity, recognizing that racism is prevalent and that a client's racial and cultural identity directly impacts how they experience being human.

Given the longstanding harm that the mental health field has caused to racialized and LGBTQIA2S+ communities, clients may not wish to disclose this information at first. Again, their autonomy and what supports the development of trust with us are what matter most.

◆ Are the forms ND-affirming?
- When you are getting to know a new client, are you asking about sensory sensitivities, accessibility, or accommodations that they might need?
- Some people may choose to ask directly about neurodivergence, as in, "are you neurodivergent? (e.g., Autistic, KCS/VAST, bipolar, traumatic brain injury, learning disabilities, posttraumatic stress)" or "has anyone ever suggested you might be neurodivergent?" Making it easy for clients to provide this information, or to get them curious if they've never been asked, can be really helpful.

One more thought. Some forms ask outright about suicidal ideation. This is especially common in community mental health and other similar settings. Personally, I don't think this is something to ask on a form without talking directly to the person about it first or being very explicit about intentionality. Because of mandatory reporting, many people identify therapists as being unsafe people to disclose their suicidal ideation to, in fear of being punished or criminalized for their honesty. This is deeply problematic and counterintuitive. If clients or prospective clients think that asking for help means that they will be hospitalized against their will and likely endure more trauma from that process, they will not ask for support. Yet when someone is struggling and feeling hopeless, they absolutely deserve support.

We live in a dominant culture that deeply stigmatizes suicide and shames people for thinking and/or talking about it. Even so, current rates of people dying by suicide are very high. Stigma can make it even more difficult for prospective clients to disclose, even if they really want support. If we are going to talk about suicide, we have to be skillful, gentle, and sensitive and normalize that sometimes being human is just too much. We all need extra support sometimes, especially if we have any marginalized identities. Remember, the systems are broken, not the individuals.

We can make it easier for prospective clients to access support by stating that being human is hard, that we live in a culture that makes it brave to admit when we are thinking about dying, that there is no shame in having suicidal thoughts, and that we are here to help if they need it. This can be in writing if an intake form is required to ask, or it can be spoken if the question is asked in session. If we are going to help people choose to live when they want to die, we need to normalize these thoughts, decriminalize them, and make them easy to talk about.

I encourage you to review the intake forms that you use. *Imagine you are a client interested in seeking counseling support...*

- How would it feel for you to complete these forms?
  - Would it make it easier or harder for you to access support?
- If you notice that the forms create barriers, could you change them, or who would you need to talk to about changing them?

As we reach the end of this topic, I invite you to pause, check in, and notice what's present for you. I can feel the intensity of all the systems of oppression present in these inquiries. This is a lot to think about, digest, and respond to. When you are ready to move on, I'll meet you in the next topic.

WHY IS OUR OFFICE SET UP THE WAY IT IS, AND WHOM DOES IT BENEFIT?

We might respond to this question differently depending on whether our work is virtual or in person, if we have our own office, or if we share a space with others.

For those who share an office with others and potentially frequently rotate spaces:

- What do you need to have with you to support your own focus, presence, attention, and sensory needs?
- Do you have a bag or container with fidgets and other objects that you enjoy?
- Are there ways to make the spaces you are in feel more cozy or homey?

For anyone who works in person (whether you have your own office or a shared office):

- When you look around the space, how do you feel?

- Does it evoke a sense of comfort, coziness, creativity, connection, or warmth?
♦ Do you like what you see?
♦ What are the seating options like?
  - Are the chairs big enough that clients of any size, including fat clients, can sit comfortably?
  - Do clients have options to sit, lie down, stand, or move?
  - Are the seating options set up in such a way that allows for playing with facing and spacing?
  - What is the texture and temperature of the floor and space like?
  - Do people have the option to take shoes off if they want to, but they are not required to?

There are many cultures and religions where it is customary to remove shoes before entering an indoor space as a form of cleanliness and respect. I'm thinking of Islam and many Asian American, Pacific Islander, and Southwest Asian and North African communities. For others outside of those cultures and religions, it may be a preference related to comfort and/or cleanliness.

At the same time, I'd like to address some reasons why clients may not want to take their shoes off. It could be related to trauma and a need to know that they can exit quickly. Dr. Carla Sherrell also teaches that it could be due to socioeconomic position concerns in which some clients with limited financial resources do not want to draw attention to their shoes and socks, attire that is often displayed to signal wealth and status. Some clients who have been financially underresourced intergenerationally may come to counseling with a history of embarrassing, traumatic experiences, over time having been teased and humiliated in childhood about whether they had socks, they had clean socks, socks and foot odor, shoe availability, and other considerations connected to socioeconomic classism. And for ND folx who find hygiene challenging, they may have been teased for having "stinky" feet and could feel self-conscious without their shoes on. For others, shoes may be a very necessary sensory support that helps them to feel safer or grounded, or they might not like the feeling of the floor on their feet.

- Is the space accessible?
  - Are there gender-neutral or all-gender bathrooms?
  - Are people with mobility issues able to access the space?
    - Are there ramps?
    - Is there an elevator?
    - Are there wheelchair-accessible bathrooms?
- If clients have sensory sensitivities with any of the textures, temperature, lighting, smells, sounds, or other visual elements, how can you accommodate them?
- Are there any adjustments you would like to make to make it more sensorially friendly for you and for your clients?
  - It might even be helpful to ask your clients how they feel in the space if you are working in person. Are there things they would change, and if so, what and why?

I recognize that for those who share an office, especially for those working in agencies or other institutions, you likely have less autonomy to change things yourself. If you notice changes that are needed, who might you need to advocate with about this?

For those who work virtually:

- When you look around your space, how do you feel?
  - Does it evoke a sense of comfort, coziness, creativity, connection, and warmth?
  - Do you like what you see, feel, hear, sense, and smell?
  - Are there any adjustments you would like to enact to make it more sensorially friendly?

For everyone:

- Take some time to look around the space from a ND-affirming, anti-oppression lens.
    - Are there objects in the space that are culturally appropriated?
        - What do you want to do with those objects to reduce harm?
        - How does the space accommodate you, who you are, and what you need?

Take as much or as little time here as you desire. Ponder away if you choose! You may even notice some creativity arise with these inquiries. No matter what is or isn't present, it's all okay. This is the end of this topic. When you are ready, I'll meet you in the next one. We're getting close to the end of this chapter.

INSURANCE COMPANIES ASIDE, WHAT AM I REALLY SAYING WHEN I CREATE TREATMENT PLANS AND GOALS?

In full disclosure, if it weren't for doing consultation with other therapists, I would not have thought about treatment plans and goals for a long time. These *scream* pathology paradigm. Sure, quantitative and qualitative measures can be helpful sometimes to assess if something we are doing is beneficial and worth the time and money investment, but treatment plans and goals were not created to be human affirming. They were created to reinforce a system that is oriented toward fixing broken humans and reinforcing white supremacy and all the other systems of oppression.

In ND-affirming, anti-oppressive care, we do not *treat*. There is no such thing as treating whole humans existing within broken systems. If we were going to treat anything, it would be the systems themselves!

If your brain works in such a way that you need a road map

of sorts to offer a framework to the work you are doing, to track what you are doing, to have some semblance that what you are doing is helpful in a field where there is rarely instant gratification, then great! I honor that you know that about yourself, and I support you working in a way that works well for you. I am in full support of you creating a road map with intentions, multiple possible offshoots, and a lack of agenda; I support co-creating possibilities with your clients and collaborating with them on their journey.

I know I get really passionate about this, and based on your training and background, you may be feeling pissed off at me right now, agitated, annoyed, or something else. It's okay to feel what you feel. I encourage you, I urge you, please don't stop at the feeling. Please let yourself look deeper, be inquisitive, and think critically about what I am saying. You don't have to like everything I write, and please consider it anyway. Do what you need to do to tend to your nervous system, to engage in sensory delight, and to take me seriously. We are not bad. We are doing the best we can, and when we know better, we do better.

It is the systems that are broken, not the individuals.

Treatment plans and planning are inherently ableist until and unless you actively dismantle them. Let's explore this a bit further. You can use these prompts with each individual client, or for now maybe pick one and explore the prompts with that person in mind. You might also prefer to reflect on these prompts in a more general way for now.

- ♦ What does your client desire for themselves or for their life?
- ♦ Is it reasonable for who they are and who they are not?
  - • Are their expectations rooted in neuronormativity

and systemic oppression, or are they a beautifully neurodivergent expression of who they are?
- Are there very real ways that they must adhere to NT expectations in order to survive?
  - How can we best support our clients, be real about the ways they sometimes *have to* conform to NT standards in order to exist, and do it as consciously as possible?
  - How can we be ND-affirming, even in the ways that their lives may require them to mask in order to have their needs met or to maintain relationships on which they rely?

Even in not ideal scenarios, in all the ways that we can, we give the autonomy back to our clients. We reconcile the paradoxes with them. We don't try to change them. We feel, grieve, rage, and celebrate *with* them.

Maybe instead of goals we can be thinking about hopes and intentions. Ever since Michelle Obama, the former First Lady and first Black First Lady in the United States, released her book *Becoming*, I've integrated that word into my vocabulary. I often think about who I am becoming and who my clients are becoming. Maybe an ND-affirming, anti-oppressive lens for goals is more a guiding star about who we're becoming or hope to become.

Here are some possibilities that come to mind. Perhaps becoming someone who:

- is gentler, kinder, more validating to ourselves;
- who actually does have needs, is allowed to have needs; and maybe even gets those needs met;
- embraces what their neurotype means for them, the beauty, the challenges, the strengths, and the disability;
- stays more regularly in connection with their autonomy versus constantly giving it away or having it taken away without their consent;

- falls in love with their humanity, knows that making mistakes is inevitable, and feels more confident to repair when they are ready.

No matter your neurotype, if you have to engage in the administrative tasks of things like treatment plans and goals, here's an experiment: read what you've come up with, but instead of your client's name, change it to your name:

- How do you feel when what is written or recorded is intended for you?
  - Does it affirm your humanity, your wholeness, your wisdom?

If it cuts you down in *any* way, if it leaves you feeling less human, less dignified, less proud of who you are, then it's *not* okay. We are just as human, just as fallible as our clients. If it wouldn't be good enough for us, then it's not good enough for them. Until you can feel your own dignity and humanity affirmed in what you write, *I implore you*, keep editing.

As we reach the end of this topic, we have another opportunity to check in with ourselves. If you notice any overwhelm showing up, a sense of "OMG, Nyck, you are giving me so much more work to do!", I hear you. That is a valid response. This does not have to happen all at once. And yes, becoming more aware of how oppressive systems are operating within our work is effortful. Hopefully, the added permission you may also be feeling to do it differently, to be more congruent with your values, to be more uniquely you can support the effort. Here is, another invitation to honor your pacing. When you are ready, I'll meet you in our final topic of this chapter.

AM I BEING THE THERAPIST I WOULD MOST WANT, NEED, OR DESIRE TO HAVE, OR AM I TRYING TO BE SOMEONE I WAS TOLD I AM SUPPOSED TO BE?

In full transparency, this question flowed out of me, and as I reread it, I'm left feeling inspired! My creativity never ceases to amaze me, hehe. Being human is a shitshow at times, I know it all too well. And I know that we are all doing the best we can with what we've got and the circumstances we are in. Trust me, I'm oozing compassion for you, for all of us. And I really want to encourage you to honestly, gently, lovingly consider the following question:

- Am I being the therapist I would most want, need, or desire to have, or am I trying to be someone I was told I am supposed to be?

To be clear, there is no set right answer, and if you say "no, I'm not," it *does not* mean you are a bad therapist or a bad person in any way. In true Nyck fashion, however, I want to encourage you to get curious. Feel free to engage in self-reflection, journal, draw or make art, move, dance, or whatever medium supports and honors your creative flow.

- What do you like, love, and/or appreciate about your unique style and way of showing up in your role as therapist?
  - Dare I even ask, what are you proud of?

If this invitation leaves you feeling uncomfortable, please be gentle with yourself. If this invitation leaves you wanting to celebrate yourself, then f*** yeah! Please do!

- When are the moments that you feel less than stellar as a therapist?
  - Do you have a sense of what precipitates or contributes to those moments?
  - Is it something you feel like you have any agency or autonomy over?
- What support might help you feel even more aligned with and in integrity with who you are and who you desire to be?

How would you respond to this question (it's similar to the one I already asked, but has some nuance):

- If I were looking for a therapist and I found someone just like me, I would schedule a consultation/session with them. ___ Yes ___ No ___ Maybe
- Second question: Why?

This isn't meant to be a trick question! Maybe you thrive with therapists who are different from you as a way to round out your perspective. Maybe there are elements about yourself that you adore and you know are your greatest assets. Maybe you desire someone with shared identities or prefer someone with different identities to offer a contrasting point of view. As with so many things I offer, there truly is no right or wrong answer to this.

My hope, however, is that you come away from this last subsection of the chapter with more self-compassion, more delight in who you are, and maybe even some celebration... that in the midst of the grand feat of being human, you are a beautiful, whole, vibrant, stellar being who is full of gifts, *and*, like me, you make plenty of mistakes, and then do your best to repair them as you are able.

If this subsection brings up grief over desiring to be someone who feels out of reach, unsafe, terrifying, or inaccessible in some way, I hope you can be as sweet and gentle with yourself as possible. If you can, I encourage you to bring this up with a trusted loved one, peer, practitioner, ancestors, nature, helping spirits, and/or your journal. May you take yourself and the obstacles seriously and shower yourself with as much compassion and tenderness as you can muster.

I am reminded of one of the many nuggets of wisdom that I gratefully received from my mentor, Dr. Carla Sherrell, who I have mentioned many times. When it comes to receiving nourishment such as positive and loving feedback, she would often say: "Take in what you can for now, and then save the rest in your back pocket for later."

With that, we have reached the end of another chapter. What a journey this has been together. Take all the time you need to honor where you are and to transition. Your pacing is just right! When you are ready, next is Chapter 9, Global Permission: Transitions, Ritual, and the Sacred. I'll meet you there!

Recap: Questions to Dismantle Normativity in the Counseling Office

- We explored a variety of considerations related to the ins and outs of counseling and ways we can keep disrupting normativity that reinforces oppression.

CHAPTER 9
Global Permission: Transitions, Ritual, and the Sacred

Throughout the course of this next chapter together, we are going to explore the themes of transitions, ritual, and the Sacred. These themes are an important albeit often less centered element of what it means to be Autistic and KCS/VAST. For some, these words may convey a spiritual or religious overtone, but I mean them as broadly and uniquely to the individual at hand as possible. While they may weave in the transpersonal, it is also about weaving in the simple with the complex, the mundane with the magnificent, the paradox of being human on Earth. To truly honor the wholeness of these neurotypes, we need to be real about the impact of transitions and honor individual transition styles. We support clients with both grounding and expansion. We provide predictability and containment or novelty and fluid structure. We encourage wonder, a gateway to seeking meaning, curiosity, creativity, and softening the suffering of the human experience.

As we continue, I invite us to be with the notion of wonder for a moment. I think Autistic/KCS/VAST folx have a propensity for maintaining wonder well beyond childhood. I think that's partly why there is a lot of stigma relating to so-called childishness among these neurotypes. Wonder sparks creativity, imagination, attention to detail, and reorienting to the so-called mundane. It allows us to see beauty and magic in the simple, maybe otherwise imperceptible moments of our existence. Wonder can be an active state or an orientation toward life. It evokes curiosity, an awareness that life is ever-changing, that we can't possibly ever know all there is to know. Not ever. Wonder knows that we are not static or fixed beings, but ever-evolving creatures who learn and adapt over time and space. Wonder allows us to not have it all figured out, and in fact, insists that we don't, can't, or won't. Wonder allows us to be beautifully and wholly human, fallible, resilient, and also delicate.

As we explore transitions, ritual, and the Sacred, may we enter an embodied state of wonder together. We have permission to explore, discover, create and co-create and to not have it all figured out. We weave together the mundane with the Sacred, simplicity with complexity, resilience with brokenness, life with death, expansion with contraction. In other words, the paradox that is the reality of what it means to be human on planet Earth. May we oscillate between the big picture and the implementation of these principles into our counseling relationships.

To support accessing an embodied state of wonder, I'm going to offer some ideas. Feel free to try them or not. Permission means your "no" is just as valid as your "yes" and "maybe." If any of these resonate for you, great! If they don't, or if you have an idea that is a better fit for you, please choose what is best for you.

- ♦ You could enter your sphere or shirt and spend some time feeling your unique, creative, brilliant differentiated self.
- ♦ You could access wonder through your sensory delight by letting yourself get enthralled by the object, movement, or sound.
- ♦ You could invoke the support of your ancestors, helping spirits, nature, pets, angels, or other form of support and be with a sense of love, support, and connection.
- ♦ You could connect with a memory of experiencing wonder or witnessing another experience wonder.

- You could think about the seasons and the wonder of birth, death, and rebirth that happens year after year in nature.
- You could connect with something from your culture or lineage that evokes a sense of wonder.
- Or something else not mentioned!

May you invite this sense of wonder and permission to come with you as we continue. May you honor the wholeness of your being, including your lived experiences, identities, places of privilege and marginalization, and your truth as it relates to this content. When you are ready, I'll meet you in the next part of this chapter's opening section.

TRANSITIONS

Transitions can be physical, emotional, mental, social, financial, or spiritual state shifts. They may be expected or unexpected, desired or unwanted. They require motor planning (the process of our body moving from one position into another), a redirection of our attention, thought, or mental process, and/or adapting to a new set of stimuli and input. Within and among the Autistic/KCS/VAST communities, we each have our own unique way of transitioning. Autistic people often prefer to have advance notice of upcoming transitions so that there is time to plan, prepare, and predict what is next. For KCS/VAST people who love novelty and spontaneity, less advanced notice may be less unsettling, sometimes even desired, unless of course it is a state shift from an area of interest to one of disinterest. Some people transition quickly; others require much more time. These neurotypes, monotropic in nature, with executive function challenges and possible slower processing or motor planning, may have very real support needs around the frequency and types of transition that they go through in a day.

Lived experience may make ND people more adaptable over time, or a buildup of trauma, oppression, and unmet needs may make them less adaptable over time. For better or worse, the one most reliable and consistent element of being human is change. I can hear singer-songwriter India.Arie's voice in my head as I write that, specifically her song "Growth" from the *Voyage to India* album. Depending on the types of transitions, they can be a very real threat to autonomy and trigger sympathetic nervous system arousal. Even when they are neutral, transitions still require the nervous system, sensory system, motor planning, and a person's energetics to adapt and orient to a new set of expectations, environmental stimuli, and input.

Dr. Carla Sherrell taught me a lot about transitions as a counselor educator. Supporting transitions is about preparation, predictability, and intentionality. It is a signaling to the body, mind, and heart that a change is coming. Some changes are in our control; some are not. When possible, we support the bodymind to know what to expect, what to plan for, and time to process the change. Being intentional about transitions when we are able to can soften the impact of how much of life is actually beyond ND people's control. This may even help soften some of the rigidity that many Autistic people navigate in order to feel safe.

Transitions abound in our daily life. They are the in between, the moments that mark a shift from one state of being to another, from one experience to the next, a stopping and starting, beginning and ending. I'll offer some examples.

- The shift from whatever is happening for a person before the start of a therapy session into the start of the therapy session.
- The ending of a session and moving onto the next part of the day (for clients). Or the ending of one session and the beginning of another (for therapists).
- Ending the day and going to sleep. Waking up and starting a new day.

- The ending of a relationship into the unknown state of life after that relationship.
- Life stages, as in the shift from adolescence into adulthood or from life into death.
- Being engaged with and enthralled in a passion and stopping to do chores, work, or homework.
- The shift from one identity into another such as passing as heterosexual to coming out as queer, from passing as cis to coming out as trans, from passing as NT to coming out as Autistic and/or KCS/VAST.

In addition to the many mundane transitions that happen on any given day, transitions can also be much bigger or significant life changes, whether wanted or unwanted, planned or unexpected. Whether of a bigger scale or seemingly more mundane, transitions can also be associated with grief. In the death-phobic and grief-phobic culture of the United States, we are taught to avoid, disregard, and quickly get over it. When a close loved one dies, most people are only allowed a maximum of one to two weeks off from work, if that. This can make it very difficult for ND people to be gentle with themselves in the midst of big feelings about seemingly silly or mundane things, let alone bigger life changes. Whether it's about the end of a favorite television show, a company changing its recipe of a favorite or safe food, losing a favorite object, or finally being safe enough to unmask, ND-affirming work means that we slow down enough to acknowledge the possible grief that may be present.

Some clients will wish to bypass their grief, invalidate their grief, and be really harsh with themselves in the midst of their grief. Others may feel totally overwhelmed by their grief. And some clients will not have grief over things they think they should feel grief about and need validation from us that their response is okay. Slowing down (with clients' consent) allows us to be present to what may need or want tending to in the moment. Other times, distraction or permission to "check out" in the presence of an unwanted transition can be deeply therapeutic. It can support much-needed titration and nervous system support. Our role is to name the transition and possible impacts and then take our clients' lead on how to best support them. Sometimes they will need more structure from us. Other times, less. Here is another place of leaning into the truth that clients are the self-expert.

RITUAL

In the midst of transition, whether neutral, joyful, or grief-ridden, ritual can be the anchor that supports us through. It may offer a sense of predictability and knowing what to expect in the midst of change. Ritual may help us access the Sacred, what evokes a sense of meaning, something bigger than ourselves, wonder, awe, or magic. Ritual can be stimming, something we look forward to, a predictable pattern of behavior or action that we engage in to mark an ending or beginning, or a practice that invokes the Divine.

A note on language. I am intentionally using the words ritual and sacred in broad terms to encompass a vast array of beliefs and orientations. For some, these words relate to organized religion, which could evoke religious trauma, so sensitivity is essential. For others, these words may be spirituality, the soul, nature, love, the Universe, Source, or a sense that "I am a mere speck in a vast night sky full of multitudes of stars, planets, and galaxies; I am both important and insignificant at exactly the same time." It can also just refer to something that is meaningful for us, like "my alone time at the end of the day is a sacred ritual that I treasure."

Another note on language. Given the prevalence of co-occurring obsessive-compulsive tendencies (what is medically known as OCD) with autism and KCS/VAST, I also want to acknowledge that the term ritual may be complex. I am using this word to refer to any practice or way of being that leaves people feeling supported, held, tended to, or honored in who they are and what they need. Through the pathology paradigm and medical model of OCD, rituals can be synonymous with compulsions, referred to as problematic behaviors that need to be extinguished and dealt with through exposure therapy. This feels very similar to how the pathology paradigm demonizes stimming. This is incredibly harmful and the antithesis to ND-affirming care. Rituals can be a lifeline, an expression of innate wisdom, and Autistic and/or KCS/VAST embodiment. It is up to the client whether or not their rituals are problematic for them. Some people have rituals that they find hinder their sense of well-being, inhibit their autonomy, and/or restrict them from living as they desire. Other clients find tremendous value, comfort, much-needed predictability, and access to life through their rituals.

Here are some examples of ritual:

- Starting each therapy session with a few moments or minutes of mindfulness, quiet, movement, or stillness to honor the transition and support both client and therapist to adjust to the presence of a new nervous system.
- Going outside after each session as a way to feel the ground beneath us, to release the client from our own energetic, emotional, or intellectual field, and to feel the support of nature in the work we do.
- Washing hands after being around other people.
- A graduation, coming-of-age event or ceremony, a wedding, a funeral or celebration of life, holidays, or traditions.
- A practice of movement, meditation, or prayer to start the day.
- Expressing gratitude before eating.
- A getting-ready-for-bed ritual.
- Taking a few deep breaths before getting out of the car or entering a new space.
- Weekly, biweekly, or monthly peer support or friend gatherings.
- Checking after meals to see if there's food in our teeth.
- Energetic clearings of our body and environment after sessions.

- Hugging a tree before a counselor education training to feel the support of the Earth and ancestors, to ground, and to access inner courage. (Yes, I absolutely use this one before I lead trainings!)
- Playing video games after school, after work, or after the kids go to bed.

Some rituals may not have anything to do with evoking a sense of the Sacred, while others may be deeply tied to accessing how we perceive and experience the Sacred, almost like a tether to the Divine/Sacred/Source. Rituals have a way of connecting us back to the present moment, to the collective, to our embodiment, to noticing how we are doing and what we might be needing.

The Sacred

Despite the ways that ableism, oppression, and trauma cause harm and can disconnect us from ourselves and our essence, my experience of Autistic and KCS/VAST people is that they have a heightened awareness of and access to energy, energetic shifts, and intuition. Their keen attention to detail, to sensory input, and to the natural world; their sensitive nervous system; and their innate culture and communication styles give them access to a dynamic, subtle, sensitive, nuanced experience of life.

While I hesitate to make any seemingly vast overgeneralizations, from my many years of experience connecting with and working with Autistic and KCS/VAST people of all ages and communication styles, a profound sensitivity, gentleness, and empathy are traits many of my clients share. For nonspeakers and PDAers, these traits seem to be even more amplified and deeply tied to how they relate to the world. I'm referring to an energetic sensitivity, intuition, and deep awareness of their environments, including human and nonhuman beings, that transcends words.

When I discovered *The Telepathy Tapes* podcast that I referenced earlier, I was thrilled to learn that the spiritual gifts of nonspeakers are being more broadly talked about and validated, even by some neuroscientists. As I listened to this, it resonated with me as profound truth and evoked a sense of "thank goodness this is being publicly addressed." Even as a speaking Autistic, I felt encouraged to take my own spiritual gifts and sensitivity more seriously.

These gifts can include telepathy (reading minds), knowing what is going to happen before it happens, communicating with people who have died, and many other forms of expanded consciousness, awareness, and perception. Their experiences are finally being taken more seriously within families and among some teachers, medical providers, scientists, and support professionals. It also feels really important to mention that oppression toward nonspeakers is still deeply pervasive. Both within Autistic communities and across NT communities, it is essential that nonspeakers are not fetishized but protected, believed, supported in their very real challenges, and honored as the whole humans that they are.

Tragically, the harshness and oppression of capitalism, colonization, white supremacy, ableism, classism, cisheteronormativity, and patriarchy that penetrate U.S. culture, institutions, and family can force people to disconnect from themselves in order to survive. Energetic attunement and awareness get deemed illegitimate. For those who have lost access, being supported to reconnect with this innate sensitivity, access to the Sacred, and deep awareness of the interconnectedness of all living beings is vital to healing, to restoring a sense of aliveness, and to well-being. This can mean decentering words or verbal processing and supporting clients to trust their bodymind's innate process of metabolizing energy and emotions through present-moment awareness. This is an essential component of decolonizing care.

Because every person is a unique individual, some with religious trauma; some who are atheists; some who are very mechanistic in nature; and some who are deeply religious, faith-based, or spiritual; it is essential that we use words like ritual and sacred with sensitivity. We need to engage in curiosity with clients about what these words mean to them or if there are other words that they prefer instead. To be ND-affirming is to not force our own agenda onto them, but to meet them where they are and honor who they are.

I've also connected with many people who do not identify with human as their origin species. I've known people who have dreams and unexplained memories of their home planet, a place that feels so viscerally familiar, yet sadly, so far away. I've had my own mystical experiences of sensing that my essence is much more closely aligned with tree than human. I resonate deeply with Earth-based, Indigenous wisdom and knowledge practices that honor and celebrate the interconnectedness of all beings and decenter humans.

While some clients will prefer a much more cognitive-centered, logic-based orientation to counseling, others will be delighted to have the transpersonal integrated into their journey. The transpersonal could include soul integration, shamanic practices, religion or spirituality, meditation, intuition, angels, helping spirits, ancestors, nature, divination cards, plant medicine, psychedelics, astrology, and so much more. It could also be an acceptance that we are all made up of energy, an energy that connects all beings and cannot be destroyed, just changed. Let's dismantle the ways that white supremacy, colonization, and capitalism have removed the soul and Earth-connection from our humanity, including from western psychology. Let's bring back the magic, the wonder, the mysticism, and the awe to our sacred work of counseling. And let's engage in this in a decolonial way, anti-racist way.

I am a strong believer that we each possess our own unique medicine in our work as therapists and that the greatest gift we can give to our clients and to ourselves is to come home to this medicine, to explore it, and to share it. No matter what our neurotype(s) may be, our innate gifts, our finely tuned nervous system, our unique ways of being, and our creativity all comprise this medicine. Being in alignment with this medicine is deeply tied to our vitality, passion, aliveness, and collective healing, and can help protect us from burnout.

This completes the opening section of this chapter. In the following sections, we will explore different types of transitions and rituals that are especially relevant to our clients and to ourselves, and we will weave in the Sacred along the way. Please take whatever time you need and care for yourself in whatever ways would be most supportive to you. When you are ready, I'll meet you in the next section.

Recap: Transitions, Ritual, and the Sacred
- Both in our day-to-day lives and in the natural world, transitions abound. Autistic and KCS/VAST people have varying relationships with and pacing needs regarding transition; acknowledging, honoring, and making space for transitions is important.
- Ritual can help us feel supported and safer in the midst of transitions. Ritual offers structure and predictability and can help us adapt to change with less distress.
- Many Autistic and KCS/VAST people have an innate sense of the Sacred, but this may have been severed within them through the impacts of colonization, oppression, and trauma. The Sacred can be anything that's meaningful to a person, but it can also be a sense of something greater than ourselves.

WORKING WITH CLIENTS
Transition Rituals to Begin the Session
Offering a transition ritual is a way of communicating to their (and our own) nervous system, "Hey, this is different. I'm not where I was before or doing what I was doing before. Now I'm here with my therapist, in this space, doing this thing together called therapy or counseling." It provides an opportunity for

their nervous system to recalibrate now that they are in the presence of another human, specifically, you. Whether we work virtually or in-person, whether this is conscious and intentional or unconscious, this recalibration happens.

For many Autistic people, the transition into the therapy space, or any social interaction for that matter, can feel a bit awkward at first. They may start wondering:

- "What am I supposed to say?"
- "How am I supposed to be?"
- "What is expected of me? ?"

A transition ritual communicates to the client, both explicitly and implicitly, "We are here now together; I am responsible for holding this therapeutic container, attuning to you and your nervous system. As you are ready, I invite you to settle into the space. I am here with you and for you."

Many clients come to therapy with some anxiety that they are supposed to have a plan and know what they want to talk about or explore. Or they are eagerly invested in being a so-called "good" client. A transition ritual, if they would like one, can help alleviate some of these nerves and remind them that they are enough, that they can be themselves, and that there is no "right" way to show up to therapy. It can also provide a much-needed sense of structure, a knowing what to expect, a sense of taking the pressure off. Alternatively, it can help them tap into their internal wisdom, intuition, and intention for the session.

Whether or not a client desires to have any particular transition ritual into and out of session, I make a point of naming the transition each session, and I offer the opportunity to insert a ritual. For some clients, our rituals stay the same over the long term; for others, the rituals may change session to session. The beauty of transition rituals, or any rituals for that matter, is that we get to choose how fluid or rigid we structure them. For instance, some clients may consistently choose to begin each session with five square breaths with me leading the counting in support of co-regulation (also known as box breathing: for example, inhale for four, hold for four, exhale for four, hold for four). Other clients may consistently choose to begin with a transition ritual, but the form of the ritual may change. Some sessions it may be a legs up the wall yoga pose with square breaths; other times it may be a human-free zone for 3–5 minutes, connecting with a pet, engaging in free-form movement or stimming, sitting quietly with attention on their breath, and/or maybe some stretching. Other clients may not want a transition ritual at all; this is just as valid!

Whenever I start with a new client, I check in with them about how I can best support them in the transition of entering the counseling space. Some clients will pretty immediately suggest an idea or a go-to strategy. Other clients may desire suggestions or options of what is possible. And again, some won't want one. I will offer some categories of rituals. The possibilities are endless, so when you notice something missing from a category, please add to this list! Here is your loving reminder to trust your wisdom and ideas.

> **IDEAS FOR TRANSITION RITUALS TO BEGIN SESSIONS**
>
> - **Movement based:** stimming, rhythmic movements, yoga poses, dance, and more.
> - **Stillness/rest based:** taking deep breaths, lying down, quiet time.
> - **Sensory based:** fidgeting with a favorite object; connecting with a pet; listening to, singing, or playing a song; looking around the space and using the eyes to orient to pleasurable or interesting objects/textures/colors.
> - **Connection based:** spending 5 minutes talking about

their passion, doing any of the above together, playing a game, watching a video, other co-regulation supports.
- **Nature based:** connecting with something from nature, whether a tree, plant, rock, shell, flower, nature image, or playing with sand.
- **Art based:** doodling or drawing, building something, crafting, crocheting, modeling clay.
- **Soul based:** calling in the support of ancestors, helping spirits, protectors, and/or nature, setting intentions for the session, pulling a card from a tarot/divination deck, chanting, prayer, connecting with sacred objects.
- **Culture based:** connecting with or engaging with cultural practices specific to the client's culture, ethnicity, lineage, and/or traditions.

Some clients may prefer more or less structure with their ritual. Less structure might involve them taking as much or as little time as they desire and letting you know when they are complete. More structure might look like setting a timer for a designated number of minutes. There is no right or wrong way to do this. Sometimes I may set a timer at a client's request and then it feels too long for them, so they let me know they'd like to end it sooner. Other times, the timer goes off and they realize they would like more time in their ritual, so we may reset it. Whatever the ritual, ideally it is supporting access to the parasympathetic nervous system.

Transition Rituals to End the Session

In a similar way that beginning transition rituals can mark the start of the session, ending transition rituals can help mark the completion of the session. Again, some clients may or may not want them, but I consistently name that our transition is coming up. Ideally, I let clients know when there are 5–10 minutes left in the session, but sometimes I lose track of time or am reluctant to interrupt! This "heads-up" helps their nervous system to know what to expect and to prepare for the upcoming ending and exiting of the space. Ending rituals can be about integration, acknowledging that the process may not be totally done, but that we need to find a done-for-now place. Or as Dr. Carla Sherrell likes to say, "non-closure."[8]

Ending rituals can be vastly creative and as unique to the client as beginning rituals. Some clients may enjoy ending the same way they began. Others might choose a different ending ritual. Like beginning rituals, these may stay the same each session or change each time. Some that I have co-created with my clients include:

> **IDEAS FOR TRANSITION RITUALS TO END SESSIONS**
>
> - Offering reassurance
> - Checking in about scheduling
> - Offering my own insight, reflections, and weaving together the themes of the session
> - Offering gratitude
> - Celebrating and validating the client's growth and insight
> - Seeking feedback from the client about what worked well for them and what they would like me to do differently next time
> - Offering containment, either with the imagination or physically: putting what is unfinished in an

---

8 This term originates from Glenn Singleton, author of *Courageous Conversations About Race: A Field Guide For Achieving Equity in Schools and Beyond*, and then I learned it from Dr. Carla Sherrell. It is generally referenced as "expect non-closure."

imaginary container and imagining it being stored somewhere safely until next time. Alternatively, using a physical container and putting inside objects/symbols representing what is unfinished to be stored somewhere safe until next time
- Requests for ongoing support or between session "homework"
- Stillness/rest
- Movement: expressing a gesture that is present, rhythmic movement, or stimming
- Taking deep breaths
- Sharing a hug (with consent!)
- Picking a card from a divination, inspiration, angel, animal or other type of deck
- Hugging a tree
- Doing some form of art or imagery to integrate the session
- Using nature objects to reflect what someone is letting go of or what they are taking with them
- Blowing out a candle

This is another opportunity to access our creativity and our unique medicine to collaboratively design rituals with our clients that leave them feeling some sense of completion, feeling cared for, or at least experiencing a sense of containment until the next session.

Transition Rituals for Coming Out in One's Neurotype

I notice a surge of energy in my body as I type out the heading for this section! I didn't know that was the next heading until the words flowed out onto the page, and I feel excited and inspired to write about this. I've had many conversations with people about the ways that gaining language for their neurotype(s) and then choosing to share it with others is very much a form of coming out. Whether a client is identified as Autistic and/or KCS/VAST as a youth or as an adult, the process of identification or realization is very much a life transition and one that deserves care and attention.

Like other coming outs, be it about sexual orientation or gender identity, coming out as Autistic and/or KCS/VAST can be liberating, grief-ridden, terrifying, enraging, and joyful all at the same time. This is a sacred time in one's life. It is an ending of who they used to identify as and a beginning of expressing a new identity. Having newly acquired language to validate a person's neurotype can be deeply life affirming, a flashing neon sign that sparkles: "I'm not broken, and I never was. I'm Autistic!" or "I'm not defective and I never was. I'm KCS/VAST!" or "It's not my fault that so much about being human doesn't make sense to me, I'm Autistic and KCS/VAST!"

The thing about coming out in an ableist dominant culture is that there are a multitude of ways it can go, some positive, some neutral, and some downright traumatic. Suddenly, a potential onslaught of permission to have needs, to be valid in one's struggles, to own one's strengths, to have fluctuating capacity can flow forth! There may also be access to a new community of shared neurotype!

Sometimes imposter syndrome is right there too: the invalidating familiar voice that wants to insist, "Yes, this very much is a *you* problem."

Sometimes, people have hidden their Autistic and KCS/VAST features for so long that people around them don't believe them, or others are uneducated about all the ways an Autistic and/or KCS/VAST person can present. From this place of ignorance, people around them might say something harmful like "but you make eye contact, or you have a job, or you have a partner, *you can't be Autistic.*" Ouch.

Often due to intergenerational trauma, some families are unable or unwilling to consider that autism and KCS/VAST are a part of the lineage, and they outright deny or reject someone's identification. Some cultures may perceive autism and KCS/VAST as shameful.

When a person already holds marginalized identities, be it due to their race, religion, gender, or sexual orientation, adding an additional marginalized identity through neurotype can feel overwhelming, daunting, or even dangerous.

Sometimes people finally feel validated in having support needs, but for all kinds of reasons, likely due to systemic oppression and intersecting marginalized identities, aren't actually able to get their needs met.

On top of all of that, the journey of reframing one's entire existence through the newfound lens of autism and/or KCS/VAST begins. This is often a huge part of the grief and/or rage that show up. Clients may be presented with the realities of how unmet they have been; how misunderstood they were by family members, the school system, the community, and other institutions; and how much trauma they endured at being expected to conform to neurotypical standards when they weren't NT.

In addition to grief or rage about the past, there may also be grief or rage about the future. Prior to coming out, clients may have had thoughts like "if I only work hard enough, I'll finally be able to do ___ (insert whatever they've been striving for that they witness NT peers doing)." Acceptance of one's neurodivergence could mean that who they've been trying to be may not ever actually happen. There can be freedom, grief, and rage here as they experience a permission to let go of NT standards and expectations. These were never meant for them in the first place, but there is also a letting go of who they won't ever be.

Coming out as Autistic and/or KCS/VAST is yet another moment of the simple meeting the complex, the mundane meeting the Sacred, the paradox of being human. It is a marker of before and after. It deserves to be acknowledged, honored, and respected for the transition that it is. There is certainly no one or right way to mark this. It is dependent on who the client is, what kind of support network they do or don't have, and how they perceive and relate to this realization. Unlike other transitions in life that can be marked in a single moment such as a graduation or a wedding, the journey of coming out is an ongoing, ever-evolving one. It certainly can be marked with a cake or a celebration with loved ones! And there are vast ways to mark and honor it. It deserves ongoing attention, care, and processing. It may mean different things at different life stages or other life transitions. It is very much a journey of undoing and of becoming. What a beautiful opportunity for you to co-create a meaningful ritual that honors both who they are and who they aren't.

Whether a client is already aware of their neurotype(s) when they first come to you, or they come into language for their neurotype(s) during the course of your counseling relationship, you can ask them how they would like to honor this transition. Our desire to celebrate with them can encourage them to honor their coming out, whether it is just with us or also with others in their life. As with all of my lists, please honor your own wisdom and experience and add your ideas. There is no way for me to capture every possible idea! Here are some suggestions that clients may be interested in for a coming out ritual:

POSSIBLE COMING OUT RITUALS

- **Movement based:** Dancing a 5Rhythms wave or other form of ecstatic dance or movement meditation; moving to a curated playlist that honors their coming out; stimming in ways they haven't allowed themselves to do before or in a long time; offering gestures that express their before, current, and future desires for themselves.
- **Stillness/rest based:** Honoring their journey through quiet contemplation or reflection; taking a nap to honor their possible exhaustion.

- **Sensory based:** Having a celebratory food or beverage; picking or buying flowers to honor themselves; baking something delicious and celebratory; making, acquiring, or buying new sensory supports.
- **Connection based:** Having a gathering with loved ones in celebration of their coming out; calling in community and connecting with other ND folx of the same neurotype; being witnessed by you in their Autistic/KCS/VAST self; joining an unmasking support or therapy or social group.
- **Nature based:** Choosing nature objects that represent who they used to be and who they are becoming; tossing nature objects into moving water as an expression of what they are letting go of that no longer serves them.
- **Art based:** Writing a letter to their past self; writing a letter to their future self; drawing, crafting, or making something to represent how they knew themselves before and who they are becoming.
- **Soul based:** Connecting with their Autistic and/or KCS/VAST ancestors; perhaps getting to know them, asking them questions, feeling their resiliency, love and support, experiencing a sense of belonging, and honoring their journey; doing a reading or pulling cards from a tarot/divination deck; having a session with a shamanic practitioner who can support the calling home of displaced/exiled soul parts, release of energetic entanglements, unravel curses, power retrievals, and help folx remember and reclaim their energetic sovereignty; journaling with their higher self and asking for support and guidance on their journey; a grief or rage ritual to honor and express a possible lifetime of unmet needs, both for them and possibly

> also for their ancestors and others who may or may not have ever had the chance to come out.
> - **Culture based:** Connecting with or engaging with cultural practices specific to the client's culture, ethnicity, lineage, and/or traditions.

No matter how a client chooses to acknowledge and honor their neurotype coming out, may we as therapists hold awareness that this is a coming home to oneself. It is a reorienting to how one may relate to their environment, to their community, and to all the different aspects of their life. It may mean a complete life overhaul in time, or an even bigger attempt to hide and shrink. Every person gets to do this in their own unique way and in their own unique timing.

There is no right way to come out.

We as therapists get to hold the Sacred, either with or for our clients, depending on where they are in their journey. We get to honor their wholeness, their strengths and challenges, their resilience, and the gift they are to the world, past, present, and future.

Transition Rituals for Honoring Major Life Changes

In our last subsection of transition, rituals, and the Sacred for clients, we'll explore big life transitions such as changes to a family system (e.g., birth of a child, marriage, divorce, death of a family member), death loss, milestones, illness, moving, starting or finishing school, getting laid off or changing jobs, or the lack of desired changes such as being single when one desires partnership. We won't possibly be able to cover all of the so-called big life changes, nor do we necessarily need to, but we'll bring awareness to how to meet the many bigger transitions a person may go through.

When it comes to these bigger life changes, we have to acknowledge that some may be chosen and desired, chosen yet not particularly desired, unexpected and desired, or unplanned and undesired. How we navigate each of these and support clients through these will vary based upon the dynamics of the change, who the client is, and their history related to change.

Since this subsection comes right after the transition of coming out subsection, I'll use examples of how unmasking journeys can influence or inspire major life changes. As people come into greater self-acceptance and embodiment of their neurodivergence, there can be many ripple effects. Sometimes these changes are desired, sometimes not. The journey to creating greater alignment in one's life with who they actually are and what they actually need can be intense for some.

Sometimes it can result in the endings of partnerships and other close relationships, be it with family members or friends. Sometimes changes in employment can happen. Sometimes massive burnout can hit and everything needs to pause in whatever ways are possible. New relationships may also form. The coming out of neurotype can also inspire other coming outs, such as sexual orientation or gender identity. Sometimes there is a desire for big changes, but a lack of access to make those changes. The possible changes that emerge can be any combination of liberating, terrifying, enraging, exciting, and grief-filled.

For many Autistic and KCS/VAST people, navigating a big transition calls for a shift to low(er) demand living. While I don't love this term, many people report skill regression when navigating major transitions. They lose access to some of the executive function capacity they previously had. Things like cooking, cleaning, eating, bathing, communication, working, parenting, emotion regulation, and managing other life responsibilities can become increasingly difficult, if not impossible. Support needs can become much more evident and perhaps greater than before. By reducing demands as much as and wherever possible, there is less pressure to maintain their previous capacity.

While it would be ideal for every Autistic and KCS/VAST person to be able to lower their demands during a big life transition, here is another area where privilege is intimately tied to access. Depending on their situation, community support, family support, and access to financial resources, not everyone has access to the support they would need to be able to do less. This is a hard one to reconcile.

That said, there are some essential questions for clients to ask themselves or for their counselors to ask them when they are going through a major life transition, whether pleasurable, traumatic, or somewhere in between. This is an invitation for both counselors and their clients to hold curiosity.

Let's get specific. Here are some examples:

- What is actually a priority, and what do they perceive is a priority but isn't actually?
- Where can they lean into permission (e.g., to do less, to have needs, to be different), delegate tasks and responsibilities if possible, and release perfectionism?
- How can they keep honoring their own unique timing and pacing, knowing that there is no such thing as a right amount of time to celebrate, to grieve, to be disappointed, to be withdrawn, or to be with whatever else they may be feeling or experiencing?

Permission. Permission. Permission.

- How can we support clients to invoke the structure, comfort, and/or creativity of ritual to help them reclaim autonomy that's been lost, have some sense of predictability and routine, and access parasympathetic states?

Remember, for our ND clients, no matter whether the change is perceived as pleasant, neutral, or unpleasant, it still may be really intense for them. Or they may be seemingly reactionless. I want to emphasize the importance of supporting clients to honor their unique ways of processing, metabolizing, and integrating big changes into their life. There is no right or wrong way for clients to respond.

Do not judge them or try to change how they relate to change.

- How can we also remind them of the wisdom of their soul's journey, expressed in such a way that resonates for them and honors their beliefs?
- What anchors or sacred rituals help them to feel held and supported by the same forces that keep the planets in rotation; that cause leaves to return in the spring; seeds to sprout and yield flowers, fruits, vegetables, or plants; and dawn and dusk to return day after day?
- Who can offer them this support whether nonphysical beings, ancestors, animals, the natural world, plant medicine or psychedelics, community, elders, mentors, or other practitioners who specialize in spiritual or soul-based support?
- How might music, ecstatic dance, art, prayer or intention, astrology, tarot, yoga, Earth-based, or other practices carry them through the crossing of the threshold that is transition?

Again, we return to creativity, accessing and sharing our unique medicine with clients, trusting them as the self-expert, honoring their inherent wisdom, and offering lots of validation. I like to remind clients that "even though this is happening, it doesn't mean you have to like it... and it's also okay to like it too."

We've reached the end of this section. Now might be a

wonderful time to check back in with yourself, to notice what you are noticing, needing, or wanting. Feel free to pause and reflect, journal, move your body, and/or take a break. When you feel ready, we'll meet back in the next section, Working With Ourselves.

Recap: Working With Clients as it Relates to Transition, Ritual, and the Sacred

- Beginning and ending rituals can help clients navigate the transition of adjusting to a new nervous system, reduce the awkwardness that may be present, and provide a structure that supports predictability.
- These rituals may stay the same every time, or there may be variation in the specific ritual that gets implemented session to session.
- Coming out as Autistic and/or KCS/VAST is a profound life transition and deserves to be tended to as such.
- Big life transitions, whether expected or unexpected, desired or undesired, may leave clients needing to lower demands, reduce expectations, honor their pacing, and access ritual and the Sacred to help cross the threshold of change.

WORKING WITH OURSELVES

As we return the focus to ourselves as counselors, you may notice a lot or a little stirring within you. May you be gentle and sweet with yourself as we explore some of the primary ways transition shows up for us. We'll begin with transition rituals before and after sessions. It may be helpful for you to have a journal, drawing, art supplies, or some other form of medium to support you in self-reflection.

Pre- and Postsession Rituals

We'll start this subsection with some self-reflection, and then I'll share more about how I engage with this. Sometimes hearing other people's ideas helps us generate our own ideas. If waiting to answer these until after you keep reading would be more helpful, please honor that. If getting to reflect on this before you hear other ideas is more useful, please honor that. I invite you to engage with these questions in whatever ways feel supportive and accessible for you.

When I think about our workday or workweek as therapists, the following curiosities come to mind:

- What transition rituals support you before heading into a session?
- What transition rituals support you once a session is over?
- How much time is ideal for you to have to transition between sessions, meetings, or tasks?
  - If that isn't accessible, what else would be supportive instead?
  - What helps you to release the work week and transition into time away from work, be it the "weekend" or extended time off? (I'm putting weekend in quotes as I realize that not all people have traditional Saturday and Sunday as their off days.)
  - How many days off do you really need in between your work weeks, and is that accessible to you?

If you have never had the chance or been encouraged to reflect on these points of inquiry, or if you have been contemplating this nearly nonstop, trying to figure out what will help you reduce burnout and make your work more sustainable, there is no one right way to approach this. Maybe what you are already doing is working just dandy for you. If that is the case, I celebrate you! I imagine this is likely not the case for most readers.

Before I share a bit about my transition rituals to offer some ideas that may spark your own creativity, I want to acknowledge that we all work in different environments with varying levels of autonomy, varying privilege, varying access to things like the outdoors or to a space that is our own that we are able to decorate ourselves. My reality may be very different from yours; I honor our differentiations and hope that you can find creative ways to get as many of your needs met as possible. Feel free to return to your sphere or custom shirt!

Rituals to Prepare for Sessions

I've learned over the years that I'm best able to focus, be present, and access my gifts when I have access to ample forms of sensory delights in each session. In addition to all of my fidgets (including a foot fidget!), a lap blanket, a chair that spins, and visual pleasure on the walls, I bring one or two beverages with me into each session. Filling my cup, slicing a lemon, heating up water, and making coffee or tea is a ritual I rely on. I tend to enjoy both a hot and cold option or a neutral option and a bubbly or flavorful option; sometimes for lack of time or other reasons, I just have one.

- ◆ What sensory support rituals have you noticed a preference for?
    - Are these accessible to you?

No matter what your neurotype, when given permission to explore this for themselves, most people find they have sensory preferences, desires, and delights. If you're not familiar with what you like or are drawn to, I encourage you to play with this and allow yourself to explore.

- ◆ Could you let yourself have two (or more!) beverages in a session?!
    - Would you even want to?!

I also tend to snack more on my workdays and may opt for something quick between sessions. It could be a protein bar, nuts, fruit, chocolate, cured meat, or whatever is available and sounds good. Especially being on testosterone, I tend toward protein-rich snacks; protein can also be really grounding for sensitive people in the helping professions.

♦ What foods do you most enjoy during and throughout your workday?

Before I log on to start my session, I also retrieve my handwritten notes from my binder for the client I am about to meet with. This way I can scan where we left off last time, notice anything specific I needed to remember or follow up on, and start to connect with their energy. At some point, either before logging on or during our beginning ritual, I try to remember to envision my sphere and/or shirt so that I can feel connected to my gifts and differentiated from my client.

Rituals to Release the Session and Client
Once the session ends, I have (again, very specific, haha) rituals that I engage with to transition out of the session. Some are consistent after every session, some I remember to do at the end of the day, and some only happen on occasion. As I said earlier in the book, to be Autistic and/or KCS/VAST is to be inconsistent! For those reading who are NT and have an easy time being consistent, I celebrate that for you! As I share my rituals, you may notice that more ideas come to you for your own possible rituals. May these ideas inspire you.

Here's what I do every time: I go to the bathroom to pee, flush, and wash my hands. As an environmentalist, on my nonwork hours, I often don't flush after each pee to conserve water. In between sessions, however, I view peeing as an energetic releasing and cleansing of my system from the client I was just with; flushing is literally flushing it away. I wash my hands not just for hygiene, but again, with a specific intention of releasing the client and wishing them well.

- ♦ How do you mark the ending of your sessions for yourself?

When I remember: sometimes I do this as or after I wash my hands, sometimes it's in a random moment when I remember, sometimes it's at the end of the day. I envision my client enveloped in some form of hammock or cozy spot with their spirit team (others may call them helping spirits) surrounding them, and safe, protected, and cared for. It's as though I'm releasing them to the Universe, the Divine, or what is bigger than me, and it reminds me where my responsibility ends. As a sensitive, empathic person, it can be all too easy to assume greater responsibility as a therapist than is actually mine.

Another ritual I sometimes engage with at the end of the day is to wash my feet. Similar to washing my hands, it is an energetic release and clearing of my sensitive system. I imagine that I'm releasing my clients and my work day as I do this. I also tend to change my clothes after my work day ends for similar reasons.

- ♦ How do you release responsibility for your clients when a session ends?

What I do on occasion: although this would be a lovely ritual to do in between every session, the reality is this happens sometimes, particularly after an emotionally intense session. I walk outside barefoot, feel my feet on the grass on the Earth, look around at the plants and trees, look up at the sky, and feel held by nature. It reminds me of my interconnectedness to all that is, and that I and my client are held by so much more than me alone.

I recognize that not everyone has access to the outside

during their workday or time that allows them to do this. Plus, what works for me may not work for you, anyway!

♦ Thinking about who you are and what is accessible to you, what helps you to feel more supported in the big picture of your work?

I haven't gotten into any consistent rituals for clearing the energetic space of my office at the end of the workday or workweek. When I sense that the energy feels heavy or stagnant, I will usually open the door. While I acknowledge the cultural appropriation of this as a non-Indigenous person, I have at times burned sage. I learned a few years back that cedar is an energetic clearing tool used by the Jewish people, so now I burn cedar instead.

♦ What clearing practices does your lineage, ancestors, or culture use?
♦ How can you partner with the land you live on to grow, tend, or forage for native plants who may desire to offer their energetic clearing and protection in exchange for your care, tending, and respect?

These are great opportunities to learn more about your own culture and the land you live on, if you are not already aware, and another step in the ever unfolding dismantling of white supremacy by engaging in decolonial practices.

Rituals Between Sessions to Support Sustainability
I was in a training once where someone also in private practice shared that they were playing with giving themselves 30 minutes between sessions. My insides thought this was brilliant! I tried it, and found that 30 minutes is way better for me than the 15 minutes in between sessions that I had previously been giving myself. My sessions are 60 minutes in duration, but my relationship to time means that we almost always start 3–5 minutes after the

scheduled start time. To make up for this, I tack on those minutes at the end. On top of that, I'm such a slow transitioner by nature (as are many of my clients), that I commonly go over time anyway. It's rare that my 30-minute break is actually 30 minutes, so when it is, it feels incredibly luxurious! It's usually just enough time to write down what I want to capture from the session and do my between-session rituals.

I realize that getting to set this type of schedule for myself is not realistic across many different environments or life circumstances. I am not a parent, so I do not have to confine my work hours to a very specific part of the day (meaning that my workday can span more hours of the day). I also have the freedom associated with private practice as it relates to autonomy over my schedule. Agency settings, school settings, certain institutions, and/or insurance reimbursement are what regulate schedules for some counselors.

- ♦ I wonder how much time you currently have, and if you desire to adjust it?
    - If you answered yes to your desire, is adjusting it an option?
- ♦ When additional time between sessions is not an option, what other possibilities are there that could support you instead?

Some ideas that come to mind are a gesture that marks the transition, a few deep breaths, a visualization, shifting your body in space to mark the ending, or telling yourself something like "that session is over, and in a moment, I will enter the next one." A ritual between sessions can be as quick or as simple as a moment of acknowledgment.

Rituals Between Workweeks to Support Sustainability

I learned early on that in order to best support my sustainability, I do best with three consecutive days off per week in a row. I recognize how inaccessible that is for a lot of therapists, especially those working in agencies or other settings, or working multiple jobs to make ends meet. I think a lack of needed time off, whether weekly time off or vacation time, is a primary cause for counselor burnout. I am so sorry if you are in a situation where you know you need more regular time off between workweeks and throughout the year, but are unable to access it. Your struggle is real, valid, and an indicator of the harm of capitalism.

While my circumstances allow for me to generally have 3 days off per week, I feel the challenge of getting the extended time off that I ideally need and want. What I experience as the biggest downside to private practice is that there's no such thing as paid sick days or paid time off. It can be tricky to save enough regularly to have a surplus available when there is no income coming in. I've heard a lot of other private practice therapists echo a similar sentiment.

Again, though, here's where privilege and access play a big role. For those who are partnered and their partner(s) makes more than enough money, saving up to take time off might be a nonissue. Another obstacle to time off can be the very real day-to-day impacts of chronic illness that cause therapists to need to cancel sessions more frequently. The unpredictability of chronic illness can make it that much more challenging to save for sick days as well as vacation time.

When we do have access to time off, either between workweeks or throughout the year, that time away from our clients can provide much-needed space and replenishment, especially of our connection to the Sacred. Sometimes the hustle and bustle of life in capitalism and colonization can make it difficult to maintain connection with our sense of purpose, wonder, meaning, and soul. If you are noticing that you are struggling to access that, it may likely be an indicator that you need a break from your work to recalibrate and focus on you. Let's engage in some self-reflection to explore this further.

- How might you be able to recalibrate and devote some time and energy to focus on you?
- Who could support you to access your needs?
- If you aren't able to access any extended amount of time off, what rituals could you implement that would foster a sense of replenishment?

Sometimes, all we have access to are small chunks of time to replenish. So called "minivacations," even if they are an hour, can be deeply restorative, especially when we are intentional about honoring them as sacred time. Bear in mind that sacred time could mean zoning out for an hour with the express purpose of powering down our bodymind. It could be anything that brings a sense of rest, relief, nourishment, decompression, pleasure, neutrality, connection to self or other (including to nature), or disconnection from self or other. I encourage you to honor your own uniqueness, knowing that what you need may likely change from day to day, week to week, or month to month. I'll leave you with these questions for the moment, knowing that we will explore this further in the section Working With Ourselves in Chapter 10 on joy. Please honor your pacing and what you need here, and when you are ready I'll meet you in the next section.

HONORING THE SACRED UNFOLDING OF OUR OWN LIFE TRANSITIONS WHILE BEING A THERAPIST

While we may love or appreciate our role as therapist when we are well resourced and in a stable place in our lives, our relationship to our work may feel very different when we are going through a hard time or a big change ourselves. Our usually focused, attentive, or present selves may be much more easily distracted, bored, checked out, or even annoyed by our clients. You've gotten to know me well enough at this point in the book to know that I do not shy away from radical honesty when that is what is needed!

If that last line wasn't enough for you, hehe, here goes: when our clients have more privilege than us, or when their struggles seem minor compared to what we are going through in our own lives, it can make it very difficult to be a therapist. I want to normalize that there may be times when you feel pissed off at your client, when you want to tell them to "shut up," or to "get a grip," or "if only you knew how good you have it." I know I am breaking all the rules by saying this out loud—more accurately, writing it. It needs to be named, because we are humans who also embody the role of therapist, and sometimes it can feel like too much to care about other people's problems when we've got plenty of our own.

I feel how radical it was for me to just share that, and I'm noticing my chest tighten a bit. I think my old friend, the fawn response, is showing up. It helps me to name that. If you have not ever felt that way toward your clients, then feel free to disregard that paragraph. And if you are someone who feels seen and validated by that paragraph, I honor you; your struggle is real.

In support of integration and curiosity, I'm going to offer some prompts for you to consider or engage with when and how you choose to.

- ♦ While we may encourage our clients to lower their demands and expectations of themselves when they are going through big changes, how can we give ourselves the same permission when we still need to show up for our clients?

I've been asked this question a number of times throughout the years. Life has given me a lot of practice at this, and I want to honor how valid and real this question is.

There are three parts to my answer. The first part relates to how often therapists (myself included) tell me that it is easier to help others than it is to receive support for themselves. I want to gently remind us that in addition to getting our needs met, the vulnerability that arises in accessing support can actually make us better therapists. It can amplify our empathy for the courage our clients have in inviting us in to support them. U.S. dominant culture is individualistic and teaches us to figure it all out on our own, by ourselves. That same culture also reinforces a false narrative that therapists have it all figured out.

No, we don't!

When we let ourselves get support, we disrupt these harmful cultural norms and honor our own humanity. Support can come in the form of working with our own therapist, coach, or practitioner; reaching out to community and other loved ones; seeking solace and wisdom from nature, journaling, or spiritual practice; calling on the ancestors; engaging in grief ritual, movement, art, or rest; and if possible, taking time off from work. If we can't reduce our workload, we can return to the inquiry from the Working With Clients section earlier in this chapter about how else in our lives we can reduce demands.

- ♦ Do you have any go-to rituals for yourself when you are having a hard time?
- ♦ Are they similar or different for when you are going through a big change?

The second part of my answer is that sometimes the familiar structure and routine of work can be its own form of resource when we are going through something big. Being with other people in their own process can be a lovely distraction from our own internal world. It can help us to shift the focus away from our own distress. Sometimes, the act of generosity of listening to and being with others in their process can be a salve to our tender hearts. It can put our challenges in perspective, or at least give us a break from having to be inundated with our own feelings. At the same time, we can give ourselves permission to be mediocre.

In response to oppression, many of us have learned that in order to be "good enough," we have to be as close to the false, colonized idea of "perfect" as possible. Similar to how racialized folx, especially Black folx, typically have to work twice as hard or more as their white peers in order to be taken seriously and given opportunities, ND people typically have to work harder than their NT peers, as do people of marginalized genders and sexual orientations in comparison to their more privileged peers. Given the very high expectations many of us have of ourselves in response to systemic and institutional pressures, it can be novel to entertain the idea of mediocrity. I certainly don't mean negligent or harmful, but also want to offer permission to not show up at or over 100%; permission to be simultaneously human *and* a therapist.

♦ While acknowledging your sociocultural identities and how you are impacted by systemic and institutional oppression in your work life, what would it even mean for you to let yourself be a mediocre therapist sometimes?

Now for the third part of my answer, and here's where it relates to my experience of the Sacred. As we navigate challenging times that grow us (whether or not we consciously consented to the growth) and release NT expectations of who and how we are supposed to be, we actually have the potential to become even better, more effective therapists. Sometimes, our own tenderheartedness softens us to be even more human, more empathetic, more patient, more humble, and less a supposed expert on life. We may find that we can relate even more to the challenges and struggles our clients are navigating. We may find that life is growing us in just the ways we need so we can show up for what our clients are bringing.

In fact, our clients' growth journeys may even start to reflect some aspects of our own growth journeys. I've been repeatedly awed and amazed at how each time I take another big step in my own growth journey, not long after, my clients seem to take the next big step in theirs. It's as if my letting go, releasing, or integrating of pain, trauma, fear, grief, the ick of being human, or even expanding my capacity for joy, readies me to be an even more equipped vessel to support them on their journey. The reverse also happens; clients may show up who reflect back to me where my continued growth is needed.

I'm so struck by the magic of it all. I'm struck by how the Sacred weaves its way into this work, even without us trying. As I open to and keep saying "yes" (however hesitant that "yes" may be at times) to the wonder, mystery, and magic of my soul's journey, something happens in the energetic field that I orbit within that seems to inspire others. It is unexplainable through the cognitive pathways of western psychology. To me, this is the role of the Sacred in action. This is the unfolding embodiment of the interconnectedness of all beings, that the people we are here to serve, show up for, and hold space for are in our lives at just the right time for mutual learning and growth.

As I finish writing that, I'm left feeling beautifully connected to my essence and to wonder. I discovered through my own therapeutic growth work a few months back that my essence has the visual expression of rainbow sparkles. I feel such sweetness as I see, sense, and feel rainbow sparkles sparkling all throughout my insides. While the earlier chapters were so necessary for the wholeness of this book and this work, I'm noticing that this chapter has been a lot more fun to write! This is the perfect segue into the last and final chapter of this book: Joy! Almost there!

But first, one more thing, hehe! I want to circle back to the importance of differentiation that we discussed in Chapter 5 on boundaries as a form of differentiation. This sacred element is another reason why it is so important that we remain differentiated from our clients. As much as we may resonate with their journey, it's essential that we don't project our learning onto theirs or think we have it all figured out for them! We get to keep honoring our similarities and differences and make ample space for their own pacing, exploration, and unfolding.

- As we prepare to transition out of this chapter, I feel curious. How does all this land for you?

Whether you are ND or NT, I think we can all relate to the ways that being a therapist can feel really challenging at times.

- Does it help to consider that we get to lower demands for ourselves, too?
- Or that our work may actually be a grounding force, a familiar structure that can help us through, while simultaneously leaning into being a bit more mediocre than we might otherwise allow? *You may notice that this requires you to keep dismantling your own ableism.*
- What is your reaction to the Sacred weaving of our growth journeys and those of our clients?

May you take some time to reflect on or bask in the ways the Sacred shows up in your life and in your work.

- How do you notice its presence?
- What helps you to access it?

You may not have answers in this moment, and that is totally okay! Even just holding the questions can spark wonder, magic, and access to our deeper wisdom when the time is right. Please tend to yourself however you choose to. When you feel complete enough for now with that, I'll meet you in the next and final chapter.

Recap: Working With Ourselves as it Relates to Transitions, Ritual, and the Sacred

- What transitions before and after the session support you? What have you noticed you need (and are able to access) relating to how much time you have between your sessions and how much time off you ideally need between your workweeks and throughout the year?
- When more time isn't available or accessible, how else might you support yourself through transitions to nourish or replenish yourself?
- How does bringing in the Sacred help you to stay connected with your gifts and to release undue responsibility that you may place on yourself as a therapist?
- It can be really challenging to be a therapist when you are going through a big change or difficult time in your own life. It's totally valid to have less patience for your clients and less capacity overall.
- Sometimes we may also notice that as we grow and evolve, our clients deepen in their growth, too. This seems directly tied to an expression of the Sacred, what is unexplainable through cognition alone.

CHAPTER 10
Pleasure/Neutrality: Joy!

As we enter our last chapter together, I notice that I am both nervous and excited. It's been a fairly difficult year for me, and I worry that writing about joy could somehow seem inauthentic or contrived. Many ND people have earned expert-level badges at suffering and struggle. And for good reason. Entertaining and yielding to joy can feel dangerous, scary, unfamiliar, or threatening. Yet I also know that, however less accessible it's been lately, I have a profound capacity for joy. In this chapter, we will orient to joy as a powerful and important act of resistance to oppression. More than a radical act of social justice, joy is a homecoming, a return to our innate wisdom, brilliance, and wholeness as ND people.

I feel curious to take a moment to check in here. Seeing the title Joy! might evoke an array of feelings or thoughts within.

- I wonder if any of the following is present for you?
  - Surprise perhaps, maybe even confusion, that a book on counseling would end with joy.
  - Anger perhaps, a belief that joy has no place in oppression work, that liberation is about "grit" and "sacrifice."
  - Excitement and curiosity perhaps, an inkling of your own inner wisdom that joy connects us to our essence, not that different from how our rage evokes our aliveness too.

- Fear perhaps, that you have been told how you relate to joy is somehow flawed or not okay, that there is a right way and then your way.
- Wonder perhaps, about what words, perspective, and insight fill the following pages that are readying to greet you.

No matter what is or isn't present for you in this moment, I encourage you to consider that it is just right for you. It is no doubt a reflection of your lived experiences, identities, places of privilege and marginalization, and perhaps your hopes and fears. I honor it all, and I encourage you to be as gentle and compassionate with yourself as you are able. As with all of the preceding chapters, please tend to yourself, your pacing, and your needs as best as you are able. I look forward to having you join me when you are ready.

Before we continue: In order to understand the why of joy as essential to ND-affirming counseling and ways of living, we have to understand why it is so radical; why it is so difficult for some people to access; why there is no one right way to experience joy, pleasure, or rest; and why it is both a privilege and an act of survival within the dominant culture. It's not going to be joyful at first, but I promise, we'll get there.

If it's helpful to have some self-care reminders, here are some ideas:

- Connect with your sphere or shirt to feel your differentiation.
- Welcome in your spiritual support such as your ancestors, helping spirits, plants, animals, or other allies.
- Engage in sensory delights, whether they are objects and/or movement.

- Rest as you need to and honor your own pacing.
- Connect with other loving, trusted humans around this content.

Please care for yourself as you need or want to, and we'll continue when you are ready.

✶ ✶ ✶ ✶

It's heartbreaking to me that capitalism and other systems of oppression make joy and rest so hard to access. For folx with more privilege, especially white privilege and class privilege, joy and rest may be more accessible. The inequity is deeply unjust.

I'm reminded of learning from Heather Clarke, introduced in Chapter 5. She teaches about the intersections of ableism and anti-Black racism and also strikes me as a person who emanates joy. Please care for yourself and engage with your sensory delights as needed as you keep reading. She introduced me to two horrific terms that were coined in the 1850s by a white, racist physician (one we learned about in Chapter 1). The first is *drapetomania*, a so-called mental illness that caused enslaved Black people to flee. The other term is *dysaethesia aethiopica*, a supposed disease or disorder characterized by laziness that only afflicted formerly enslaved people who lived in Black communities. White supremacy, capitalism, and colonization equated being Black with enslavement, labor, production at all costs, and a complete lack of autonomy. A desire for autonomy and rest was criminalized. This is the origin story of ableism as it exists today.

I know we are here to explore joy, and at the moment I notice an impulse to throw something as rage pulsates through me. Both rage and joy are expressions of aliveness, and right now, I feel very alive. I am profoundly aware of the intersections of my privileged and marginalized identities.

I'm going to take a moment to tend to my internal experience and then I will return. Please tend to what is present in you as well, no matter what is or isn't arising.

* * * *

As we return, I'm very aware of the fullness of my human experience. I gave myself permission to engage in big movement. I honored my impulse to go outside and sensed myself expand as far and wide as I could imagine; this historical trauma is way too big for my body to hold. Imagining that the Earth is holding it with me helps it to move through me, rather than get compressed and stuck. I said hello to the trees and honored our connection. I tended to the heartbreak and grief, allowing the energy and emotion to flow. Tending to the Sacred rage and grief is an essential part of dismantling how whiteness lives in me. It is also necessary in order to create space for joy.

Now we are going to shift our attention to present-day advocacy that is rooted in joy, pleasure, and rest.

The Black Liberation Movement teaches about the power of pleasure and rest as forms of resistance. As a white person, I feel sensitive to and aware of what it means to "borrow" from this movement that has faced and continues to face profound oppression and opposition from white supremacy.

adrienne maree brown (she/they) describes herself as a "growing garden of healing ideas." The author of multiple books, including the *New York Times* bestseller *Pleasure Activism*, adrienne is a deeply creative Black leader. In their book, they explore pleasure as an act of resistance that is paramount to Black liberation and queer liberation. Pleasure may be sensory based or sexual, involve an intimate partner or solo practice, and is even more expansive than that brown honors the many thought leaders and activists who came before her, who birthed and grew this movement and created a space for her wisdom and brilliance to be shared.

Tricia Hersey, a Black activist, speaker, educator, performance artist, and author of multiple books, including the *NY Times* bestseller *Rest as Resistance: A Manifesto*, calls herself a Nap Bishop. Her work centers on the powerful and radical notion that rest is a liberatory act, especially for Black, Indigenous, and

Brown people. She curates collective napping experiences as part of her work toward community healing. She encourages people to interrupt grind culture, to stop producing for the capitalist system, and to prioritize rest as a necessary and often inaccessible form of medicine and healing.

I'm also thinking about Pride, an honoring of LGBTQIA2S+ identities. Pride became an international movement after the Stonewall uprising and the activism of Marsha P. Johnson, a Black transwoman, and Sylvia Rivera, a Latinx transwoman, in particular. Queerness and transness had historically been criminalized and policed; it was not safe for queer and transgender people to openly love who they loved or express themselves authentically. Erasure or attempted erasure of queer and trans folx was the norm. Unfortunately, much of this still exists today, particularly for trans folx. Pride exists as we know it today because of Black and Brown women, who are frequently at the forefront of liberation movements.

Pride is a celebration! It is an invitation to live and love out loud, to be bright, expressive, colorful, and authentic. It is a reminder that queer and trans people do exist and have a right to exist. That queer and trans love is beautiful, is equally valid as cis-heteronormative love, and deserves to be protected. As much as Pride is also about advancing rights for queer and trans people, it is about joy, pleasure, and rest. Joy is absolutely fundamental to LGBTQIA2S+ liberation.

As a trans person, as a queer person, and as a multiply-ND person, my cells know this wisdom to be profound truth: joy, pleasure, and rest are essential to reclaiming our wholeness and our sovereignty. In the United States, a colonized, capitalist nation that was built upon the labor and lives of primarily Black folx and Indigenous folx, to disengage from the act of producing and consuming, to prioritize pleasure and joy for the mere sake of the experience, and to connect to wonder is a radical act.

The dominant culture is centered around neurotypicality, white supremacy, able-bodied supremacy, cis-heteronormativity, capitalism, colonization, Christian supremacy, and patriarchy. To exist outside of these identities is to be faced with structural hate, fear, confusion, and pain. To embody joy, to glimpse wonder, to revel in pleasure, and to rest are radical expressions of justice, of aliveness, of self-love.

As I mentioned in Chapter 1, according to the pathology paradigm, "there is no such thing as a joyful Autistic person." I'm putting that in quotes to make sure there is no room to misinterpret those as my words or my perspective. According to the dominant culture, to be Autistic is to only know suffering, struggle, and deficit. In fact, not being in a state of persistent distress is a common reason for not being identified as Autistic. This narrative is similar for KCS/VAST people.

And yet, Autistic and KCS/VAST people's potential for joy is profound. Increased neural connections contribute to heightened sensory sensitivity, attention to detail, creativity, and passion. While many NT people tend to exist on the black-gray-white color spectrum of normalcy, many ND people have access to every shade of every color in the rainbow in their internal world! Their breadth, depth, and the vibrancy of their daily life can be vast. How ironic that Autistic people are so often described as being such black-and-white thinkers!

In a world filled with unwanted sensory stimulation or lacking the right amount and types of desired stimulation, sensory delight as a form of pleasure is a powerful antidote. I am referring to pleasure related to input from visual (sense of sight), tactile (sense of touch), auditory (sense of hearing), olfactory (sense of smell), gustation (sense of taste), proprioception (sense of the body in space), interoception (inner body awareness), and/or vestibular (sense of balance) senses. What is sensory delight to one person may be sensory assault to another, so honoring individuality and uniqueness is essential.

In the field of occupational therapy, the term sensory diet is often used to describe important daily or regularly engaged with sensory input and activities that nourish the sensory and nervous systems. Similar to brushing your teeth or flossing, tending to a sensory diet is thought of as a daily hygiene habit that is an important part of health and wellness. A sensory diet could include: daily skin brushing, dedicated time with a weighted object or self-massage to access proprioception, or a habit of rhythmic movement to stimulate vestibular input, just to name a few ideas.

I appreciate the perspective that specific and desired sensory input are essential for Autistic and KCS/VAST people. I want to expand upon this, though. Just as teeth brushing and flossing can feel like a demand or one more thing on a seemingly never ending to-do list of daily tasks, what if we adjusted the language and lens? Feel free to take a moment to reflect on this, or you can let it percolate in the background while you keep reading.

- What if we showed our clients how tending to their sensory needs and desires can be an honoring of themselves as the god, goddess, or goddex that they innately are?
- What if engaging in sensory delight were viewed as a sacred offering of nectar to the Source that sustains us?

I'm thinking about this as:

- A recognition that our human form is as much of the Earth and the natural world as are trees, plants, and all the nonhuman animals.
- A returning to Indigenous wisdom.
- A reminder that our sensitive bodies are not merely a source of punishment in a NT world, however true that might feel in moments, but also a sacred, bountiful gift.
- A source of profound pleasure that is our own unique gateway to joy.
- What if we held this orientation for and with our clients?

I'd like for us to consider that accessing joy through sensory pleasure is a profound act of ND resistance. Let's consider that finding pleasure in the sensitive ND sensory and nervous system inherently dismantles and deconstructs the diseases of colonization, capitalism, white supremacy, cis-heteronormativity, and neurotypicality. It is not about more doing, but about being who it is natural for us to be. This includes allowing ourselves to curate experiences and environments that engage our senses and evoke delight. Allowing ourselves to be delighted is an expression of the holy, a returning to wholeness, a radiating of our magnificence. Being delighted unites us with our Autistic and/or KCS/VAST culture and lineage, embodies pride, and celebrates our bodies as a source of resilience. Being in delight and pleasure restores right relationship with our ND selves; it is an expression of self-acceptance, self-compassion, and self-love.

- ♦ What if we prioritized sensory pleasure and joy, not just in the counseling space but in our day-to-day living?
- ♦ What if it was as important, as basic, and perhaps even as complex as hydrating and eating can be for some ND people?

As we continue with this chapter, we will explore how we can support clients and ourselves to learn about and access our sensory delight and joy. As sensate beings, this chapter is inherently somatic in nature; like all emotions, joy is expressed in and through the body. Some people may experience joy as:

- o a felt sense or visual image of rainbow sparkles throughout their insides (as I do);
- o a warm, comforting sensation in their belly;
- o an awareness of being totally present in the moment;
- o an absence of discomfort;
- o flapping their arms;

- a big energy that is loud, animated, and takes up a lot of space;
- or happy hands (to name only a few).

No matter what our interoception is like, we can all get acquainted with how joy lives in and through us.

At the same time, I want to remind us that there is no right way to experience or to express joy. All too often, from an ableist lens Autistic and/or KCS/VAST people are told they don't express emotions correctly. Ouch! Some people will experience profound internal joy and it may be unrecognizable to an unknowing stranger. Others will have loud, happy, excited hands. Others will be vocal and big in their energy. Any and all ways of expressing joy (or other emotions) are valid and to be accepted! For many Autistic and/or KCS/VAST clients, letting others witness them in their authentic expression of joy can be deeply vulnerable and a form of unmasking. It is essential that you hold reverence and respect for your client's joy, *not judgment*.

May this chapter provide a gateway to joy, a reminder of our inherent wisdom and life force that is vital to our survival. May our connection to joy, whether newfound or reinvigorated, be like nectar to the ancestors, to nature, to our communities, and to ourselves. While it is easy to connect with and explore intergenerational trauma, may this invitation to joy be a reminder of the intergenerational resilience and wisdom that lives within our cells, too.

As we conclude this section, I invite you to check back in with yourself. Perhaps take a moment to notice how you are doing and what you are noticing. Do you need anything before you continue? Please take your time as you desire to, explore what's present for you, and I'll meet you in the next section when you are ready.

Recap: An Introduction to Joy as a Form of Resistance
- In order to understand why joy is an essential part of this work, we have to acknowledge that ableism originates from anti-Black racism, white supremacy, cis-heteronormativity, capitalism, and colonization and that systemic oppression makes access to joy profoundly complex.
- Joy, like pleasure and rest, is a form of resistance. The Black liberation movement has many teachings on this, including those of adrienne maree brown and Tricia Hersey, along with many others throughout time.
- The LGBTQIA2S+ liberation movement also centers joy as a form of resistance and social justice. Pride began as an uprising and we owe much to Marsha P. Johnson, a Black transwoman, and Sylvia Rivera, a Latinx transwoman.
- Autistic and KCS/VAST people have innately sensitive sensory and nervous systems that, trauma and oppression aside, make sensory pleasure a profound source of joy.
- Rather than another demand or thing to do, accessing sensory pleasure and joy regularly can be explored through the lens of spiritual practice, radical self-love, social justice, reclaiming wholeness, and being essential to daily life.

WORKING WITH CLIENTS

When I think of neurodivergent joy, I think about monotropism and regular connection with passions. Some people like the term special interests or SPINs, and other people find that language offensive, so I'll use the word passion as an attempt to be the most inclusive. If joy is one way to access our aliveness, then devoted time to passions is essential to survival. Passions may be body based, intellectually based, emotionally based, socially based, and/or spiritually based. They are deeply connected to sensory pleasure. While we talked about the value of prioritizing parasympathetic states in Chapter 4, Pleasure/Neutrality: Prioritizing Parasympathetic States, this chapter takes it a step further. Helping our clients to center joy and passions transcends the counseling space and supports an orientation to life that includes their relationship to joy.

In terms of language, I see joy as the overarching catchall word that includes pleasure, passions, creativity, and even rest. Rest does not have to mean sleep, but what supports us to disengage from production for profit and from stimulating the capitalist economy. What evokes joy in a person could be as unique as the individual themself.

While a need for devoted time to exist in a monotropic state centered on something so interesting or creative is universal to the Autistic and KCS/VAST neurotypes, the source of that passion is deeply individualized. Any topic, however broad or specific, can be a passion. For some, it's learning about people, relationships, and self-growth (think therapists and other practitioners, wink wink). For others, it can be topics related to the natural world, Earth-based sciences, gaming, crafting, history, space, the future, art, animals, architecture, food, travel, computers and technology, medicine, spirituality or religion, outdoor adventure, sexuality, gender, culture, pop culture, theater, sports (either playing or watching) or collecting. Really, the list is endless and there's no way for me to capture it all.

In Chapter 1, we explored infodumping or monologuing as a ND love language and a valuable means of rapport building with clients. The topics that our clients love to share about are usually sources of passion. We can help clients create rituals or practices that center investing time and energy into their passion(s) outside of the counseling space (or help them to discover what their passions may be). Clients may need our encouragement to take their passions seriously—*to take themselves seriously*—as they relate to their passions. Unless of course that passion is also a source of generating income and building wealth; then capitalism encourages spending time on said passions. Some passions may require spending money, while others less so. Here is where financial privilege can make accessing one's passion a bit tricky. This is an important part of the conversation.

To help illustrate my point, I'm going to share a story that depicts an experience of an Autistic person taking their passions seriously. This story was shared during an episode of *The Autistic Culture* podcast with Dr. Angela Kingdon and Matt Lowry. While not all of us can feasibly make this happen, I loved hearing this. Matt (he/him) is a white, Autistic mental health professional who specializes in autism evaluations. He was going to have his son for the weekend, the same week that a new *Legend of Zelda* game came out. He was so excited about this game and couldn't wait to get to play it. He also was really invested in being a present father and wanted to be able to center his son's passions during their weekend together. Knowing that he would be distracted thinking about and wanting to play the new game over the weekend, which was in direct contradiction to his values for parenting, he took time off from work at the start of the week to play the game. He prioritized his passion and took himself seriously.

From a capitalist, ableist lens, there could be so many judgments about this choice.

From a ND-affirming, anti-ableist joy is a form of resistance lens, this blew my mind in the most amazing way.

From an intersectional, anti-oppressive lens, I thought about how many people don't have access to the financial and other resources they would need to take days off from work to devote to their passion.

Matt's actions are a pinnacle example of an ideal mental health day for ND folx (except for clients in burnout whose passions may be temporarily inaccessible to them). This leads me to a place of curiosity. I'll offer some prompts that we will then explore throughout the rest of this section. You may wish to engage directly with these now or read them and keep going while they percolate.

- How can we support our clients to begin to take their passions more seriously?
- And then, how can we support them from an executive function standpoint to help turn this idea into action? Work and school could be interchangeable here. This idea isn't just for adults or even just for those people with jobs.

Now let's say we're talking about a daily, weekly, or other regularly scheduled interval devoted to engaging in sacred, uninterrupted time with their passion. Here is a list of questions that can help clients explore this.

> **QUESTIONS TO HELP CLIENTS CREATE A PASSION RITUAL: ADDRESSING LOGISTICS**
>
> - If you work, do you have paid time off, or can you afford to take time off from work? Or to miss school?
> - Are there any caregiving needs (e.g., child care, elder care, pet care) that would be required in order to take time for your passions?
> - What other logistics would be required in order to take time to devote to passions?
> - What responsibilities can wait so that your passions can be prioritized?
> - What responsibilities can't wait or have to come before your passions?
> - Is there a time of day/week/month that works best for your energy level, responsibilities, and other people you may need to coordinate with?

- How much time do you need to feel satisfied, knowing that life isn't always predictable and sometimes unexpected things happen?
- How do you want to mark the beginning and ending of your passion time to account for the transition into and out of the experience? (e.g., put a do not disturb sign on the door if you live with others and take it down when done; set a timer if that adds containment or helps you honor a potential time boundary; put on your headphones to begin and take off your headphones to end; play a beginning and ending song; stimming ritual; the possibilities are endless).
- How often would you like to engage in this ritual? Is that realistic? If not, how can we be creative to help you get your needs met?
- Does this ritual require you to spend money? If so, how much? Do you need support with budgeting for that?
- What obstacles might get in the way of you accessing or prioritizing this ritual? How might you navigate those obstacles? (Together, you can brainstorm a list of potential obstacles and potential work-arounds or solutions.)

Depending on one's neurotype, especially with needs for novelty, passions may change over time. This does not make a person's passions any less valid or important. It may require creative budgeting, but the ritual doesn't necessarily have to be passion specific. And the ritual can evolve and change over time and as the passion shifts.

We can then help our clients to integrate the value of connecting with their passions by connecting it to somatic markers and sensory input. Perhaps the client engages in their passion in session and you explore this together in the moment. Perhaps they imagine engaging in their passion and share what they notice. Or they might do this on their own the next time they are engaging in their passion in their own time. Here are some prompts:

- What do you notice in your present-moment experience when you are engaging with your passion?
- What indicators help you know you are experiencing joy? Some examples include (these may seem familiar from Chapter 4, Pleasure/Neutrality: Prioritizing Parasympathetic States):
    - Body sensation (presence of sensation *or* absence of sensation)
    - Focus/presence
    - Imagery
    - Internal speed or volume
    - Quality of breath
    - Mood
    - Stimming
- What is the sensory experience of engaging with your passion?
- What, if anything, have you noticed is the impact of this time on the rest of your day, week, and so on? (Consider impact on sleep, relationships, energy level, pain levels, focus, emotional state, regulation, overall sense of well-being.)
- How does your passion ritual help connect you with your wholeness?
- Is there anything that would make this experience or ritual *even better*? (Thank you to the somatic sex educators who taught me to think about and ask this question!)

Given that the body can be such a source of discomfort and distress for many ND clients, this passion ritual helps bring awareness to and magnify the body as a source of pleasure.

Here are some examples of how clients can amplify sensory delight while curating a passion ritual:

Example 1

A ritual for someone who loves gaming: playing a favorite game, and the graphics and design are a source of such visual pleasure. The sound or music may be a source of auditory pleasure, especially when set to just the right volume. If it's a multiplayer game, the collaboration and connection may be a source of social and emotional pleasure. All the while, favorite snacks and beverages are easily accessible when desired, and the gaming chair allows for spinning, rocking, and other desired movement to support vestibular input. Comfy clothes are worn and the lighting is set just right.

Example 2

A ritual for someone who loves nature: exploring a trail in the forest, by the ocean, through a garden, or in the neighborhood. Options abound, including having barefoot time on the earth, noticing all the plants, trees, creatures and sounds, having a conversation with the trees to support external processing, or connecting with fairies, plant spirits, or other nature magic. Touching nature objects adds tactile pleasure. Tree hugging, push-ups against a tree, yoga poses, agility movements on the beach or grass, or climbing a tree all add proprioceptive input. Swaying or swinging on a swing adds vestibular input. Noticing how the temperature of the air feels on your body adds interoception.

Example 3

A ritual for someone who loves architecture: browsing through books, magazines, catalogues, or websites looking at structures and taking in sheer visual delight at the artistry or uniqueness. Add to that the intellectual stimulation of gathering new ideas and possibilities. Intellectual stimulation inspires creativity and a desire to draw or paint ideas. There's a preferred utensil or medium, be it pencil, markers, pens, pastels, or watercolors, that provides tactile pleasure. Noise-cancelling headphones create an absence of auditory stimulation, or there's a background of favorite music playing at just the right volume. This all happens while wearing the most comfy of clothes (or their birthday suit), with easy access to a preferred beverage or snack, with just the right amount of light in the space. The chair spins, and in the joy of it all, there may be rocking, too. A weighted blanket on the lap adds proprioceptive input.

In these rituals, the details are considered and taken seriously. There is an effort, but not a demand, to incorporate as much of the sensory experience as one may desire, have the bandwidth for, and have access to. There is tending to the entire system. There is also permission to be less embodied if that is needed. Pleasure is prioritized, and unwanted sensory input gets removed where possible, adding in even more delightful sensory input where possible. There's no such thing as doing this right or wrong. It's about savoring, delighting, and self-validation in a vortex of focused attention on something that is so interesting, novel, and/or inspiring.

Pleasure for the sake of pleasure.

For some, this level of presence and engagement may even evoke a sense of spiritual connection or union with what is greater than ourselves.

In support of digesting and integrating this, I'm going to offer some prompts for self-reflection. Please consider this an invitation to engage however you wish to or not to.

- As clients go about their daily life, how might this orientation toward joy, pleasure, and passion inform their moment-to-moment experience?
- How might this orientation support them to feel less

isolated or less alone and more connected to the vastness that we all exist within?
- Would prioritizing moments each day, where and when possible, to curate or engage in environments that provide desired sensory input and omit unwanted sensory input help them to remember their innate brilliance and wisdom?

As we reach the end of this section, I encourage you to check back in with yourself. Perhaps you choose to notice what's present within you.

- How might you want to make this moment *even better* for yourself?

Lingering and savoring are encouraged if that is what you desire. When you're ready, I look forward to greeting you in the next section, Working With Ourselves.

Recap: Working With Clients as it Relates to Joy!
- Engaging in passions (some like the term special interests, also known as SPINS) is a necessary and important means of accessing aliveness and joy.
- We can help clients create rituals where they engage in monotropic passion time on a regular basis. This may require executive function support.
- We can help them integrate the value of this ritual by exploring its impact on their present-moment state and the rest of the day or week.
- Engaging in passions is deeply sensate in nature and offers an important alternative to the often uncomfortable or distressing experience of existing within a ND human body.

WORKING WITH OURSELVES

As counselors and helping practitioners, we have a very meaningful role. We get to help people come home to themselves, discover and connect with their more authentic selves, and be a safe enough, trusting human who can help mend the damage caused by other humans.

How sacred.

At the same time, our role doesn't typically offer much instant gratification. As social justice counselors and advocates, we are plenty aware of the broken and oppressive systems and structures within which we and our clients exist. For those with justice sensitivity, it can get even harder. Meaning alone often isn't enough to prevent burnout.

This is why I believe, in addition to executive function support and being intentional about our relationship with the Sacred or what is bigger than us, we can derive much-needed joy from permission to have moments of *taking a break from it all*.

As much as we care about our clients, about doing good in the world, and about leaving this world better than we found it, we are also human beings who have our own thresholds, capacities, limitations, and needs. Sometimes that need, however effortful it may feel in the moment, is to take a break from it all and prioritize our own joy and pleasure. Maybe you agree that joy is important, but knowing that other people are suffering while you take a break pains you. Maybe your marginalized identities don't allow much space to take a break. I feel you. I see you.

For those therapists who are ND, you may feel deeply seen by the Working With Clients section and that may be how you choose to integrate more intentional joy into your life. You may know that you have passions that mean a lot to you, and maybe you now feel that extra permission to prioritize them more than you previously thought you could or was acceptable. Or maybe you already were prioritizing them and you feel affirmed in your choices and actions!

For those who are NT, especially those with multiple privileged identities, you may feel surprised by the notion of joy being a radical act. Maybe joy is easy for you to access. Or maybe it isn't, but for reasons not having to do with your sociocultural identities.

For therapists with one or more marginalized identities who regularly revel in your joy and know it is medicine, both for you and for the people you share your gifts with, let's celebrate!

We live in a world where suffering abounds. We know this, witness this, sense this, and feel this on the regular. This leads me to some inquiry. Please take a moment to read through these inquiries, even if you choose not to engage with them right now.

- What if honoring and validating this suffering is only part of the process?
- What if we also get to prioritize parasympathetic states to support resilience?

We can do this by consciously and intentionally inviting joy, pleasure, creativity, and rest into our lives.

- In fact, what if we were as intentional about our joy, pleasure, creativity, and rest as we are about holding space for those who are suffering?
- What might it be like to engage in joy, pleasure, creativity, and/or rest *just for the sake of it?*

For some people, these will be easy to answer. For others, it may evoke a sense of a blank stare, an "I don't know," maybe even a feeling of confusion, overwhelm, annoyance, or frustration. I want to be mindful that accessing joy can exist anywhere on the spectrum of simple, easeful, and/or accessible to downright hard, daunting, grief inducing, and/or inaccessible. If you identify with it feeling hard, here's an idea (this might be supportive even if joy is fairly accessible to you).

- Think about a moment or moments that make you smile or laugh (whether internally or externally), when you feel present, or when you feel neutral, alive, radiant, hopeful, creative, or inspired. Maybe you even get happy hands to show for it!

As you reflect on this moment(s), notice your present-moment experience.

- Are there any body sensations that arise?
- Perhaps an absence of body sensation?
- Do you notice any images or colors that show up?
- What happens to your focus, temperature, speed, volume, breath, or movement?

I'm offering lots of possible prompts to support your individuality as it relates to interoception and accessibility.

Notice what arises. Whatever shows up could be considered your *joy anchor* or joy indicator. This anchor can act as an indicator that joy, as you experience or relate to it, is present. When you reflect on that anchor, it may evoke a sense of joy and parasympathetic states. You can use your anchor to help identify what evokes that sense, image, or experience and what doesn't.

I'll offer an example to make it more tangible. When I'm in touch with my joy, which feels parallel to how I experience my sense of essence, I notice rainbow sparkles. Sometimes they radiate throughout my whole body; other times they are specific to an area of my insides. When I want to access joy, I can visualize my rainbow sparkles. Sometimes that sparks an inspired idea or puts me in touch with a desire that is connected to feeling, expressing, and/or amplifying my joy. Other times, when I engage in a particular something, I may notice that rainbow sparkles appear inside of me. The somatic marker of joy can help to make joy more accessible or noticeable when it arises.

Let's play with this together.

Using your joy anchor (if that was helpful for you), I invite you to explore your joy with me. You could create a mental list, a written or typed list, a drawing, a movement, a song, anything at all. I'll share some ideas to get us thinking. As you read through this list, you can track your joy anchor and notice if it shows up at all.

If these feel true for you, great, keep adding to it. If these don't feel true for you, that's okay, too; please create your own list!

- Enjoying flowers
- Being in nature
- Taking naps
- Playing with pets
- Dancing
- Gardening
- Trying a new food or restaurant
- Having sex (self-sex or sex with others)
- Playing video games
- Binge watching a favorite show
- Making art
- Evoking gender euphoria
- Watching cute cat videos
- Sitting in the dark with noise-cancelling headphones on
- Being spontaneous
- Enjoying happy hour
- Taking a bath
- Scrolling social media
- Watching the sunrise or sunset
- Having alone time
- Sharing quality time with loved ones

- Solving crossword puzzles
- Reading a book and getting all cozy
- Having two desserts
- Saying "no" to unwanted demands and prioritizing autonomy
- And from the previous section, getting enthralled in your passion(s)

Take as much or as little time here as you choose. There's no right or wrong way to do any of this. Your list may be a combination of seemingly simple moments and bigger experiences. I purposely chose ideas that are less consumer driven. So much of the pop culture self-care movement is about spending a lot of time on expensive and elaborate things. That is not accessible to many people and also isn't anti-capitalist. There is nothing wrong with spending money on self-care when you have it, but I want to illustrate how much more broad and accessible self-care actually can be.

When you feel ready, I have some follow-up curiosities and prompts. Whether from the list above or your own list that you created:

- How does it feel to make this list?
  - Do you notice a shift in internal state or thoughts?
- How often do you currently engage with or experience the things on your list?
  - Do you feel satisfied with how often you engage, or would you like the frequency to change?
- What obstacles might be in the way of increasing the frequency if that's your desire?
  - What might help you navigate or overcome the obstacles you thought of?
- How might your life and your work be different if prioritizing pleasure were as important as helping others?

Of all the chapters and all the sections I've written, I'm appreciating how being in this inquiry with you is evoking a feeling of such aliveness within me. My rainbow sparkles are very present. I'm reminded of a magical hike I went on in the Colorado mountains several years ago. I was drawn to a particular tree near the end of the hike, and I stopped to share a hug. The tree shared a message with me: *your purpose is pleasure.*

In some ways, that message was hard to receive, but it was also very poignant for me. By that point in time, I was a couple years into learning how to orient toward pleasure. Suffering had been such a baseline, such a primary orientation for so much of my life. It was so novel and enlivening to discover that pleasure could be as much a catapult for growth as my suffering had been.

On the tough days and in the midst of collective suffering, it's easy to forget that tree wisdom. Pleasure is an ongoing practice and a dedication, and it can take effort to remember. I suspect it is a part of our birthright, though, given that we were born with both a sympathetic *and* parasympathetic nervous system. Indigenous wisdom seems to know this. It is so rooted in gratitude and reciprocity, and both gratitude and reciprocity strike me as direct access points to joy.

As we reach the end of this journey together, I am overflowing with gratitude for the opportunity to share my passion with you. Thank you so deeply for receiving me, these words, and all these ideas. May you feel even more connected to your innate brilliance and wisdom, in touch with your creativity and curiosity, and supported in the areas of your continued growth.

Inspired by the wisdom of Robin Wall Kimmerer, a Citizen Potawatomi woman, scientist, keeper of Indigenous wisdom, educator, and author of *Braiding Sweetgrass: Indigenous Wisdom, Scientific Knowledge, and the Teaching of Plants*, may this book be a seed that sprouts in abundance for many generations to come. May neurodiversity be such common and integrated knowledge for our future ancestors that there is no such thing as coming out.

May there be ample spaciousness for everyone to exist as they are, with their needs, wants, offerings, strengths, challenges, and uniqueness cared for. May everyone be generously supported by a loving and accepting community. And may everyone have access to their wholeness, innate wisdom, creativity, and capacity for thriving.

Recap: Accessing Our Joy as Counselors

- In addition to applying the previous section as it feels appropriate, we can support our joy by having permission for moments to *take a break from it all*.
- Our work is deeply meaningful and steeped in social justice. We can prioritize pleasure, joy, and rest in support of our resilience and our wholeness.
- Using your joy anchor if that's helpful, create a list of what brings you joy, pleasure, creativity, and/or rest. However seemingly trivial, simple, or elaborate, this is just about experiencing pleasure, joy, creativity, and/or rest for the sake of it.
- Explore how present joy is or isn't in your life right now, what you may want to change, how you might change it, and what obstacles you may need to overcome.
- Thank you so much for going on this journey with me!

APPENDIX

ND-AFFIRMING, ANTI-OPPRESSIVE GROUP AGREEMENTS

1. **Honoring autonomy:** I don't have to do anything I don't want to do.
2. **Permission:** I care for myself as, how, and when I need/want to (even when that looks, feels, or sounds different from other cohort members).
3. **Boundaries as differentiation:** I recognize that I come to this group with my own unique brilliance, challenges, history, identities, and perspective. I am both similar to and different from my fellow cohort members. I belong here, I am plenty as I am, and I am a valued member of this community.
4. **Curiosity:** I have a lot of wisdom already, and there is always more to learn. I will do my best to stay open-hearted and gentle with myself and others in this learning process. It may not always be comfortable (stims and sensory delights encouraged)! I don't have to have it all figured out, I am still becoming...
5. **Brave space:** Being human is a big feat! I will tend to my vulnerability and gauge what level of risk I am up for in any given moment. Some examples of risk: leaning into self-permission, speaking when I might typically be quiet, slowing down when I might typically go fast (or vice versa), letting myself be cared for by the group, trying out more authentic-to-me ways of relating

or engaging, saying "no" when I might typically force myself to say "yes," and so on.

6. **Mutual respect:** I recognize that each of us is entering into this space with our own sociocultural locations/identities, some marginalized, some privileged. I will do my best to remain openhearted and open-minded, knowing that my perspective and my lived experience may be very different from others in the group.

7. **Repair:** Whenever two or more humans come together, rupture is a possibility. Rejection sensitivity can make this step the hardest part of being in a group. It is likely that as a group member, I might say or do something that has a negative impact on another. I will do my best to stay connected with my and others' humanity and be accountable for my impact. I will practice not shaming myself or others. If I'm on the receiving end of an "ouch," I can say or type in the chat, "ouch"; this will express that a rupture has happened and that there is a need for repair. *I can make a mistake and still be accepted and loved.*

8. **Expect nonclosure*:** The work of ND-affirming, anti-oppression counseling and living is a lifelong journey. And we have a *(insert duration of group, e.g., 1 hour)* container per session. There may be times when we feel unfinished. I will tend to myself and my process, and advocate for my needs as I'm able.

9. **Confidentiality:** In support of this being a safer and brave space, I will *not* share anyone's personal information or content with anyone outside of the group. I will *not* share the session recording with anyone. I can freely share my own process or impact with people outside of this cohort.

10. **Accessing accommodations:** I will notice what support I may be needing or wanting, and as I'm able, I will advocate for and access that support.

11. **Staying engaged*:** I will be present, knowing that my

sense of being present may be unique. If or when I notice I'm not present, I will reengage as I'm able. Staying engaged could mean that I need to take a break from the group experience in order to stay connected to myself.

*These terms come from the work of Glenn Singleton, Black thought leader and strategist, author of *Courageous Conversations About Race: A Field Guide for Achieving Equity in Schools and Beyond*. They were then taught to me through Dr. Carla Sherrell, one of my mentors, a Black, same gender loving scholar, social justice leader, counselor educator, clergy candidate, and my graduate school professor. This list was inspired by her teachings about dismantling power, privilege, and oppression, and then expanded upon with my ND-affirming lens.

Also a note on language: I used this for a cohort-based learning lab with fellow therapists. You will notice I reference the word "cohort" or "cohort member." The wording can be updated to reflect the specific group involved. If you use these agreements, please include a credit line that attributes them to Glenn Singleton, Dr. Carla Sherrell, and Nyck Walsh, and if you're discussing them, please acknowledge us.

FOR CONTINUED LEARNING

A by no means exhaustive list, but hopefully a helpful start!

Books and Articles
- *Unmasking Autism: The New Faces of Neurodiversity* by Devon Price
- *Toward a Neuroqueer Future: An Interview with Nick Walker* by Nick Walker
- *Neuroqueer Heresies: Notes on the Neurodiversity Paradigm, Autistic Empowerment, and Postnormal Possibilities* by Nick Walker
- *All the Weight of Our Dreams: On Living Racialized Autism*

edited by Lydia X. Z. Brown, E. Ashkenazy and Morénike Giwa Onaiwu
- *Autistic and Black: Our Experiences of Growth, Progress, and Empowerment* by Kala Allen Omeiza
- *A Day with No Words* by Tiffany Hammond
- *Neurotribes: The Legacy of Autism and How to Think Smarter for People Who Think Differently* by Steve Silberman
- *Divergent Mind: Thriving in a World That Wasn't Designed for You* by Jenara Nerenberg
- *Spectrum Women: Walking to the Beat of Autism* edited by Barb Cook and Dr. Michelle Garnett
- *The Autistic Brain* by Temple Grandin
- *A Different Sort of Normal* by Abigail Balfe (geared to Autistic girls, but I have heard it's wonderful for adults and people of all genders, too)
- *Sincerely, Your Autistic Child: What People on the Autism Spectrum Wish Their Parents Knew About Growing Up, Acceptance, and Identity* by Autistic Women and Nonbinary Network
- *Supporting Autistic Transgender Youth and Adults* by Finn Gratton
- *Unmasked: The Ultimate Guide to ADHD, Autism, and Neurodivergence* by Ellie Middleton
- *Autistic Masking: Understanding Identity Management and the Role of Stigma* by Amy Pearson and Kieran Rose
- *How to ADHD: An Insider's Guide to Working with Your Brain, Not Against It* by Jessica McCabe
- *The Rainbow Brain* by Sandhya Menon (Neurodiversity-affirming picture book)

Websites
- autastic.com—for late-identified, racialized Autistic adults, community connection and resources
- aspergerexperts.com—founded by two Autistic adults

who provide advocacy, education, resources (outdated name, but quality work)
- embrace-autism.org—affirming resource that has some really good self-assessments for autism, such as CAT-Q for camouflaged/masked adults and the RAADS, also for KCS/VAST
- aucademy.co.uk—lots of educational info about autism
- additudemag.com—resource on KCS/VAST. I have mixed feelings on its neurodivergent-affirming stance, but there's enough value here and good content to make it worthwhile
- neuroclastic.com—Autistic people writing about all things autism
- aane.org, lots of resources including social and support groups for people of all ages
- awnnetwork.org—Autistic Women and Non-binary Network
- autismlevelup.com—lots of great resources for helping kids to understand themselves, very affirming, great tools for schools, too
- divergentminds.org—Autistic-run organization that embraces intersectionality

Social Media

Many of these on Instagram (IG) and Facebook (FB) may also be on other platforms.

- Fidgets and Fries (IG, FB); author of NYT Bestselling children's book *A Day With No Words*
- Black Girl, Lost Keys (KCS/VAST focus, has a podcast, FB, and more)
- autisticamente_marcela (FB, IG,)
- Supernova Momma (Natasha Nelson) (IG, FB)
- Autism in Black (FB, IG); has annual conference called Autism in Black and also a podcast

- AutisHim Black Fathers and Autism (FB, YouTube, all socials, have a podcast)
- Nigh.functioing.Autism (FB, IG)
- Parenting Decolonized (FB, IG)
- @jtknoxroxs Jen White Johnson (IG)
- NeuroWild (IG, FB) incredible art that makes complex ideas really digestible
- The Autisticats (IG)
- How to ADHD by Jessica McCabe (YouTube, also other social media)
- The Neurodivergent Rebel (IG, FB)
- Kristy Forbes (FB), _kristyforbes Autism and ND specialist (IG)
- The Autistic Advocate-Kieran Rose (FB, IG)
- At Peace Parents (FB, IG) about raising PDA kids
- Trauma Geek: Trauma and Neurodiversity Education (FB, IG)
- Therapists Supporting Neurodiversity (FB group for therapists)

Podcasts

Because of how I take in information and my auditory processing, I rarely listen to podcasts; because I want to personally vouch for what I recommend, this list is quite small.

- *The Telepathy Tapes*
- *Neurodivergent Narratives Podcast*
- *The Autism in Black Podcast*
- *The Autistic Culture Podcast*
- *Divergent Conversations*
- *The Neurodiversity Podcast*

EPILOGUE

Tears are starting to flow as I write this. As I've said many times throughout this text, I love my career so much and am deeply passionate about the work that I do. And in full disclosure, my role as a therapist has never been harder. I've often been reminded of what being a therapist was like when the pandemic began. So frequently, I thought to myself and also said to clients, "I didn't learn how to be a therapist in a pandemic!" It was wild to be navigating such a similar reality as my clients, knowing that I didn't have any more "answers" than they did. None of us had lived through a pandemic before!

The same is so bizarrely true in 2025. For me and my clients, living in what many, including myself, see as the rise of a dictatorship is a new experience. I recognize that this is not true for many people throughout the world. Yet again, I don't have any more so-called "answers" than my clients do. The best I can do is to keep showing up, lean into realness, validate their experience, feel our solidarity, hold the paradoxes, tend to collective grief and Sacred rage, zoom out to feel the bigger Ancestral and Earth-based supports available to us, and acknowledge the ways our continued growth and unlearning of oppressive systems is in service to collective healing. Outside of the therapy space, I engage in my own practices.

These days, my practices include continued trauma and growth work, staying connected to the collective, providing mutual aid and donating money in support of collective liberation, advocacy work, rest, grief ritual, and Earth-based practice. I'm deeply grateful to have recently and serendipitously discovered the work of Doctora (Dra.) Rocío Rosales Meza (she/her), a

Xicana Medicine Woman, Seer, and counseling psychology PhD. Her teachings are helping me to better meet the present moment. As a student of the decolonial movement with her as my teacher, I continue to unlearn my white colonized mind.

Through Dra. Rocío's teachings, I learned that I have precolonial healed ancestors (ancestors who lived before the times of colonization and are in a state of healed wholeness), and I am growing relationship with them. They have helped me to access a love I never knew existed for me before. I am also deepening into right relationship with Mother Earth. As a trans person who likes to disrupt binary language, I previously used a more gender neutral term for our precious Earth, but recently I discovered that leaning into Mother Earth is profoundly healing for my mother wounds. I've been enthusiastically recommending Dra. Rocío's work to my clients.

In my white body and as a U.S. citizen with English as my first language, I have built-in privilege. My heart regularly breaks for Latinx communities and immigrants. My heart also regularly breaks for Palestinian folx, Black folx, Indigenous folx, Muslim folx, trans folx, Autistic folx, VAST folx, and disabled folx. Grief ritual is a big part of my life these days.

As a trans person, I often live in fear. Even in a so-called "sanctuary" state, I have developed a deep mistrust of humans and have to effort to keep my heart soft. As an Autistic and VAST person, I feel grateful for the privilege I have to mask and use spoken language, and my heart breaks for all those in our community whose access to care, food, health insurance, housing, and basic human needs are currently being or about to be stripped away.

Being human has always felt like a big feat for me, and lately I frequently hear myself think, feel, and say "existing just feels like too much these days." And that sentiment comes from someone who isn't in direct, present-moment danger. I don't know how our fellow humans are doing it.

I have other moments when I can deeply sense, on a cellular or soul level, that my whole life has been preparing me for this moment. There's a knowingness in me that I am here, at this time, for a reason.

It's become pretty common for clients and me to talk about our mortality these days: to address the paradox of trying to live in the present, engage in growth and unlearning, and continue to dream, while at the same time, feeling like there may not be a future for us to exist in. Being a therapist in 2025 means not shying away from these conversations. In fact, sometimes I actually prefer them, because of their realness. Pretending that the world isn't collapsing actually takes a lot more effort for me. And, I'm so grateful for my custom sphere and shirt; leaning into parasympathetic states; permission to have needs and get them met when, where, and as I can; and my relationship to ritual, the Sacred, and joy as resistance.

My tears haven't stopped flowing since beginning to write this epilogue. It feels like my raw, real, transparent self is an offering to you—a final sharing of my heart before we go our separate ways.

As time passes, more and more people will lose access to health insurance. Less people will be able to afford the cost of therapy. Less people will access Autism evaluations due to the danger of having a medical diagnosis on file, unless it is absolutely necessary for the purpose of accessing life-saving services. If you are already feeling the brunt of that and worry about how you will afford to make ends meet, that is so real. I can't predict how the future will unfold, and there is a tremendous amount of real-life evidence that points to continued—and even worsening—suffering before things get better.

It feels profoundly brave to write this. I am well aware of the risk I'm taking. I know my white body offers me some protection, and for the last many months, my trans, queer, Autistic, VAST, pro-Palestine self has prayed that I live long enough to witness the release of this book out into the world, and that I get to experience its impact. I know that is not a guarantee.

I cannot thank you enough for taking this journey of

Neurodivergent Somatics in Therapy with me. It gives me strength and courage to know that there are so many others invested in this work too. I saw a meme a few months ago of a predator fish eating a school of smaller fish. Next to it was an image of the same predator fish, only this time there was a GIANT school of smaller fish surrounding the predator, so giant that the predator became the prey.

Inspired by the teachings of Dra. Rocío, I've been engaging in a daily morning ritual with Mother Earth. I greet all of her creations, offer gratitude, give thanks for the gift of waking up to a new day, sing to her, and offer a prayer. It seems futile to pray for evil to disappear, so instead my prayer is inspired by the fish meme:

May enough of us rooted in love and unlearning wake up and do our part so that the evil in this world no longer has power.

With love and gratitude, and in solidarity,
Nyck

REFERENCES

Botha, M., Chapman, R., Giwa Onaiwu, M., Kapp, S. K., Stannard Ashley, A., & Walker, N. (2024). The neurodiversity concept was developed collectively: An overdue correction on the origins of neurodiversity theory. *Autism, 28*(6), 1591–1594. https://doi.org/10.1177/13623613241237871

Brom, D., Stokar, Y., Lawi, C., Nuriel-Porat, V., Ziv, Y., Lerner, K., & Ross, G. (2017), Somatic experiencing for posttraumatic stress disorder: A randomized controlled outcome study. *Traumatic Stress, 30*, 304–312. https://doi.org/10.1002/jts.22189

brown, a. m. (2019). *Pleasure activism: The politics of feeling good*. AK Press.

Caldwell, C., & Leighton, L. B. (2018). *Oppression and the body: Roots, resistance, and resolutions*. North Atlantic Books.

Xie, C., Xiang, S., Shen, C., Peng, X., Kang, J., Li, Y., Cheng, W., He, S., Bobou, M., Broulidakis, M. J., van Noort, B. M., Zhang, Z., Robinson, L., Vaidya, N., Winterer, J., Zhang, Y., King, S., Banaschewski, T., Barker, G. J., . . . & ZIB Consortium. (2023). A shared neural basis underlying psychiatric comorbidity. *Natural Medicine, 29*(5), 1232–1242. https://doi.org/10.1038/s41591-023-02317-4

Eames, C., & O'Connor, D. (2022). The role of repetitive thinking and spirituality in the development of posttraumatic growth and symptoms of posttraumatic stress disorder. *PLoS ONE, 17*(8), Article e0272036. https://doi.org/10.1371/journal.pone.0272036

Guy, L., Souders, M., Bradstreet, L., DeLussey, C., & Herrington, J. D. (2014). Brief report: Emotion regulation and respiratory sinus arrhythmia in autism spectrum disorder. *Autism & Developmental Disorders, 44*, 2614–2620. https://doi.org/10.1007/s10803-014-2124-8

Hallowell, E. M., & Ratey, J. J. (2022). *ADHD 2.0: New science and essential strategies for thriving with distraction—from childhood through adulthood*. Random House Publishing Group.

Hersey, T. (2022). *Rest is resistance: A manifesto*. Little, Brown Spark.

Himmerich, S. J., & Orcutt, H. K. (2021). Examining a brief

self-compassion intervention for emotion regulation in individuals with exposure to trauma. *Psychological Trauma: Theory, Research, Practice, & Policy, 13*(8), 907–910. https://doi.org/10.1037/tra0001110

Jones, R., Quigney, C., & Huws, J. (2003) First-hand accounts of sensory perceptual experiences in autism: A qualitative analysis, *Journal of Intellectual & Developmental Disability, 28*(2), 112–121, https://doi.org/10.1080/1366825031000147058

Leedham, A., Thompson, A., Smith, R., & Freeth, M. (2020). "I was exhausted trying to figure it out": The experiences of females receiving an autism diagnosis in middle to late adulthood. *Autism 24* (1), 135–146. https://doi.org/10.1177/1362361319853442

Lohrasbe, R. S,. & Ogden, P. (2017). Somatic resources: Sensorimotor psychotherapy approach to stabilizing arousal in child and family treatment. *Australian & New Zealand Journal of Family Therapy, 38*, 573–581. https://doi.org/10.1002/anzf.1270

McCabe, J. (2024). *How to ADHD: An insider's guide to working with your brain, not against it.* Rodale Books.

Menakem, R. (2017). *My grandmother's hands: Racialized trauma and the pathway to mending our hearts and bodies.* Central Recovery Press.

Milton, D. (2012). On the ontological status of autism: The "double empathy problem." *Disability and Society, 27* (6), 883–887.

Mullen, J. (2023). *Decolonizing therapy: Oppression, historical trauma, and politicizing your practice.* Norton Professional Books.

Payne, P., & Crane-Godreau, M. (2013). Meditative movement for depression and anxiety. *Frontiers in Psychiatry, 4.*

Payne, P., Levine, P., & Crane-Godreau, M. (2015). Somatic experiencing: Using interoception and proprioception as core elements of trauma therapy. *Frontiers in Psychology, 6.* https://doi.org/10.3389/fpsyg.2015.00093

Payne, P., & Crane-Godreau, M. (2015). The preparatory set: A novel approach to understanding stress, trauma, and the bodymind therapies. *Frontiers in Human Neuroscience, 9.* https://doi.org/10.3389/fnhum.2015.00178

Pearson, A., & Rose, K. (2021). A conceptual analysis of autistic masking: Understanding the narrative of stigma and the illusion of choice. *Autism in Adulthood, 3* (1), 52–60.

Pearson, A., & Rose, K. (2023). *Autistic masking: Understanding identity management and the role of stigma.* Pavilion Publishing.

Piepzna-Samarasinha, L. L. (2018). *Care work: Dreaming disability justice*. Arsenal Pulp Press.

Poole, D., Gowen, E., Warren, P. A., & Poliakoff, E. (2018). Visual-tactile selective attention in autism spectrum condition: An increased influence of visual distractors. *Experimental Psychology: General, 147*(9), 1309–1324. https://doi.org/10.1037/xge0000425

Price, D. (2022). *Unmasking autism: Discovering the new faces of neurodiversity*. Harmony Books.

Price, M. (2015). The bodymind problem and the possibilities of pain. *Hypatia, 30*(1), 268–284. http://www.jstor.org/stable/24542071

Rose, K. (2022). *An introduction to monotropism* [Video]. YouTube. https://www.youtube.com/watch?v=qUFDAevkd3E

Rumball, F., Happe, F., Grey, N. (2020). Experience of trauma and PTSD symptoms in autistic adults: Risk of PTSD development following DSM-5 and non-DSM-5 traumatic life events. *Autism Research, 13*(2), 2122–2132.

Sherrell, C. (2018). The oppression of Black bodies: The demand to simulate white bodies and white embodiment. In C. Caldwell & L. B. Leighton (Eds), *Oppression and the body: Roots, resistance, and resolutions* (pp. 141–155). North Atlantic Books.

Silberman, S. (2015). *Neurotribes: The legacy of autism and how to think smarter about people who think differently*. Allen & Unwin.

Singleton, G. E. (2021). *Courageous conversations about race: A field guide for achieving equity in schools and beyond* (3rd ed.). Corwin Press.

SMIL Autism Resources. (2022, April 20). *Problems that lead to poor outcomes for autistic people-with foundations for divergent minds* [Video]. YouTube. www.youtube.com/watch?v=BzcJhmdh4vo

Straiton, D., & Sridhar, A. (2022). Short report: Call to action for autism clinicians in response to anti-Black racism. *Autism, 26*(4), 988–994. https://doi.org/10.1177/13623613211043643

van der Kolk, B. A. (2002). Beyond the talking cure: Somatic experience and subcortical imprints in the treatment of trauma. In F. Shapiro (Ed.), *EMDR as an integrative psychotherapy approach: Experts of diverse orientations explore the paradigm prism* (pp. 57–83). American Psychological Association. https://doi.org/10.1037/10512-003

Walker, N., & Raymaker, D. M. (2021). Toward a neuroqueer future: An interview with Nick Walker. *Autism Adulthood, 3*(1), 5–10. https://doi.ord/10.1089/aut.2020.29014.njw

Walker, N. (2021). *Neuroqueer heresies: Notes on the neurodiversity paradigm, the autistic experience, and postnormal possibilities.* Autonomous Press.

Wall Kimmerer, R. (2013). *Braiding sweetgrass: Indigenous wisdom, scientific knowledge, and the teachings of plants.* Milkweed Editions.

White, S., Conner, C., Beck, K., & Mazefsky, C. (2021) Clinical update: The implementation of evidence-based emotion regulation treatment for clients with Autism. *Evidence-Based Practice in Child and Adolescent Mental Health, 6*(1),1–10. https://doi.org/10.1080/23794925.2020.1796551

INDEX

In this index, *n* stands for note.

5Rhythms, 105

ableism
  diet culture and, 177
  double empathy problem and, 40–42
  engagement expectations and, 215
  and internalized rules, 76
  language expectations and, 207, 210
  racism and, 103–104
  strategies for dismantling, 57–58, 130–161
  as a threat for ND people, 61
  treatment plans and goals and, 229
  See also normativity, dismantling, in the counseling office
ableist statements, 131–140
accessibility, for attending therapy, 170–172
accessibility, for bathroom use, 171, 198
accommodations and supports
  for accessing therapy, 170–172
  for assorted EF, 163, 180–186
  autonomy as, 184, 214
  for challenges with linear time, 143–144
  engagement styles as, 215
  for extending past therapeutic hours, 206
  for therapists, 186–200
  validation of struggles in accessing, 164–165
  See also sensory input
activities of daily living, 185
  See also eating; hand washing
ADH (attention deficit hyperactivity), 21
  See also KCS/VAST people
ADHD 2.0 (Hallowell & Ratey), 21
administrative tasks, 186–194
  See also appointment reminders; documentation
advocacy, 9, 90–91
  See also accommodations and supports
AFAB. *See* assigned female at birth (AFAB) people
alexithymia, 37, 78
allistic people, 41
  See also *neurotypical entries*
AMAB (assigned male at birth) people, 33
amygdala. *See* threat responses

anti-racism work, 116, 127–128
anxiety scales, 91
appointment reminders, 47
apps, 180, 181
artwork, 88
Asasumasu, K., 8, 9
ASD (Autism Spectrum Disorder), 15
Asmus, K., 63, 83
Asperger, H., 16–17
Asperger's, 16
assigned female at birth (AFAB) people
　ableist statements affecting, 136, 139
　effects of easy influence among, 36–37
　effects of masking in, 106–107, 136
　responses to stress by, 33
assigned male at birth (AMAB) people, 33
asynchronous learning, 180–181
attachment, disorganized, 74n
attention deficit hyperactivity (ADH), 21
　See also KCS/VAST people
attention-seeking, as an ableist statement, 139
attunement. *See* telepathy
Attunement through the Body (Nagatomo), 6n
autigender, 51
autism, *DSM* depiction of, 25
Autism Spectrum Disorder (ASD), 15
Autisticamente Marcela. *See* Gonzalez, M.
The Autistic Brain (Grandin), 33n

The Autistic Culture Podcast (Kingdon & Lowry), 285
Autistic Masking (Rose), 13
Autistic people
　ableist statements and, 132–139
　characteristics of, 31–39, 242
　child custody issues for, 29
　comfort versus discomfort in, 70–71
　coming out as, 251–255
　co-occurring conditions in, 134, 240–241
　culture and communication overview of, 42–44, 45–48
　and EFs during threat responses, 162–163
　engagement styles in, 215
　gender-affirming care denial for, 29
　governmental offenses toward, 29
　highly sensitive neurotype versus, 9
　language preferences among, 13–15, 16
　ND versus, 9
　pacing in, 183
　potential for joy in, 279
　sensitivity and permeability in, 105–106
　task sequence and completion in, 174
　threat response in, 59, 60–61
　transitions and, 237, 238, 256–257
　as whole, 13, 119
　wonder and, 235
autonomy
　as an accommodation or support, 184, 214

Index

anxiety scales and, 91
celebration of, 75–76, 84–85, 123
differentiation of self and, 109, 127–128
oppression's effects on, 102, 104
racism's effects on, 276
transitions and, 238
See also Persistent Demand Avoidance or Persistent Drive for Autonomy (PDA)

baseline resumption, 90–92
bathrooms. *See* gender-neutral bathrooms
Becoming (Obama), 230
bio breaks, 87–88
Black Liberation Movement, 277–278
body doubling, 180
body language, 43, 95, 214
See also non-spoken communication
bodymind, 6–7, 13, 31, 34, 167
See also Client as Self-Expert
The Body Remembers (Rothschild), 6n
body sensation, 79, 88
See also indicator tracking; proprioceptive input
bookkeeping and taxes, 193–194
boundaries
oppression and, 101–105
and reduction of enmeshment, 122–123
as safety, 101
sensitivity and permeability and, 105–109
visualization exercises, 109–117
See also differentiation

Braiding Sweetgrass (Kimmerer), 297
breaks
focus, or lack thereof, during, 172–174
human-free zone break, 88
for physiological needs, 87–88, 195–199
for prioritizing joy, 292
validation of, 90–91, 181
See also pausing; sensory input
breathing, 77, 89, 247
brown, a., 277
Buirski, J., 22

Caldwell, C., 211
cancellation policy, 216–218
capitalism, 148, 187–188, 219, 266, 284–285
See also dominant culture
changes. *See* transitions
Chapman, G., 45
child custody issues, 29
chronic illness, 61, 216, 217, 266
Clarke, H., 103, 276
Client as Self-Expert
about, 57–58
boundaries as form of differentiation, 100–109
boundaries visualization exercises, 109–117
dismantling ableism, 130–161
therapeutic relationship and, 118–129, 142–151
client release, therapist rituals for, 262–264
client rituals
about, 240–242
beginning the session, 245–248
ending the session, 248–250

client rituals (*continued*)
    honoring major life changes, 255–259
    for neurotype coming out, 250–255
    the Sacred, 242–245
clients. *See* Autistic people; "good" clients; KCS/VAST people
clinical practice improvement. *See* therapeutic relationship
coexisting in same space, 46–47
colonization, 148, 266
    See also dominant culture
colors, 80
comfort versus discomfort, 70–71
coming out, as neurotype, 250–255
common sense, appearance of lacking, 138–139
communication, explicit, 181
    See also culture and communication styles
communication differences, 171–172, 183–184, 207–211
    See also culture and communication styles; double empathy problem
compatibility challenges, 172
confidence scales, 91–92
consent, 43, 57, 75–77, 84–85
co-occurring conditions, in ND people, 134, 240–241
co-regulation, 46–47, 68–69, 89
counseling offices, dismantling normativity in, 201–234
    See also accessibility, for attending therapy
counseling relationship, dismantling ableism within, 151–161
    See also therapeutic relationship

countertransference, 96–97, 120–122
Courageous Conversations About Race (Singleton), 249*n*, 301
cubing, 88–89
culture and communication styles
    Autistic people, 42–44, 45–49
    confusion with, 61
    counseling and awareness of, 44–45
    invalidation of struggles, 60
    KCS/VAST people, 44
custom shirt boundary exercises, 113–116
custom sphere boundary exercises, 110–113

Dana, D., 89
dancing/movement, 87
    See also stimming
Davis-Pierre M., 87*n*
A Day With No Words (Hammond), 14
deep pressure, 47–48
defiance, as an ableist statement, 135–136
demands, reduction of, 182–183
diagnosed versus identified/realized/discovered, 19
Diagnostic and Statistical Manual (*DSM*), 11, 20, 25
Dickens, K., 19
diet culture, 176–177
differentiation, 109, 127–129, 271–272
    See also boundaries
discomfort versus comfort, 70–71
disorganized attachment, 74*n*

doctoral level identification, of
    autism, 27–28
documentation, 189–191, 262
    See also intake paperwork;
    treatment plans and goals
dominant culture
    about, 243, 278–279
    communication rules in, 42–43
    facing, pacing, and spacing, 211
    pacing, 69, 183, 205
    pausing, 83
    suicidal ideation, 224
    window of tolerance in, 68
    See also ableism; capitalism;
    neurotypical entries; white
    supremacy
dopamine, 22–23
double empathy problem, 40–42
drapetomania, 11
drinks, 86, 196–197
DSM. *See Diagnostic and Statistical Manual* (DSM)
DSM-V, 16
dysaethesia aethiopica, 276

Earth contact, 86–87
    See also nature, connection to
eating, 196, 261–262
    See also food acquisition,
    preparation, and consumption sequences
EF. *See* executive function (EF)
emails, responding to, 192–193
emotionality, as an ableist statement, 135, 138
emotional regulation, 37
empaths, autism versus, 9–10
energy levels, honoring, 79, 198–199
engagement expectations, 215–216
enmeshment, reduction of, 122–123

executive function (EF)
    about, 36, 162–163
    accommodations and supports for generalized, 163, 180–186
    accommodations and supports for therapists, 186–200
    taking breaks, 172–174
    task sequence and completion, 174–179
    expectations, 44, 181, 182–183
    See also ableism; dominant culture; "good" clients; "good" therapists
explicit communication, 149–150, 181, 214, 215–216
    See also culture and communication styles
eye contact, 26, 33, 215
    See also facing, pacing, and spacing

facing, pacing, and spacing, 207–214
feedback. *See* positive feedback
feedback rituals, 149
fidgeting, 34
    See also stimming
fidgets, 87
Fidgets and Fries. *See* Hammond, T.
financial privilege, 170, 218, 219–221, 266, 285
5Rhythms, 105
The Five Love Languages (Chapman), 45
"The Five Neurodivergent Love Languages," 45–48
focus and attention, 79
    See also monotropism

food acquisition, preparation, and consumption sequences, 174–179
  See also eating
four I's of oppression, 142, 146
functioning labels, 16–18

game playing, 88
gaslighting, 139
gender-affirming care, 29
gender identity, 49–52, 223
gender-neutral bathrooms, 171, 198
genetic effects, 38
gift giving, 48
glimmers, 89
Global Permission
  about, 58
  breaks, 172–174, 181
  cancellation policy, 216–218
  client rituals, 240–259
  communication expectations, 207–211
  EF accommodations and supports, 180–186
  EF challenges, identifying and supporting, 162–169
  EF therapist accommodations and supports, 186–200, 202
  engagement expectations, 215–216
  facing, pacing, and spacing, 207–214
  financial access, 219–221
  intake paperwork, 221–225
  office space set up, 171, 225–228
  the Sacred, 240, 242–245, 255, 267–272
  session lengths, 203–206
  task sequence and completion, 174–179

therapist authenticity, 231–233
therapist rituals, 259–267
therapy access accommodations and supports, 170–172
transitions, 183, 237–240, 256–257
treatment plans and goals, 228–231
Gonzalez, M., 45
"good" clients, 144, 151, 157, 161, 246
"good" therapists, 57, 147–149, 158, 269
grief, 239–240
group agreements, 299–301
"Growth" (India.Arie), 238

Hallowell, E., 21
Hammond, E., 40
Hammond, T., 14, 102, 207–208
hand washing, 185, 241, 262–263
happy hands, 282
  See also stimming
Hersey, T., 277–278
high-functioning/low-functioning, 16–18
highly sensitive neurotype, autism versus, 9
homosexuality, as deviant, 11
hopes and intentions, 230–234
How to ADHD (McCabe), 133, 136
human-free zone break, 88
hydrating, 86, 196–197
hygiene, 263
  See also hand washing

identification, external, 24–28
identification of autism, by self, 26–31
identity-first language, 13–23

imagery, 79–80, 88
imposter syndrome, 27
indicator tracking
  for clients, 64–65, 77–82, 91
  for therapists, 95, 97–98
Indie.Arie, 156, 238
Indigenous wisdom, 280, 297
indirectness, 14, 43
influence, easy target for, 36–37
infodumping, 46, 88, 284
in-person location challenges, 170–171, 225–228
in-person sessions, communication differences during, 171, 210
intake paperwork, 221–225
interconnectedness. *See* the Sacred
interest levels, 21
  See also focus and attention
internalized gaslighter, 139
internalized rules, 76, 145–146, 157, 158–159
  See also ableism; "good" clients; "good" therapists
internal speed, 78
internal volume, 79
interoception. *See* indicator tracking
intersectionality
  and effects on racialized clients, 61, 102–103, 106–107, 135
  and effects on transgender and ND people, 49–52, 61

Janae Elisabeth, 22
Johnson, J., 103
Johnson, M., 278
joy
  feelings or thoughts about, 274–275
  as a form of resistance, 277–279, 283
  inequity of, 276
  manifestations of, 281–282
  as part of therapist self-care, 292–298
  See also passions; pleasure/neutrality
joy anchors, 294–295
justice, expressions of, 278–279
justice sensitivity, 37–38, 105–106, 205

KCS (kinetic cognitive style), 21–23
KCS/VAST people
  ableist statements and, 132–139
  about, 21–23
  characteristics of, 32–33, 34, 35, 242
  comfort versus discomfort in, 70–71
  coming out as, 251–255
  co-occurring conditions in, 134, 240–241
  culture and communication overview of, 44
  engagement styles in, 215
  external identification of, 24
  motivation strategies for, 133
  potential for joy in, 279
  RSD and, 38, 44
  sensitivity and permeability in, 105–106
  task sequence and completion in, 174
  threat responses in, 59–61, 162–163
  transitions and, 237
  as whole, 119
  wonder and, 235

KCS/VAST tax, 175
key, for symbols and tools, xviii
Kimmerer, R., 297
kinespheres, 111
kinesthetic learning
    as an accommodation or support, 181–182
    indicator tracking during, 77–82
    for parasympathetic state prioritization, 62–66
    pausing during, 82–84
    scale creation in, 82
    sensory delight choices/stimming in, 63, 64, 84–90
    See also proprioceptive input
Kingdon, A., 285

language and terminology, xvi–xvii, 13–23, 240
    See also ableist statements; communication differences; culture and communication styles
Lawson, W., 22
laziness, as an ableist statement, 133–134
learning, asynchronous, 180–181
learning difficulties, as an ableist statement, 134
Lesser, M., 22
linear time challenges, 143–144
literal communication. *See* communication, explicit; culture and communication styles
location challenges, 170–171
love languages. *See* "The Five-Neurodivergent Love Languages"

low-functioning/high-functioning, 16–18
Lowry, M., 285

manipulativeness, as unmet need, 134
marginalized groups
    autonomy over identity of, 14
    effects of indirect language on, 14, 43
    feelings of danger in, 61–62, 67
    neurotypes as, 59, 252
    oppression and, 101–103, 106–107
    therapist understanding of, 94, 127–128
    See also racialized clients
masking
    ableist statements and, 140
    and effects in AFAB people, 106–107, 136
    effects of being easily influenced and, 36–37
    and others' denials of autism, 26
    threat response and, 61–62
McCabe, J., 133, 136
medications or supplements, 184
mediocrity, entertaining the idea of, 95, 119, 270
Milton, D., 41
monologuing, 46, 284
monotropism, 22, 173–174, 183, 237
    See also passions
movement. *See* dancing/movement; stimming
Mullan, J., 30
Murray, D., 22

Nagatomo, S., 6*n*
nature, connection to, 87, 263
    See also Earth contact

Index

neurocosmopolitan, 155–156
neurodivergent (ND) people
   autism versus, 9
   comfort versus discomfort in, 70–71
   and disclosure on intake paperwork, 223
   importance of connection with other, 41–42
   sensory sensitivity in, 279, 280
   sexual orientations of, 50
   task sequence and completion in, 174–179
   threat response in, 59–61
   time obstacles for, 143–144, 170, 182, 183
   transitions and, 183, 238, 239
   See also Autistic people; KCS/VAST people
neurodivergent (ND) therapists
   documentation strategies, 189
   enmeshment reduction by, 122
   pendulation and supports for, 152–153
   productivity requirements and, 187–188
   self-disclosure by, 123
Neurodivergent Somatics, 55–58
neurodiverse, defined, 9
neurodiversity paradigm, 7–10, 12, 169
neurological curiosity, 38
Neuroqueer Heresies (Walker), 14
Neurotribes (Silberman), 16
neurotypes
   importance of connection with same, 41–42
   as innate, 19
   and journey to change their narrative, 35–36

   overview, 8, 9–10
   relief of validation of, 26
   transition rituals for coming out in one's, 250–255
   See also specific neurotypes
neurotypical (NT) privilege, 9, 12, 154, 252
neurotypical (NT) therapists, 120, 122, 153–155
neurotypicality, 8, 9, 11, 41
Neurowild. *See* Hammond, E.
Neurowonderful. *See* Schaber, A.
neutrality. *See* Pleasure/Neutrality
Nili, M., xviii
"non-closure," 249, 249*n*
nonspeakers, 242–243
non-spoken communication, 207–211
   See also body language
nonverbal versus nonspeaking, 18–19
normativity, dismantling, in the counseling office, 201–234
   See also ableism

Obama, M., 230
obsessive-compulsive tendencies, 240–241
office space set up, 170–171, 225–228
oppression
   boundaries and, 101–105
   four I's of, 142, 146
   of joy, 276, 283
   of knowledge and wisdom, xv
   marginalized groups and, 101–103, 106–107
   neurodiversity paradigm and, 8
   of nonspeakers, 243

oppression (*continued*)
  perfectionism and, 270
  pervasiveness of, 151
  of the Sacred, 243
  strategies for dismantling, 221
  toward ND people, 29, 35, 59–60
  See also dominant culture
oscillation of attention, 67
  See also pendulation
overstimulation, reduction of, 182

pacing
  about, 69–70
  as an accommodation or support, 183, 205
  consent and, 75, 76
  engagement styles in, 215–216
  See also facing, pacing, and spacing; pausing
parallel play, 46–47
parasympathetic nervous system, prioritization of, 62–66
passion rituals, 286–290
passions, 34–35, 283–286
pathology paradigm, 10–12, 20, 228, 240–241, 280–281
pattern recognition, 38
pausing
  for clients, 82–84, 85
  for therapists, 98
payment for care, 148, 170
  See also financial privilege
PDA (Persistent Demand Avoidance or Persistent Drive for Autonomy), 20
pendulation
  about, 66–67, 68, 90
  for therapists, 95, 98–99, 152–153

perfectionism, 183, 270
permission. *See* consent; Global Permission
perseverance, lack of, as an ableist statement, 137–138
Persistent Demand Avoidance or Persistent Drive for Autonomy (PDA), 20
pets, 87
physiological needs, of therapists, 195–199
Pleasure Activism (brown), 277
Pleasure/Neutrality
  about, 56–57, 277
  baseline resumption and next steps, 90–92
  consent, 75–77, 84–85
  indicator tracking, 64–65, 77–82, 91
  kinesthetic learning of, 62–66
  pausing, 82–85
  psychoeducation, 73–74
  as the Sacred, 290–291
  scale creation, 63–64, 72–73, 82
  sensory delight choices/stimming, 84–90
  sensory input as identity-affirming, 280–281
  somatic psychology concepts in, 66–72
  sympathetic responses and, 59–62, 74, 147
  See also joy; passion rituals; passions
positive feedback, 44, 181
potential, not living up to, as an ableist statement, 136–137
prefrontal cortex, 162–163
Price, M., 6
Pride, 278

private practice benefits, 189, 217, 219, 264–265
private practice downfalls, 187, 266
privilege
    access and, 166–167, 257, 266
    author's journey in, xiv, 104, 189, 208, 306
    joy and rest and, 276
    power to change and, 155
    therapeutic relationship and, 268
    See also financial privilege; neurotypical (NT) privilege
productivity requirements, 187–188
proprioceptive input, 47–48, 86
psychoeducation, 73–74

racial identity, 223
racialized clients
    effects of intersectionality for, 61, 102–103, 106–107, 135
    reparations for, 219–220
    as terminology choice, xvi
    therapist need for differentiation with, 127
    white therapist ignorance of issues of, 76, 103–104, 154–155
racism
    ableism and, 103–104
    and allowed responses to stress, 33
    autonomy and, 276
    drapetomania and, 11
    and saying "no," 76
    unidentified Autistic peers and, 25
    See also dominant culture

rage. *See* Sacred rage
Ratey, J., 21
regulation. *See* co-regulation; self-regulation; temperature regulation
rejection sensitivity dysphoria (RSD), 38, 44
reminders, 47
resourcing, 66, 85–86, 95–96
    See also sensory input
Rest as Resistance (Hersey), 277
rituals. *See* client rituals; passion rituals; the Sacred; stimming; therapist rituals
Rivera, S., 278
Rosales Meza, R., ,306–307
Rose, K., 13
Rothschild, B., 6*n*
routines, 35
    See also rituals
RSD. *See* rejection sensitivity dysphoria (RSD)

the Sacred, 240, 242–245, 255, 267–272
Sacred rage, 30, 205–206
scaffolding, 75
scale creation, 63–64, 72–73, 82
scents, 80
Schaber, A., 45
schedule flexibility, 182, 198–199, 264–265
    See also session lengths; working from home
scheduling, 186–189
self-care. *See* activities of daily living; breaks; resourcing; therapist self-care
self-compassion, 230–234
self-disclosure, 96–98, 123–126

self-growth, 121
self-identification of autism, 26–31
selfishness, as an ableist statement, 136
self-regulation, 34, 37, 68
   See also temperature regulation
sensitivity and permeability, 105–109, 135, 138
   See also wonder
sensory diet, 279–280
sensory input
   as an accommodation or support, 182
   deep pressure, 47–48
   examples for readers, 7
   for kinesthetic learning, 63, 64, 84–90
   and office space set up, 227
   pleasure and, 279–280
   session preparation therapist rituals and, 261–262
   through passion rituals, 289–290
sensory profiles, 32
session lengths, 203–206
session-related therapist rituals, 261–264
sexual orientations, 50
Sharpe, G., 23
Sherrell, C., 142, 233, 249, 301
shirt boundary exercises, 113–116
shoe removal, 226
Siegel, D., 67
Silberman, S., 16
Singleton, G., 249n, 301
smart watches, 78
snacks and drinks, 86
social power, 127–128
somatic psychology concepts, in Pleasure/Neutrality, 66–72

Somatic Soul-Based Trauma Training (Asmus), 63
Somé, S., 125
sounds, 87
Southwest Asian and North African (SWANA), xviii
spacing. *See* facing, pacing, and spacing; office space set up
special interests/SPINs, 34, 283
   See also passions
special needs, 169
sphere boundary exercises, 110–113
spiritual activities, 89
   See also nature, connection to; the Sacred
spiritual gifts, 242–243
spoken language, expectations for, 207–211
square breaths, 89, 247
stimming, 34, 43–44, 80, 282
stress, responses to, 33
   See also threat responses
structure, 184
sucking it up, as an ableist statement, 138
   See also sensitivity and permeability
suicidal ideation, 224
supplements or medications, 184
supports and accommodations. *See* accommodations and supports
support swapping, 47, 180
sustainability, therapist rituals to support, 264–267
SWANA (Southwest Asian and North African), xviii
Sykes, W., 19
symbols and tools key, xviii

sympathetic nervous system, 59–62, 74, 147
synaptic pruning, 59
systemic injustice, 62
See also marginalized groups

task sequence and completion, 174–179
tax filing. See bookkeeping and taxes
telehealth, 171
See also virtual sessions
telepathy, 19, 243
The Telepathy Tapes (Dickens), 19, 242–243
temperature regulation, 87
terminology and language, xvi–xvii, 13–23
therapeutic hours, 203–206
therapeutic relationship
  and antithesis of intake paperwork, 222
  in Client as Self-Expert, 118–129
  compatibility challenges, 172
  dismantling ableism within, 135, 141–151
  dismantling white supremacy, 103–105
  factors affecting quality of, 235
  in Global Permission, 58
  infodumping as rapport building, 46, 284
  in Pleasure/Neutrality, 56–58, 65–66
  privilege and, 268
  self-disclosure, 96–97, 123–126
therapist authenticity, 231–233
therapist rituals, 259–267
therapists, 230–234
See also "good" therapists; neurodivergent (ND) therapists; neurotypical (NT) therapists; white therapists
therapist self-care
  ableism and, 151–161
  accommodations and supports for, 186–200, 202
  breaks, 195–199, 292
  differentiation, 127–129, 271–272
  and difficulties getting support, 268–269
  and getting support through helping clients, 269–271
  integration of joy into, 292–298
  mediocrity, entertaining the idea of, 95, 119, 270
  self-examination in, 93–95
  See also physiological needs, of therapists; therapist rituals
threat responses
  about, 59–61
  to being witnessed, 84
  and choice for indicator tracking, 81
  during EFs, 162–163
  as individual, 80
  masking and, 61–62
  psychoeducation about, 73–74
  to therapists, 74n
time obstacles, 143–144, 170, 182
See also transitions
titration, 67
toileting, 171, 197–198, 262–263
tracking nervous system states, 67
See also indicator tracking
trans Autistic people, gender-affirming care denial for, 29

transition rituals
  to begin the session, 245–248
  to end the session, 248–250
  for honoring major life changes, 255–259
  for neurotype coming out, 250–255
  therapist reflections on their own, 259–260
transitions, 183, 237–240, 256–257
Trauma Geek. *See* Janae Elisabeth
trauma healing, 36, 74
treatment plans and goals, 228–231
trusting the client as self-expert, 118–120

unmasking
  author's journey in, 27, 107–108
  therapist support for, 36, 58, 108, 282
  transition rituals for, 250–255

validation, of autism identification, 27–28
VAST (variable attention stimulus trait), 21–23
  See also KCS/VAST people
vestibular input, 86
vigilance, 61–62
  See also threat responses
virtual sessions, 171, 208–209, 210, 214, 227
visualization exercises, 109–117

Wakefield, D., 44
Walker, N., 14, 21, 50, 156
Walsh, K., 56
white supremacy
  anti-ableism and, 94
  as basis for ND oppression, 8, 65, 78, 83, 125
  DSM and, 11
  facing, pacing, and spacing, 211
  racialized clients and danger of, 76, 154–155, 219–220, 276
  spoken language, expectations for, 207
  stimming and, 34
  and view of transgender people, 50–51
wholeness, caring for one's, 6–7
window of tolerance, 67–68, 83–84
wonder, 156, 235–237, 271
  See also sensitivity and permeability
working from home, 180–181

ABOUT THE AUTHOR

Nyck Walsh (he/they) brings a whole person, anti-oppressive, intersectional, somatic lens to working with Autistic and KCS/VAST folx. A white, Autistic, VAST, queer, and trans counselor, Nyck is the director of Nyck Walsh Counseling & Training Center and creator of the Neurodivergent Somatics model. He curates reparative experiences for late-identified Autistic and KCS/VAST folx to connect with their innate wisdom, dismantle ableism, be supported in their challenges, and unpack their lives through their unidentified and often misunderstood neurodivergent (ND) experience. His counselor education programs have created an international following, with both ND and neurotypical counselors alike reporting that they feel deeply supported and validated by his approach. While being human presents no shortage of complexity, Nyck delights in frolicking in nature and living among the trees with his four-legged bestie in the mountains of what is colonially known as Colorado.